COOPERATION IN THE CLASSROOM

David W. Johnson

Roger T. Johnson

Edythe Johnson Holubec

Seventh Edition

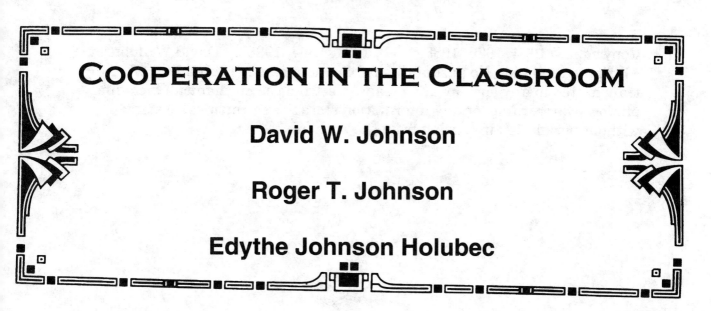

Interaction Book Company

7208 Cornelia Drive

Edina, Minnesota 55435

(612) 831-9500

FAX: (612) 831-9332

This book is dedicated to the thousands of teachers who have taken our
training in cooperative learning and created classroom environments where
students care about each other and each other's learning.

TABLE OF CONTENTS

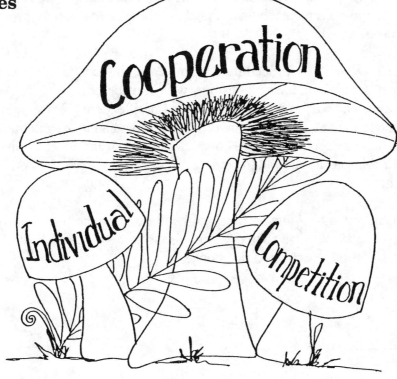

PREFACE

How students interact with each other as they learn has been a relatively ignored variable in teaching despite its powerful effects on a wide range of instructional outcomes. Extensive research indicates that cooperation among students produces greater effort to learn, more positive relationships among students, and greater psychological health than do competition or working individualistically. At the same time, teachers have been taught and encouraged to prevent students from helping each other, talking to each other, or encouraging each other.

This book is about structuring learning situations cooperatively, so that students work together. Cooperative learning is an old idea. Shifting the emphasis from working alone to caring about whether classmates are learning is a relatively simple idea. Implementing it is not. This book is a practical guide for using cooperative learning. Gaining a high level of expertise in implementing cooperative learning takes training, perseverance, and support. The training that has been planned to go with this book will provide a good start, but it may take a year or two of actual experience in the classroom before cooperative learning becomes an integrated and natural part of your teaching. Persisting until you can use cooperative learning procedures and strategies at a routine-use level will benefit your students in numerous ways. It is well worth your effort.

It has taken us nearly 30 years to build the theory, research, and practical experience required to write this book. Our roots reach back through Morton Deutsch to Kurt Lewin. We wish to acknowledge our indebtedness to the work of both of these social psychologists. In the 1960s we began reviewing the research, conducting our initial research studies, and training teachers in the classroom use of cooperation. Since then our work has proliferated.

Many teachers have taught us procedures for implementing cooperative learning and have field tested our ideas in their classrooms with considerable success. We have been in their classrooms and we have sometimes taught beside them. We appreciate their ideas and celebrate their successes. In addition, we have had many talented and productive graduate students who have conducted research studies that have made significant contributions to our understanding of cooperation. We feel privileged to have worked with them.

We wish to thank Linda M. Johnson for all of her hard work, help, and assistancework in completing this book. We wish to thank Thomas Grummett, Nancy Waller, and Tim Johnson for most of the drawings in this book.

CHAPTER ONE:

WHAT IS COOPERATIVE LEARNING?

Introduction

There is a power to working in groups. A group of staff and trustees at the Bronx Educational Services shaped the first nationally recognized adult literacy school. A group of citizens in Harlem founded and operated the first Little League there in over forty years. Motorola used small manufacturing groups to produce the world's lightest, smallest, and highest-quality cellular phones (with only a few hundred parts versus over a thousand for the competition). Ford became America's most profitable car company in 1990 on the strength of the use of small groups to build its Taurus model.

Groups have existed for as long as there have been humans (and even before). Groups have been the subject of countless books. Every human society has used groups to accomplish its goals and celebrated when the groups were successful. It was groups that built the pyramids, constructed the Temple of Artemis at Ephesus, created the Colossus of Rhodes, and the hanging gardens of Babylon. It is obvious that groups outperform individuals, especially when performance requires multiple skills, judgments, and experiences. Many educators, however, overlook opportunities to use groups to enhance student learning and increase their own success.

The opportunity to capitalize on the power of groups in schools begins with understanding the answers to the following questions (see Figure 1.1):

1. What is cooperative learning?

2. What are the differences among cooperative, competitive, and individualistic efforts?

3. Why use cooperative learning? What are the expected outcomes resulting from cooperative efforts?

4. What are the basic elements of cooperative learning that make it work? How do you structure the basic elements into cooperative lessons?

5. What are the ways positive interdependence may be structured into a cooperative lessons?

1 : 1

Cooperation In The Classroom, Interaction Book Company, 7208 Cornelia Drive, Edina, MN 55435, (612) 831-9500, FAX (612) 831-9332

FIGURE 1.1 CIRCLES OF LEARNING

SOCIAL INTERDEPENDENCE

Cooperative	Competitive	Individualistic

RESEARCH: WHY USE COOPERATIVE LEARNING

Effort To Achieve	Positive Relationships	Psychological Health

FIVE BASIC ELEMENTS

Positive Inter-dependence	Individual Accountability	Promotive Interaction	Social Skills	Group Processing

COOPERATIVE LEARNING

Formal Coop Learning	Informal Coop Learning	Coop Base Groups
Make Preinstructional Decisions	Conduct Introductory Focused Discussion	Opening Class Meeting To Check Homework, Ensure Members Understand Academic Material, Complete Routine Tasks Such As Attendance
Explain Task And Cooperative Structure	Conduct Intermittent Pair Discussions Every Ten Or Fifteen Minutes	Ending Class Meeting To Ensure Members Understand Academic Material, Homework Assignment
Monitor Learning Groups And Intervene To Improve Taskwork & Teamwork	Conduct Closure Focused Discussion	Members Help And Assist Each Other Learn In-Between Classes
Assess Student Learning And Process Group Effectiveness		Conduct Semester Or Year Long School Or Class Service Projects

COOPERATIVE SCHOOL

Teaching Teams	Site-Based Decision Making	Faculty Meetings

CONSTRUCTIVE CONFLICT

STUDENTS		FACULTY	
Academic Controversy	Negotiating, Mediating	Decision-Making Controversy	Negotiating, Mediating

CIVIC VALUES

Work For Mutual Benefit, Common Good	Equality Of All Members	Trusting, Caring Relationships	View Situations From All Perspectives	Unconditional Worth Of Self, Diverse Others

1 : 2

Cooperation In The Classroom, Interaction Book Company, 7208 Cornelia Drive, Edina, MN 55435, (612) 831-9500, FAX (612) 831-9332

	THE CAUSES OF THE MISSED OPPORTUNITIES TO CAPITALIZE ON THE POWER OF GROUPS
_____	1. **Belief that isolated work is the natural order of the world.** Such myopic focus blinds educators to the realization that no one person could have built a cathedral, achieved America's independence from England, or created a supercomputer.
_____	2. **Resistance to taking responsibility for others.** Many educators do not easily (a) take responsibility for the performance of colleagues or (b) let colleagues assume responsibility for their work. The same educators may resist letting students take responsibility for each other's learning.
_____	3. **Confusion about what makes groups work.** Many educators may not know the difference between cooperative learning groups and traditional groupwork.
_____	4. **Fear that they cannot use groups effectively to enhance learning and improve teaching.** Not all groups work. Most adults have had personal experiences with very ineffective and inefficient committees, task forces, and clubs and know firsthand how bad groups can be. When many educators weigh the potential power of learning groups against the possibility of failure, they choose to play it safe and stick with the status quo of isolated work.
_____	5. **Concern about time and effort required to change.** Using cooperative learning requires educators to apply what is known about effective groups in a disciplined way. Learning how to do so and engaging in such disciplined action may seem daunting.

Directions: Consider the five sources of resistance to using cooperative learning given above. Rate yourself from "1" to "5" on each source.

1----------------2----------------3------------4----------------5

Low	Middle	High
Not A Concern Of Mine	Somewhat A Concern	Consistently And Strongly A Concern

6. How do you teach students the social skills they need to work effectively in groups?

7. How do you structure group processing to ensure cooperative groups continuously improve their functioning?

1 : 3

Cooperation In The Classroom, Interaction Book Company, 7208 Cornelia Drive, Edina, MN 55435, (612) 831-9500, FAX (612) 831-9332

8. How do you assess the quality and quantity of students' work in cooperative groups?

9. How do you structure cooperation among faculty and staff to ensure that cooperative efforts are institutionalized throughout school life?

DEFINITIONS EXERCISE

Given below are three concepts and three definitions taken from Deutsch (1962) and Johnson and Johnson (1989). Match the correct definition with the correct concept. Find a partner and (a) compare answers and (b) explain your reasoning for each answer.

_____	1. Competitive Efforts	a. Exists when there is positive interdependence among students' goal attainments; students perceive that they can reach their goals if and only if the other students in the group also reach their goals.
_____	2. Individualistic Efforts	b. Exists when there is negative interdependence among goal achievements; students perceive that they can obtain their goals if and only if the other students in the class fail to obtain their goals.
_____	3. Cooperative Efforts	c. Exists when there is no interdependence among goal achievements; students perceive that the achievement of their goals is unrelated to what other students do.

This book explains how to use the power of groups to maximize each student's learning. Doing so requires educators to apply the basics of how groups work with discipline and diligence. While the power of cooperative learning is obvious to many educators, the discipline needed to use cooperative learning effectively is not. The basic elements that make cooperation work cannot be taken for granted or treated lightly. They must be carefully and precisely structured into every learning group. Understanding how to use cooperation effectively begins with knowing the difference between cooperative, competitively, and individualistic efforts.

1 : 4

Cooperation In The Classroom, Interaction Book Company, 7208 Cornelia Drive, Edina, MN 55435, (612) 831-9500, FAX (612) 831-9332

Learning Together Versus Learning Alone

Teachers may structure lessons so that students:

1. Work together in small groups, ensuring that all members complete the assignment.

2. Engage in a win-lose struggle to see who is best in completing the assignment.

3. Work independently to complete the assignment.

Students' learning goals may be structured to promote cooperative, competitive, or individualistic efforts. In every classroom, instructional activities are aimed at accomplishing goals and are conducted under a goal structure. A **learning goal** is a desired future state of demonstrating competence or mastery in the subject area being studied. The **goal structure** specifies the ways in which students will interact with each other and the teacher during the instructional session. Each goal structure has its place (Johnson & Johnson, 1989a, 1994). In the ideal classroom, all students would learn how to work cooperatively with others, compete for fun and enjoyment, and work autonomously on their own. The teacher decides which goal structure to implement within each lesson. The most important goal structure, and the one that should be used the majority of the time in learning situations, is cooperation.

Definitions

Cooperation is working together to accomplish shared goals. Within cooperative situations, individuals seek outcomes that are beneficial to themselves and beneficial to all other group members. **Cooperative learning** is the instructional use of small groups so that students work together to maximize their own and each other's learning. It may be contrasted with **competitive** (students work against each other to achieve an academic goal such as a grade of "A" that only one or a few students can attain) and **individualistic** (students work by themselves to accomplish learning goals unrelated to those of the other students) learning. In cooperative and individualistic learning, you evaluate student efforts on a criteria-referenced basis while in competitive learning you grade students on a norm-referenced basis. While there are limitations on when and where you may use competitive and individualistic learning appropriately, you may structure any learning task in any subject area with any curriculum cooperatively.

1 : 5

Cooperation In The Classroom, Interaction Book Company, 7208 Cornelia Drive, Edina, MN 55435, (612) 831-9500, FAX (612) 831-9332

WHAT IS IT?

Given below are twelve statements. Form a pair and agree on whether each statement reflects a cooperative, competitive, or individualistic situation. Place each statement in the appropriate column in the table given below.

Statements

1. Strive for everyone's success.
2. Strive to be better than others.
3. Strive for own success only.
4. What benefits self does not affect others.
5. Joint success is celebrated.
6. What benefits self benefits others.
7. Only own success is celebrated.
8. Motivated to help and assist others.
9. What benefits self deprives/hurts others.
10. Motivated only to maximize own productivity.
11. Own success and other's failure is celebrated.
12. Motivated to ensure that no one else does better than oneself.

COOPERATIVE	COMPETITIVE	INDIVIDUALISTIC

Why Use Cooperative Learning?

The conviction to use cooperative learning flows from knowing the research. Since the first research study was published in 1898, there have been over 600 experimental and over 100 correlational studies conducted on cooperative, competitive, and individualistic efforts (see Johnson & Johnson, 1989 for a complete review of these studies). The multiple outcomes studied can be classified into three major categories (see Figure 1.3): efforts to achieve, positive relationships, and psychological health. From the research,

1 : 6

Cooperation In The Classroom, Interaction Book Company, 7208 Cornelia Drive, Edina, MN 55435, (612) 831-9500, FAX (612) 831-9332

we know that cooperation, compared with competitive and individualistic efforts, typically results in:

1. **Greater Efforts To Achieve:** This includes higher achievement and greater productivity by all students (high-, medium-, and low-achievers), long-term retention, intrinsic motivation, achievement motivation, time-on-task, higher-level reasoning, and critical thinking.

2. **More Positive Relationships Among Students:** This includes esprit-de-corps, caring and committed relationships, personal and academic social support, valuing of diversity, and cohesion.

3. **Greater Psychological Health:** This includes general psychological adjustment, ego-strength, social development, social competencies, self-esteem, self-identity, and ability to cope with adversity and stress.

The powerful effects of cooperation on so many important outcomes separates it from other instructional methods and makes it one of your most important instructional tools.

Types Of Cooperative Learning Groups

These problems are endemic to all institutions of education, regardless of level. Children sit for 12 years in classrooms where the implicit goal is to listen to the teacher and memorize the information in order to regurgitate it on a test. Little or no attention is paid to the learning process, even though much research exists documenting that real understanding is a case of active restructuring on the part of the learner. Restructuring occurs through engagement in problem posing as well as problem solving, inference making and investigation, resolving of contradictions, and reflecting. These processes all mandate far more active learners, as well as a different model of education than the one subscribed to at present by most institutions. Rather than being powerless and dependent on the institution, learners need to be empowered to think and learn for themselves. Thus, learning needs to be conceived of as something a learner does, not something that is done to a learner.

Catherine Fosnot (1989)

There are three types of cooperative learning groups. **Formal cooperative learning** groups last from one class period to several weeks. You may structure any academic assignment or course requirement for formal cooperative learning. Formal cooperative learning groups ensure that students are actively involved in the intellectual work of organizing material, explaining it, summarizing it, and integrating it into existing conceptual structures. They are the heart of using cooperative learning. **Informal cooperative learning** groups are ad-hoc groups that last from a few minutes to one class

Cooperation In The Classroom, Interaction Book Company, 7208 Cornelia Drive, Edina, MN 55435, (612) 831-9500, FAX (612) 831-9332

period. You use them during direct teaching (lectures, demonstrations, films, videos) to focus student attention on the material they are to learn, set a mood conducive to learning, help set expectations as to what the lesson will cover, ensure that students cognitively process the material you are teaching, and provide closure to an instructional session. **Cooperative base groups** are long-term (lasting for at least a year), heterogeneous groups with stable membership whose primary purpose is for members to give each other the support, help, encouragement, and assistance each needs to progress academically. Base groups provide students with long-term, committed relationships.

In addition to the three types of cooperative learning, **cooperative learning scripts** are standard cooperative procedures for (a) conducting generic, repetitive lessons (such as writing reports or giving presentations) and (b) managing classroom routines (such as checking homework and reviewing a test). Once planned and conducted several times, scripted repetitive cooperative lessons and classroom routines become automatic activities in the classroom.

When you use formal, informal, and cooperative base groups repeatedly, you will gain a routine-level of expertise in doing so. **Expertise** is reflected in your proficiency, adroitness, competence, and skill in doing something. Expertise in structuring cooperative efforts is reflected in your being able to:

1. Take any lesson in any subject area with any age student and structure it cooperatively.

2. Use cooperative learning (at a routine-use level) 60 to 80 percent of the time.

3. Describe precisely what you are doing and why in order to (a) communicate to others the nature and advantages of cooperative learning and (b) teach colleagues how to implement cooperative learning.

4. Apply the principles of cooperation to other settings, such as colleagial relationships and faculty meetings.

You usually gain such expertise through a progressive-refinement procedure of (a) teaching a cooperative lesson, (b) assessing how well it went, (c) reflecting on how cooperation could have been better structured, and then (d) teaching an improved cooperative lesson, (b) assessing how well it went, and so forth. You thus gain experience in an incremental step-by-step manner. The **routine-use level of teacher expertise** is the ability to structure cooperative learning situations automatically without conscious thought or planning. You can then use cooperative learning with fidelity for the rest of your teaching career.

Cooperation In The Classroom, Interaction Book Company, 7208 Cornelia Drive, Edina, MN 55435, (612) 831-9500, FAX (612) 831-9332

TYPES OF COOPERATIVE LEARNING

Form a pair. In the spaces below, write out the definition of each type of cooperative learning in your own words.

FORMAL	INFORMAL	BASE GROUPS

What Kind Of Group Am I Using?

There is nothing magical about working in a group. Some kinds of learning groups facilitate student learning and increase the quality of life in the classroom. Other types of learning groups hinder student learning and create disharmony and dissatisfaction with classroom life. To use cooperative learning effectively, you must know what is and is not a cooperative group.

There are many kinds of groups that can be used in the classroom. Cooperative learning groups are just one of them. When you use instructional groups, you have to ask yourself, "*What type of group am I using?*" The following checklist may be helpful in answering that question.

1. **Pseudo-Learning Group:** Students are assigned to work together but they have no interest in doing so. They believe they will be evaluated by being ranked from the highest performer to the lowest performer. While on the surface students talk to each other, under the surface they are competing. They see each other as rivals who must be defeated, block or interfere with each other's learning, hide information from each other, attempt to mislead and confuse each other, and distrust each other. The result is that the sum of the whole is less than the potential of the individual members. Students would achieve more if they were working alone.

1 : 9

Cooperation In The Classroom, Interaction Book Company, 7208 Cornelia Drive, Edina, MN 55435, (612) 831-9500, FAX (612) 831-9332

2. **Traditional Classroom Learning Group:** Students are assigned to work together and accept that they have to do so. Assignments are structured, however, so that very little joint work is required. Students believe that they will be evaluated and rewarded as individuals, not as members of the group. They interact primarily to clarify how assignments are to be done. They seek each other's information, but have no motivation to teach what they know to their groupmates. Helping and sharing is minimized. Some students loaf, seeking a free ride on the efforts of their more conscientious groupmates. The conscientious members feel exploited and do less. The result is that the sum of the whole is more than the potential of some of the members, but the more hard working and conscientious students would perform higher if they worked alone.

3. **Cooperative Learning Group:** Students are assigned to work together and they are happy to do so. They believe that their success depends on the efforts of all group members. There are five defining characteristics. **First**, the group goal of maximizing all members' learning provides a compelling common purpose that motivates members to roll up their sleeves and accomplish something beyond their individual achievements. Members believe that "they sink or swim together," and "if one of us fails, we all fail." **Second**, group members hold themselves and each other accountable for doing high quality work to achieve their mutual goals. **Third**, group members work face-to-face to produce joint work-products. They do real work together. Students promote each other's success through helping, sharing, assisting, explaining, and encouraging. They provide both academic and personal support based on a commitment to and caring about each other. **Fourth**, group members are taught social skills and are expected to use them to coordinate their efforts and achieve their goals. Both taskwork and teamwork skills are emphasized. All members accept the responsibility for providing leadership. **Finally**, groups analyze how effectively they are achieving their goals and how well members are working together. There is an emphasis on continuous improvement of the quality of learning and teamwork processes. The result is that the group is more than a sum of its parts and all students perform higher academically than they would if they worked alone.

4. **High-Performance Cooperative Learning Group:** This is a group that meets all the criteria for being a cooperative learning group and outperforms all reasonable expectations, given its membership. What differentiates the high-performance group from the cooperative learning group is the level of commitment members have to each other and the group's success. Jennifer Futernick, who is part of a high-performing, rapid response team at McKinsey & Company, calls the emotion binding her teammates together *"a form of love"* (Katzenbach & Smith, 1993). Ken Hoepner of the Burlington Northern Intermodal Team (also described by Katzenbach and Smith, 1993) stated: "*Not only did we trust each other, not only did we respect each other, but we gave a damn about the rest of the people on this team. If we saw somebody vulnerable, we were there to help.*" Members' mutual concern for each other's personal growth enables high-performance cooperative groups to perform far above

Cooperation In The Classroom, Interaction Book Company, 7208 Cornelia Drive, Edina, MN 55435, (612) 831-9500, FAX (612) 831-9332

expectations, and also to have lots of fun. The bad news about high-performance cooperative groups is that they are rare. Most groups never achieve this level of development.

TYPES OF GROUPS

Demonstrate your understanding of the different types of groups by matching the definitions with the appropriate group. Check your answers with your partner and explain why you believe your answers to be correct.

TYPE OF GROUP	DEFINITION
_____ Pseudo Group	a. A group in which students work together to accomplish shared goals. Students perceive they can reach their learning goals if and only if the other group members also reach their goals.
_____ Traditional Learning Group	b. A group whose members have been assigned to work together but they have no interest in doing so. The structure promotes competition at close quarters.
_____ Cooperative Learning Group	d. A group that meets all the criteria for being a cooperative group and outperforms all reasonable expectations, given its membership.
_____ High- Performance Cooperative Learning Group	c. A group whose members agree to work together, but see little benefit from doing so. The structure promotes individualistic work with talking.

To use cooperative learning effectively, you must realize that not all groups are cooperative groups. The learning group performance curve illustrates that how well any small group performs depends on how it is structured (Figure 1.1) (Katzenbach & Smith, 1993). Placing people in the same room and calling them a cooperative group does not make them one. Study groups, project groups, lab groups, home rooms, reading groups are groups, but they are not necessarily cooperative. Even with the best of intentions, you may find traditional classroom learning groups on your hands rather than cooperative learning groups. Your job is to form students into learning groups, diagnose where on the group performance curve the groups are, keep strengthening the basic elements of cooperation, and move the groups up the performance curve until they are truly cooperative learning groups.

Cooperation In The Classroom, Interaction Book Company, 7208 Cornelia Drive, Edina, MN 55435, (612) 831-9500, FAX (612) 831-9332

FIGURE 1.1 THE LEARNING GROUP PERFORMANCE CURVE

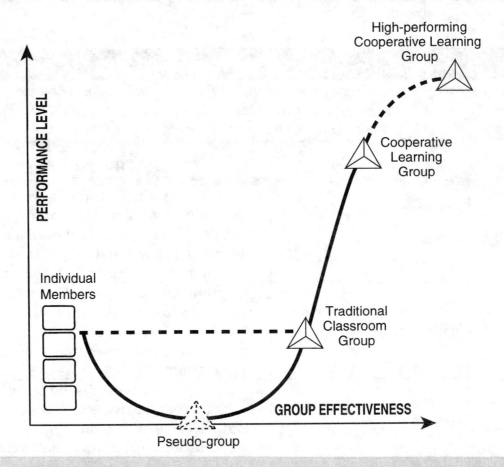

TABLE 1.1 COMPARISON OF LEARNING GROUPS

TRADITIONAL LEARNING GROUPS	COOPERATIVE LEARNING GROUPS
Low interdependence. Members take responsibility only for self. Focus is on individual performance only.	High positive interdependence. Members are responsible for own and each other's learning. Focus is on joint performance.
Individual accountability only.	Both group and individual accountability. Members hold self and others accountable for high quality work.
Assignments are discussed with little commitment to each other's learning.	Members promote each other's success. They do real work together and help and support each other's efforts to learn.
Teamwork skills are ignored. Leader is appointed to direct members' participation.	Teamwork skills are emphasized. Members are taught and expected to use social skills. All members share leadership responsibilities.
No group processing of the quality of its work. Individual accomplishments are rewarded.	Group processes quality of work and how effectively members are working together. Continuous improvement is emphasized.

1 : 12

Cooperation In The Classroom, Interaction Book Company, 7208 Cornelia Drive, Edina, MN 55435, (612) 831-9500, FAX (612) 831-9332

What Makes Cooperation Work

Together we stand, divided we fall.

Watchword Of The American Revolution

On July 15, 1982, Don Bennett, a Seattle businessman, was the first amputee ever to climb Mount Rainier (reported in Kouzes & Posner, 1987). He climbed 14,410 feet on one leg and two crutches. It took him five days. When asked to state the most important lesson he learned from doing so, without hesitation he said, "*You can't do it alone.*"

What did he mean? During one very difficult trek across an ice field in Don Bennett's hop to the top of Mount Rainier, his daughter stayed by his side for four hours and with each new hop told him, "*You can do it, Dad. You're the best dad in the world. You can do it, Dad.*" There was no way Bennett would quit hopping to the top with his daughter yelling words of love and encouragement in his ear. The encouragement of his daughter kept him going, strengthening his commitment to make it to the top. The classroom is similar. With members of their cooperative group cheering them on, students amaze themselves and their teachers with what they can achieve.

To structure lessons so students do in fact work cooperatively with each other, you must understand the basic elements that make cooperation work. Mastering the basic elements of cooperation allows you to:

1. Take your existing lessons, curricula, and courses and structure them cooperatively.

2. Tailor cooperative learning lessons to your unique instructional needs, circumstances, curricula, subject areas, and students.

3. Diagnose the problems some students may have in working together and intervene to increase the effectiveness of the student learning groups.

For cooperation to work well, you explicitly have to structure five essential elements in each lesson (see Figure 1.2). **The first and most important element is positive interdependence.** You must give a clear task and a group goal so that students believe they "*sink or swim together.*" You have successfully structured positive interdependence when group members perceive that they are linked with each other in a way that one cannot succeed unless everyone succeeds. If one fails, all fail. Group members realize, therefore, that each person's efforts benefit not only him- or herself, but all other group members as well. Positive interdependence creates a commitment to other people's success as well as one's own and is the heart of cooperative learning. If there is no positive interdependence, there is no cooperation.

1 : 13

Cooperation In The Classroom, Interaction Book Company, 7208 Cornelia Drive, Edina, MN 55435, (612) 831-9500, FAX (612) 831-9332

© Johnson, Johnson, & Holubec

The second essential element of cooperative learning is individual and group accountability. The group must be accountable for achieving its goals. Each member must be accountable for contributing his or her share of the work (which ensures that no one can "hitch-hike" on the work of others). The group has to be clear about its goals and be able to measure (a) its progress in achieving them and (b) the individual efforts of each of its members. **Individual accountability** exists when the performance of each individual student is assessed and the results are given back to the group and the individual in order to ascertain who needs more assistance, support, and encouragement in completing the assignment. The purpose of cooperative learning groups is to make each member a stronger individual in his or her right. Students learn together so that they can subsequently perform higher as individuals.

The third essential component of cooperative learning is promotive interaction, preferably face-to-face. Students need to do real work together in which they promote each other's success by sharing resources and helping, supporting, encouraging, and praising each other's efforts to learn. Cooperative learning groups are both an academic support system (every student has someone who is committed to helping him or her learn) and a personal support system (every student has someone who is committed to him or her as a person). There are important cognitive activities and interpersonal dynamics that can only occur when students promote each other's learning. This includes orally explaining how to solve problems, discussing the nature of the concepts being learned, teaching one's knowledge to classmates, and connecting present with past learning. It is through promoting each other's learning face-to-face that members become personally committed to each other as well as to their mutual goals.

The fourth essential element of cooperative learning is teaching students the required interpersonal and small group skills. In cooperative learning groups students are required to learn academic subject matter (taskwork) and also to learn the interpersonal and small group skills required to function as part of a group (teamwork). Cooperative learning is inherently more complex than competitive or individualistic learning because students have to engage simultaneously in taskwork and teamwork. Group members must know how to provide effective leadership, decision-making, trust-building, communication, and conflict-management, and be motivated to use the prerequisite skills. You have to teach teamwork skills just as purposefully and precisely as you do academic skills. Since cooperation and conflict are inherently related (see Johnson & Johnson, 1991, 1992), the procedures and skills for managing conflicts constructively are especially important for the long-term success of learning groups. Procedures and strategies for teaching students social skills may be found in Johnson (1991, 1993) and Johnson and F. Johnson (1997).

The fifth essential component of cooperative learning is group processing. Group processing exists when group members discuss how well they are achieving their goals and maintaining effective working relationships. Groups need to describe what member actions are helpful and unhelpful and make decisions about what behaviors to continue or

1 : 14

Cooperation In The Classroom, Interaction Book Company, 7208 Cornelia Drive, Edina, MN 55435, (612) 831-9500, FAX (612) 831-9332

change. Continuous improvement of the process of learning results from the careful analysis of how members are working together and determining how group effectiveness can be enhanced.

Your use of cooperative learning becomes effective through disciplined action. The five basic elements are not just characteristics of good cooperative learning groups, they are a discipline that you have to rigorously apply (much like a diet has to be adhered to) to produce the conditions for effective cooperative action.

UNDERSTANDING COOPERATIVE LEARNING

Types Of Groups	Cooperative Groups	Essential Elements	Outcomes
Pseudo Groups	Formal Cooperative Learning	Positive Interdependence	Effort To Achieve
Traditional Groups	Informal Cooperative Learning	Individual Accountability	Positive Relationships
Cooperative Groups	Cooperative Base Groups	Promotive Interaction	Psychological Health
High-Performing Cooperative Groups		Interpersonal And Small Group Skills	
		Group Processing	

Managing Conflicts Constructively

Cooperation and conflict go hand-in-hand (Johnson & Johnson, 1970). The more group members care about achieving the group's goals, and the more they care about each other, the more likely they are to have conflicts with each other. How conflict is managed largely determines how successful cooperative efforts tend to be. In order to ensure that conflicts are managed constructively, students must be taught two procedures and sets of skills.

First, students must be taught the procedures and skills needed to manage the academic/intellectual conflicts inherent in learning groups (Johnson & Johnson, 1995b). Intellectual challenge is created by structuring academic controversies, Students are placed in cooperative groups of four, divided into two pairs, and each pair is given

1 : 15

Cooperation In The Classroom, Interaction Book Company, 7208 Cornelia Drive, Edina, MN 55435, (612) 831-9500, FAX (612) 831-9332

either the "pro" or "con" position on an issue being studied. Students then research and prepare their position, present the base case possible for their position, refute the opposing position, try to see the issue from both sides, and create a synthesis that incorporates the best reasoning from both sides. Such "intellectual disputed passages" create higher level reasoning, and higher achievement, and greater long-term retention.

EXTRAORDINARY ACHIEVEMENT

Sandy Koufax was one of the greatest pitchers in the history of baseball. Although he was naturally talented, he was also unusually well trained and disciplined. He was perhaps the only major-league pitcher whose fastball could be heard to hum. Opposing batters, instead of talking and joking around in the dugout, would sit quietly and listen for Koufax's fastball to hum. When it was their turn to bat, they were already intimidated. There was, however, a simple way for Koufax's genius to have been negated. By making the first author of this book his catcher. To be great, a pitcher needs an outstanding catcher (his great partner was Johnny Roseboro). David is such an unskilled catcher that Koufax would have had to throw the ball much slower in order for David to catch it. This would have deprived Koufax of his greatest weapon. Placing Roger and Edythe at key defensive positions in the infield or outfield, furthermore, would have seriously affected Koufax's success. Sandy Koufax was not a great pitcher on his own. Only as part of a team could Koufax achieve greatness. In baseball and in the classroom it takes a cooperative effort. Extraordinary achievement comes from a cooperative group, not from the individualistic or competitive efforts of an isolated individual.

Second, students must be taught the procedures and skills needed to negotiate constructive resolutions to their conflicts and mediate classmates' conflicts (Johnson & Johnson, 1995a). Students are trained to be peacemakers in a two-step process. The **first** step is to train students to negotiate constructive resolutions to their conflicts of interests. When two students want the same book or want to use the computer at the same time, for example, they must negotiate an agreement that is acceptable to both. Once students know how to negotiate, the **second** step is to train students to be mediators. A peer mediation program is then implemented where students take the conflicts they cannot negotiate successfully to a mediator who helps then do so.

The combination of knowing how to manage intellectual disagreements and how to negotiate/mediate conflicts among students' wants, needs, and goals ensures that the power of cooperative efforts will be maximized. The productivity of groups increases dramatically when members are skilled in how to manage conflicts constructively.

1 : 16

Cooperation In The Classroom, Interaction Book Company, 7208 Cornelia Drive, Edina, MN 55435, (612) 831-9500, FAX (612) 831-9332

TABLE 1.2 CONFLICT RESOLUTION PROCEDURES

ACADEMIC CONTROVERSY	PEACEMAKER PROGRAM	
	PROBLEM-SOLVING NEGOTIATIONS	PEER MEDIATION
Research And Prepare Positions	State What You Want	End Hostilities
Present And Advocate Position	State How You Feel	Ensure Commitment To Mediation Process
Open Discussion: Advocate, Refute, Rebut	State Your Reasons For Wanting And Feeling As You Do	Facilitate Problem-Solving Negotiations
Reverse Perspectives: Present Opposing Position	Reverse Perspectives: Summarize Opposing Position	Formalize Contract
Reach Consensus On Best Reasoned Judgment: Synthesize	Create Three Optional Agreements That Maximize Joint Outcomes	
	Choose One And Formalize Agreement	

The Cooperative School

W. Edwards Deming, J. Juran, and other founders of the quality movement have stated that more than 85 percent of the behavior of members of an organization is directly attributable to the organization's structure, not the nature of the individuals involved. Your classroom is no exception. If competitive or individualistic learning dominates your classroom, your students will behave accordingly, regardless of whether you have temporarily put them in cooperative groups. If cooperative learning dominates your classroom, your students will behave accordingly and a true learning community will result.

The issue of cooperation among students is part of a larger issue of the organizational structure of schools (Johnson & Johnson, 1994). For decades schools have functioned as "*mass production*" organizations that divided work into component parts (first grade, second grade; English, social studies, science) to be performed by teachers who are isolated from their colleagues and work alone, in their own room, with their own set of students, and with their own set of curriculum materials. Students can be assigned to any teacher because students are considered to be interchangeable parts in the education

Cooperation In The Classroom, Interaction Book Company, 7208 Cornelia Drive, Edina, MN 55435, (612) 831-9500, FAX (612) 831-9332

machine. By using cooperative learning the majority of the time you are changing the basic organizational structure of your classroom to a team-based, high-performance one. In other words, cooperation is more than an instructional procedure. It is a basic shift in organizational structure that will affect all aspects of classroom life.

In a **cooperative school**, students work primarily in cooperative learning groups, teachers and building staff work in cooperative teams, and district administrators work in cooperative teams (Johnson & Johnson, 1994). The organizational structure of the classroom, school, and district are then congruent. Each level of cooperative teams supports and enhances the other levels.

A cooperative school structure begins in the classroom with the use of cooperative learning the majority of the time (Johnson & Johnson, 1994). Work teams are the heart of the team-based organizational structure and cooperative learning groups are the primary work team. Cooperative learning is used to increase student achievement, create more positive relationships among students, and generally improve students' psychological well-being. Having teachers advocate cooperation to their students, furthermore, changes their own attitudes toward working collaboratively with colleagues.

The second level in creating a cooperative school is to form colleagial teaching teams, task forces, and ad hoc decision-making groups within the school (Johnson & Johnson, 1994). Teacher teams are just as effective as student teams. The use of cooperation to structure faculty and staff work involves (a) colleagial teaching teams, (b) school-based decision making, and (c) faculty meetings. Just as the heart of the classroom is cooperative learning, the heart of the school is the colleagial teaching team. **Colleagial teaching teams** are small cooperative groups (two to five teachers) whose purpose is to increase teachers' instructional expertise and success (Johnson & Johnson, 1994).

A school-based decision-making procedure is implemented through the use of two types of cooperative teams (Johnson & Johnson, 1994). A **task force** considers a school problem and proposes a solution to the faculty as a whole. The faculty is then divided into **ad hoc decision-making groups** and considers whether to accept or modify the proposal. The decisions made by the ad hoc groups are summarized, and the entire faculty then decides on the action to be taken to solve the problem.

The third level in creating a cooperative school is to implement administrative cooperative teams within the district (Johnson & Johnson, 1994). Administrators are organized into colleagial teams to increase their administrative expertise as well as task forces and ad hoc decision making groups.

Willi Unsoeld, a mountain climber and philosopher, gave this advice "*as the secret to survival*" to all those who set off to climb a mountain: "*Take care of each other, share*

1 : 18

Cooperation In The Classroom, Interaction Book Company, 7208 Cornelia Drive, Edina, MN 55435, (612) 831-9500, FAX (612) 831-9332

your energies with the group, no one must feel alone, cut off, for that is when you do not make it." The same may be said for everyone entering a school.

GAINING EXPERTISE IN COOPERATIVE LEARNING

Year	Training And Application
One	Teachers (and administrators) are organized into colleagial teaching teams that meet weekly and are trained in the fundamentals of cooperative learning. The teachers become an inhouse demonstration project for other teachers to view and then emulate.
Two	Teachers are trained in the integrated use of (a) formal, informal, and base groups, (b) cooperative, competitive, and individualistic learning, as well as the teaching of advanced social skills. Administrators receive six days of training on the cooperative school.
Three	Teachers are trained in how to (a) create academic conflicts to intellectually challenge students, and (b) use a peer mediation program to manage classroom and school discipline problems. The "superstar" teachers receive leadership training on how to (a) conduct the training on cooperative learning, (b) give inclassroom help and support to the teachers being trained, and (c) organize colleagial teaching teams. The leaders are then given responsibility for conducting the training in their district.
Four	Continued functioning of colleagial support groups supported by the teachers trained to be leaders.

The Third C: Civic Values

Some historians claim that the decline and fall of Rome was set in motion by corruption from within rather than by conquest from without. Rome fell, it can be argued, because Romans lost their civic virtue. **Civic virtue** exists when individuals meet both the letter and spirit of their public obligations. For a community to exist and be sustained, members must share common goals and values aimed at increasing the quality of life within the community. No one should be surprised that in a community where competitive and individualistic values are taught, people will behave in accordance with such values. When that happens in a society, for example, people may stop obeying the law. Running stoplights may become a common occurrence as the individualist thinks it is rational to do so as he or she will arrive at the destination sooner. If someone is killed,

Cooperation In The Classroom, Interaction Book Company, 7208 Cornelia Drive, Edina, MN 55435, (612) 831-9500, FAX (612) 831-9332

it will be a pedestrian, not the driver. But each of us is at some time a pedestrian. Community cannot be maintained unless members value others and the community as a whole, as well as themselves.

School and classroom management requires that all members of the school community adopt a set of civic values (Johnson & Johnson, 1996b, in press). To create the common culture that defines a community, there must be common goals and shared values that help define appropriate behavior. A learning community cannot exist in schools dominated by (a) competition where students are taught to value striving for their personal success at the expense of others or (b) individualistic efforts where students value only their own self-interests. Rather, students need to internalize values underlying cooperation and integrative negotiations, such as commitment to the common good and to the well being of other members, a sense of responsibility to contribute one's fair share of the work, respect for the efforts of others and for them as people, behaving with integrity, caring for other members, compassion when other members are in need, and appreciation of diversity. Such civic values both underlie and are promoted by the cooperation and constructive conflict resolution that take place in the school.

Nature Of This Book And How To Use It

This is not a book you can read with detachment. It is written to involve you with its contents. By reading this book you will not only be able to learn the theoretical and empirical knowledge now available on cooperative learning, but you will also learn to apply this knowledge in practical ways within your classroom and school. Often in the past, practitioners concerned with cooperative learning did not pay attention to the research literature, and cooperation researchers neglected to specify how their findings could be applied. Thus, the knowledge about effective use of cooperation was often divided. In this book we directly apply existing theory and research to the learning and application of effective cooperative learning procedures and skills. In other words, this book combines theory, research, and practical application to the classroom. In using this book, diagnose your present knowledge and skills, actively participate in the exercises, reflect on your experiences, read the chapters carefully, discuss the relevant theory and research provided, and integrate the information and experiences into your teaching repertoire. In doing so, you will bridge the gap between theory and practice. You should then plan how to continue your skill- and knowledge-building activities after you have finished this book. Most important of all, you should systematically plan how to implement the material covered in each chapter into your classroom.

Summary

In this chapter we have seen that there are three types of social interdependence: competitive, individualistic, and cooperative, Of the three, cooperation tends to promote

Cooperation In The Classroom, Interaction Book Company, 7208 Cornelia Drive, Edina, MN 55435, (612) 831-9500, FAX (612) 831-9332

the highest achievement, most positive relationships, and greatest psychological health. In order to harness the power of cooperation, however, it is necessary to know what makes it work and apply those elements with discipline and diligence. Like Sandy Koufax, natural talent is not enough to make a great teacher. Being well trained in how to use cooperative learning and unusually well disciplined in structuring the five basic elements in every lesson are also necessary. The five essential components are positive interdependence, individual accountability, promotive interaction, social skills, and group processing. From structuring these five elements into lessons, teachers can create formal cooperative learning lessons, informal cooperative learning lessons, and cooperative base groups. Repetitive lessons and procedures may be turned into cooperative scripts. The use of cooperative learning takes place within an organizational context. If the organizational context emphasizes mass production of educated students, it works against the use of cooperative learning. If the organizational context is a team-based, high-performance structure, then it encourages and supports the use of cooperative learning. In a high-performance school, the five basic elements of cooperation are used to structure teaching teams, faculty meetings, and site-based decision making. Finally, the long-term success of cooperative efforts depends on members having frequent conflicts that are managed constructively.

The next chapter focuses on the teacher's role in using formal cooperative learning. This provides the foundation for using all types of cooperative learning.

Implementation Assignment One

Each week you will plan in your base group how to apply to your classroom and school what you have learned. This implementation assignment functions as a learning contract with your base group. In planning how to implement what you have learned, it is important to be as specific as possible about implementation plans and to keep a careful record of your implementation efforts. There are three forms connected with the implementation assignments: the cooperative learning contract, cooperative learning progress report, and cooperative lessons log sheet.

1. Read Chapters One and Two.

2. Write down your feelings about competing, working individualistically, and cooperating with others. Think back over the years. What memories are most vivid about competing, cooperating, and working individualistically.

3. Examine the subject areas, curriculums, and lessons you teach and decide on ten places where cooperative learning may be (or is being) fruitfully used in your classroom.

Cooperation In The Classroom, Interaction Book Company, 7208 Cornelia Drive, Edina, MN 55435, (612) 831-9500, FAX (612) 831-9332

COOPERATIVE LEARNING CONTRACT

Write down your major learnings from reading this chapter and participating in training session one. Then write down how you plan to implement each learning. Share what you learned and your implementation plans with your base group. Listen carefully to their major learnings and implementation plans. You may modify your own plans on the basis of what you have learned from your groupmates. Volunteer one thing you can do to help each groupmate with his or her implementation plans. Utilize the help groupmates offer to you. Sign each member's plans to seal the contract.

MAJOR LEARNINGS	IMPLEMENTATION PLANS

Date: _____ Participant's Signature: _____

Signatures Of Group Members: _____

_____

1 : 22

Cooperation In The Classroom, Interaction Book Company, 7208 Cornelia Drive, Edina, MN 55435, (612) 831-9500, FAX (612) 831-9332

COOPERATIVE LEARNING PROGRESS REPORT

Name: _____ School: _____

Subject Area: _____ Grade: _____

Date	Lesson	Successes	Problems

Describe Critical Or Interesting Incidents:

1 : 23

Cooperation In The Classroom, Interaction Book Company, 7208 Cornelia Drive, Edina, MN 55435, (612) 831-9500, FAX (612) 831-9332

COOPERATIVE LEARNING LOG SHEET

Name: _____ School: _____

Subject Area: _____ Grade: _____

Week	Lessons Planned, Taught	Social Skills Included	Planned With	Observed By	Given Away To
1					
2					
3					
4					
5					
6					
7					
8					
9					
10					
11					
12					
13					
14					
15					
Group					
Total					

1 : 24

Cooperation In The Classroom, Interaction Book Company, 7208 Cornelia Drive, Edina, MN 55435, (612) 831-9500, FAX (612) 831-9332

EXERCISE

MATERIALS

1 : 25

Cooperation In The Classroom, Interaction Book Company, 7208 Cornelia Drive, Edina, MN 55435, (612) 831-9500, FAX (612) 831-9332

EXPECTATIONS FOR PARTICIPANTS

1. **Attend and actively participate in all class sessions**. Attending each session is only half the battle. Each participant needs to be active and not only concerned about his or her own work, but also concerned about the work of the other people in the class. Expect to be actively working during most of the session and to be able to improve your skill in working with others during the course.

2. **Do all the weekly implementation assignments**. The weekly Implementation Assignments are the heart of the course and are designed to be practical in getting cooperative learning started in your classroom. Keep in mind that each class session begins with a chance to share what you have done with the implementation assignment and to hear what the others in your base group have done. They are counting on you to bring back your results.

3. **Read the material in <u>Cooperation in the Classroom</u> with care**. Each chapter of Cooperation in the Classroom contains reading material that should be read with care. It is sometimes helpful to underline or highlight important points, write questions in the margin, and add your own thoughts to what is written.

4. **Plan and teach at least one cooperative lesson each week**. Except perhaps for the first week, you should try as many cooperative learning procedures and lessons as you can. Planning and implementing at least one lesson each week is the way that this course will become powerful for you. Part of the sharing in the base groups will center on what is happening in the teaching of cooperatively structured lessons and the use of cooperative learning strategies and skills.

5. **Plan and teach at least five specific cooperative skills over the course**. One of the most interesting and productive parts of the course is to teach students to be more effective in the way they cooperate with one another. The cooperative skills include basic behaviors like using quiet voices and staying with your group, to more complex leadership and communication skills like disagreeing while confirming other's competence. There are many reasons why teaching students cooperative skills is important. One of them is that students' efforts to work together become even more effective and, therefore, achievement continues to grow.

Cooperation In The Classroom, Interaction Book Company, 7208 Cornelia Drive, Edina, MN 55435, (612) 831-9500, FAX (612) 831-9332

6. **Monitor the behaviors of your students with care while they are working cooperatively with special attention to at least two key students**. While it is important to monitor all students who are working cooperatively, you should pick out two particular students in whom you have a high interest. Perhaps it will be a student who is handicapped in some way, a very bright student, or a student who had real difficulty in working with others. Whoever you pick, you should regularly monitor him or her several times while he or she works in cooperative learning groups and keep track of your observations for a Case Study.

7. **Keep a journal analyzing your implementation of cooperative learning**. From this journal will be developed assumptions about cooperative learning and your most frequently used cooperative learning strategies.

8. **Develop a colleagial relationship with at least one person in your school who is interested in what you are doing and perhaps even willing to try some cooperative lessons**. There is good evidence that people who innovate in their classrooms need the support of at least one colleague to persevere. Think about your staff and select at least one colleague who would be interested in cooperative learning and would interact with you about what you are doing. If you are participating in the training as part of a team from the same school, you may still want to think about keeping other colleagues informed and interested.

9. **Take an active and supportive interest in the work of the other members of your base group and assist them in accomplishing the course requirements**. The base group is only one of several groups you will be a part of during this course, but it is important. At the beginning of each session the base group will meet and share their experience from the week before. They are expected to provide encouragement for each other and assist each group member to get the most from this course. The assignments will be reviewed by the base group and direct communication with the instructor is provided by the base group file folder (a folder where implementation assignments are stored and instructor feedback is written).

10. **Enjoy yourself and help those around you enjoy themselves during the course sessions**.

1 : 27

Cooperation In The Classroom, Interaction Book Company, 7208 Cornelia Drive, Edina, MN 55435, (612) 831-9500, FAX (612) 831-9332

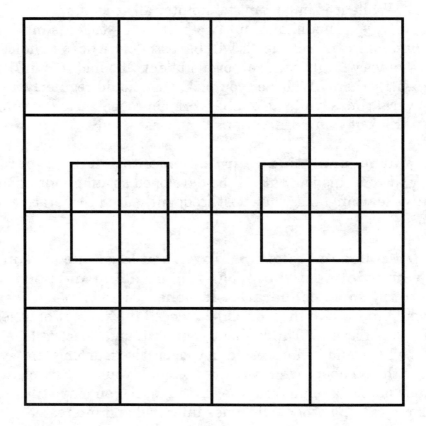

HOW DO I FEEL?

WHAT DID I NOTICE?

1 : 28

Cooperation In The Classroom, Interaction Book Company, 7208 Cornelia Drive, Edina, MN 55435, (612) 831-9500, FAX (612) 831-9332

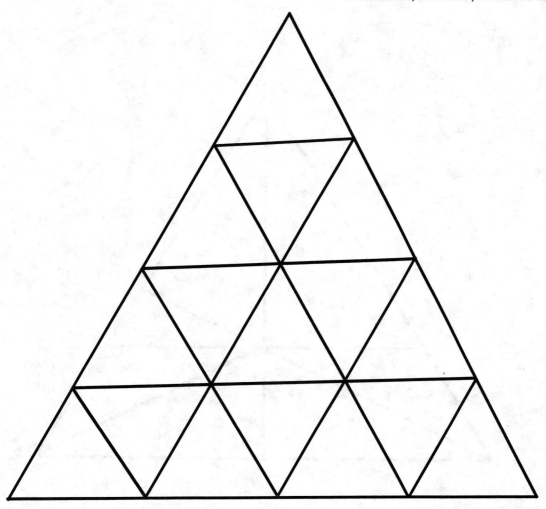

How Do I Feel?

What Did I Notice?

Cooperation In The Classroom, Interaction Book Company, 7208 Cornelia Drive, Edina, MN 55435,
(612) 831-9500, FAX (612) 831-9332

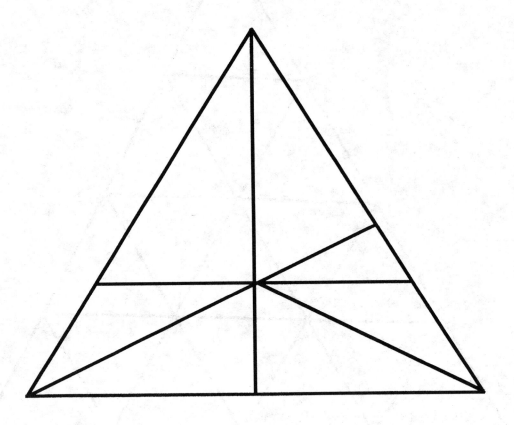

HOW DO I FEEL?

WHAT DID I NOTICE?

Cooperation In The Classroom, Interaction Book Company, 7208 Cornelia Drive, Edina, MN 55435, (612) 831-9500, FAX (612) 831-9332

Definitions

A **learning goal** is a desired future state of competence or mastery in the subject area being studied. A **goal structure** specifies the type of interdependence among individuals as they strive to accomplish their goals. Interdependence may be positive (cooperation), negative (competition), or none (individualistic efforts).

COOPERATION: WE SINK OR SWIM TOGETHER

Individuals work together to achieve shared goals. Individuals work together to maximize their own and each other's learning.

    Work in small, often heterogeneous groups
    Strive for all group members' success
    What benefits self benefits others
    Joint success is celebrated
    Rewards are viewed as unlimited
    Evaluated by comparing performance to preset criteria

COMPETITION: I SWIM, YOU SINK; I SINK, YOU SWIM

Individuals work against each other to achieve a goal only one or a few can attain.

    Work alone
    Strive to be better than classmates
    What benefits self deprives others
    Own success and others' failure is celebrated
    Rewards are limited
    Graded on a curve or ranked from "best" to "worst"

INDIVIDUALISTIC: WE ARE EACH IN THIS ALONE

Individuals work by themselves to accomplish learning goals unrelated to those of other individuals.

    Work alone
    Strive for own success
    What benefits self does not affect others
    Own success is celebrated
    Rewards are viewed as unlimited
    Evaluated by comparing performance to preset criteria

Cooperation In The Classroom, Interaction Book Company, 7208 Cornelia Drive, Edina, MN 55435, (612) 831-9500, FAX (612) 831-9332

BASIC ELEMENTS OF COOPERATIVE TEAMS

POSITIVE INTERDEPENDENCE

Team members perceive that they need each other in order to complete the group's task ("sink or swim together"). Leaders may structure positive interdependence by establishing **mutual goals** (maximize own and each other's productivity), **joint rewards** (if all group members achieve above the criteria, each will receive bonus points), **shared resources** (members have different expertise), and **assigned roles** (summarizer, encourager of participation, elaborator).

INDIVIDUAL ACCOUNTABILITY

Assessing the quality and quantity of each member's contributions and giving the results to the group and the individual.

FACE-TO-FACE PROMOTIVE INTERACTION

Team members promote each other's productivity by helping, sharing, and encouraging efforts to produce. Members explain, discuss, and teach what they know to teammates. Leaders structure teams so that members sit knee-to-knee and talk through each aspect of the tasks they are working to complete.

INTERPERSONAL AND SMALL GROUP SKILLS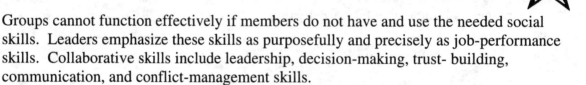

Groups cannot function effectively if members do not have and use the needed social skills. Leaders emphasize these skills as purposefully and precisely as job-performance skills. Collaborative skills include leadership, decision-making, trust- building, communication, and conflict-management skills.

GROUP PROCESSING

Groups need specific time to discuss how well they are achieving their goals and maintaining effective working relationships among members. Leaders structure group processing by assigning such tasks as (a) list at least three member actions that helped the group be successful and (b) list one action that could be added to make the group even more successful tomorrow. Leaders also monitor the groups and give feedback on how well the groups are working together.

1 : 32

Cooperation In The Classroom, Interaction Book Company, 7208 Cornelia Drive, Edina, MN 55435, (612) 831-9500, FAX (612) 831-9332

BASIC ELEMENTS OF COOPERATION

Task: Learn the five basic elements of a well-structured cooperative lesson so that you never forget them for as long as you live. For each element:
1. Read the paragraph defining it.
2. Restate its definition in your own words and write it down.
3. Rate from 1-to-10 the extent to which your group experienced the element while you completed the previous cooperative task.
4. Write down at least two things your instructor did to ensure that the element was structured into the previous cooperative task.

Cooperative: Ensure that all members complete the assignment by coming to agreement on the answers and ensuring that everyone can explain each answer. To assist in doing so, each member takes one of the following roles: Reader, Recorder, Checker.

Expected Criteria For Success: Everyone must be able to name and explain the basic elements.

Individual Accountability: One member from your group will be randomly chosen to name and explain the basic elements.

Expected Behaviors: Active participating, checking, encouraging, and elaborating by all members.

Intergroup Cooperation: Whenever it is helpful, check procedures, answers, and strategies with another group.

Your Definition	Rating	Ways It Was Structured

Cooperation In The Classroom, Interaction Book Company, 7208 Cornelia Drive, Edina, MN 55435, (612) 831-9500, FAX (612) 831-9332

COOPERATIVE LEARNING LESSON STRUCTURES

During the training sessions you will participate in a number of cooperative lessons. These lessons are generic in that they can be used daily (or at least several times a week). The cooperative lesson structures modeled in this training may be used repeatedly with any curriculum in any subject area. They are content free. During the training sessions each of these cooperative lesson structures will be modeled. They will then be explained. Your **tasks** are to:

1. Attend to the structure of the activities as well as the content.

2. For each cooperative learning structure complete the chart given below.

3. Plan how to use each cooperative learning structure in your classes. Translate each structure to make it useable with your students, curricula, and circumstances.

4. Use each cooperative lesson structure and adapt and fine-tune it until it produces the results you wish.

WHAT I LIKE ABOUT THE STRUCTURE	WHAT TO WATCH OUT FOR	WHERE AND WHEN I WILL USE IT

1 : 34

Cooperation In The Classroom, Interaction Book Company, 7208 Cornelia Drive, Edina, MN 55435, (612) 831-9500, FAX (612) 831-9332

PROBLEM SOLVING LESSON

Task: Solve each problem correctly.

Cooperative: One set of answers from the group, everyone has to agree, everyone has to be able to explain the strategies used to solve each problem.

Expected Criteria For Success: Everyone must be able to explain the strategies used to solve each problem.

Individual Accountability: One member from your group will be randomly chosen to explain (a) the answer and (b) how to solve each problem. Alternatively, use the simultaneous responding procedure of having each group member explain the group's answers to a member of another group.

Expected Behaviors: Active participating, checking, encouraging, and elaborating by all members.

Intergroup Cooperation: Whenever it is helpful, check procedures, answers, and strategies with another group.

1 : 35

Cooperation In The Classroom, Interaction Book Company, 7208 Cornelia Drive, Edina, MN 55435, (612) 831-9500, FAX (612) 831-9332

CONCEPT INDUCTION

Concept formation may be done inductively by instructing students to figure out why the examples have been placed in the different boxes. A procedure for doing so is as follows:

1. Draw two (or three) boxes on the chalkboard. Label them Box 1, Box 2, or Box 3.
2. Place one item in each box.
3. Instruct students to use the **formulate, explain, listen, create** procedure to discuss how the items are different.
4. Place another item in each box and repeat. Tell students not to say outloud to another group or the class how the items are different. Each pair must discover it.
5. Once a pair "has it," the members are to make a definition for each box. They then create new examples that may be placed in the boxes.

Tasks: Analyze the examples the teacher places in each box. Identify the concept represented by each box. Then create new examples that may be placed in the boxes.

Cooperative: Students turn to the person next to them and create an answer they can agree on. Students:
1. **Formulate** an individual answer.
2. **Share** their answer with their partner.
3. **Listen** carefully to their partner's answer.
4. **Create** a new answer that is superior to their initial formulations through the processes of association, building on each other's thoughts, and synthesizing.

Expected Criteria For Success: Each student must be able to identify the concept represented by each box.

Individual Accountability: One member from the pair will be randomly chosen to explain the answer.

Expected Behaviors: Explaining, listening, synthesizing by all members.

Assignment
Think of a concept you will teach in the near future. Script out exactly what you will say to your class in using the **Concept Induction** procedure.

Cooperation In The Classroom, Interaction Book Company, 7208 Cornelia Drive, Edina, MN 55435, (612) 831-9500, FAX (612) 831-9332

COOPERATION IN THE CLASSROOM: CHAPTER ONE SUMMARY

1. One Example Of A Group Being More Powerful Than Separate Individuals Is:

   _____

2. Give Two Reasons Why Many Teachers Fail To Utilize The Power Of Groups:

   a. _____

   b. _____

3. Define Cooperative, Competitive, And Individualistic Learning:

   Cooperative: _____

   Competitive: _____

   Individualistic: _____

4. Give three reasons based on the research why cooperative learning should be

   used:

5. Define the types of cooperative learning:

   Formal: _____

   Informal: _____

   Base Groups: _____

6. Define the five different types of groups?

   a.

   b.

   c.

   d.

   e.

1 : 37

Cooperation In The Classroom, Interaction Book Company, 7208 Cornelia Drive, Edina, MN 55435, (612) 831-9500, FAX (612) 831-9332

7. Name and define the basic elements that make cooperation work?

    a.

    b.

    c.

    d.

    e.

8. Why do collaborators need to learn how to manage conflict constructively?

9. What is the cooperative school?

Cooperation In The Classroom, Interaction Book Company, 7208 Cornelia Drive, Edina, MN 55435, (612) 831-9500, FAX (612) 831-9332

CHAPTER TWO:

THE TEACHER'S ROLE

Teacher's Role: Being "A Guide On The Side"

At age 55, after his defeat by Woodrow Wilson for President of the United States, Teddy Roosevelt took a journey to South America. The Brazilian Government suggested he lead an expedition to explore a vast, unmapped river deep in the jungle. Known as the River of Doubt, it was believed to be a tributary to the Amazon. Roosevelt accepted instantly. *"We will go down the unknown river,"* he declared, and the Brazilian government organized an expedition for the trip. *"I had to go,"* he said later, *"it was my last chance to be a boy."* Roosevelt, with his son Kermit and a party of eighteen, headed into the jungle. *"On February 27, 1914, shortly after midday, we started down the River of Doubt into the unknown,"* Roosevelt wrote. The journey was an ordeal. Hostile Indians harassed them. Five canoes were shattered and had to be rebuilt. Their food ran short and valuable equipment was lost. One man drowned when his canoe capsized. Another went berserk and killed a member of the expedition and then disappeared into the wilderness. Roosevelt, ill with fever, badly injured his leg when he tried to keep two capsized canoes from being smashed against rocks. Unable to walk, he had to be carried. Lying in a tent with an infected leg and a temperature of 105, he requested to be left behind. Ignoring such pleas, Kermit brought his father to safety with the help of the other members of the expedition. Teddy Roosevelt barely survived, but he and his companions accomplished their mission. The party mapped the 1000 mile River of Doubt and collected priceless specimens for the Museum of Natural History. The river was renamed in his honor, **Rio Theodore**.

An expedition such as Roosevelt's consists of four phases:

1. You make a series of pre-journey decisions about the number of people needed, the materials and equipment required, and the route to be taken.

2. You brief all participants on the goals and objectives of the journey, emphasize that members' survival depends on the joint efforts of all, and the behaviors you expect of members of the expedition.

3. You make the journey, carefully mapping the area traveled and collecting the targeted specimens.

Cooperation In The Classroom, Interaction Book Company, 7208 Cornelia Drive, Edina, MN 55435, (612) 831-9500, FAX (612) 831-9332

4. You report your findings to interested parties, reflect on what went right and wrong with fellow members, and write your memoirs.

Conducting a cooperative lesson is done in the same way. You, the teacher, make a number of preinstructional decisions, explain to students the instructional task and the cooperative nature of the lesson, conduct the lesson, and evaluate and process the results. More specifically, you:

1. **Make Preinstructional Decisions:** In every lesson you (a) formulate objectives, (b) decide on the size of groups, (c) choose a method for assigning students to groups, (d) decide which roles to assign group members, (e) arrange the room, and (f) arrange the materials students need to complete the assignment.

2. **Explain the Task and Cooperative Structure:** In every lesson you (a) explain the academic assignment to students, (b) explain the criteria for success, (c) structure positive interdependence, (d) explain the individual accountability, and (e) explain the behaviors you expect to see during the lesson.

3. **Monitor and Intervene:** While you (a) conduct the lesson, you (b) monitor each learning group and (c) intervene when needed to improve taskwork and teamwork, and (d) bring closure to the lesson.

4. **Evaluate and Process:** You (a) assess and evaluate the quality and quantity of student achievement, (b) ensure students carefully process the effectiveness of their learning groups, (c) have students make a plan for improvement, and (d) have students celebrate the hard work of group members.

In each class session teachers must make the choice of being "a sage on the stage" or "a guide on the side." In doing so they might remember that **the challenge in teaching is not covering the material for the students, it's uncovering the material with the students.**

The purpose of this book is to provide detailed and specific practical guidance for conducting cooperative lessons. Each chapter explains an important step in structuring cooperative learning and gives detailed practice help for implementing it.

2 : 2

Cooperation In The Classroom, Interaction Book Company, 7208 Cornelia Drive, Edina, MN 55435, (612) 831-9500, FAX (612) 831-9332

TEACHER'S ROLE

MAKE DECISIONS
Objectives
Group Size
Assign Students To Groups
Assign Roles
Arrange Room
Plan Materials

EXPLAIN TASK & COOPERATIVE STRUCTURE
Explain Academic Task
Specify Criteria For Success
Explain Positive Interdependence
Explain Individual Accountability
Specify Expected Behaviors
Structure Intergroup Cooperation

MONITOR & INTERVENE
Arrange Face-To-Face Promotive Interaction
Observe Students' Interactions
Intervene To Improve Taskwork
Intervene To Improve Teamwork
Provide Closure

ASSESS, EVALUATE, & PROCESS
Assess Student Learning
Evaluate If Appropriate
Structure Group Processing
Structure Group Celebration

2 : 3

Cooperation In The Classroom, Interaction Book Company, 7208 Cornelia Drive, Edina, MN 55435, (612) 831-9500, FAX (612) 831-9332

Preinstructional Decisions

Specifying the Instructional Objectives

The Roman philosopher Seneca once said, "*When you do not know to which port you are sailing, no wind is favorable.*" The same may be said for teaching. To plan for a lesson you must know what the lesson is aimed at accomplishing. You need to specify **academic objectives** (based on a conceptual or task analysis) and **social skills objectives** that detail what interpersonal and small group skills you wish to emphasize during the lesson. You choose social skills by:

1. Monitoring the learning groups and diagnosing the specific skills needed to solve the problems students are having in working with each other.

2. Asking students to identify social skills that would improve their teamwork.

3. Keeping a list of social skills you teach to every class. The next one on the list becomes the skill emphasized in today's lesson.

4. Analyzing what social skills are required to complete the assignment.

The most sophisticated way to determine the social skills students need to complete a lesson is through creating a flow chart. A **Flow Chart** is a simple yet powerful visual tool to display all the steps in a process. Creating a flow chart involves six steps.

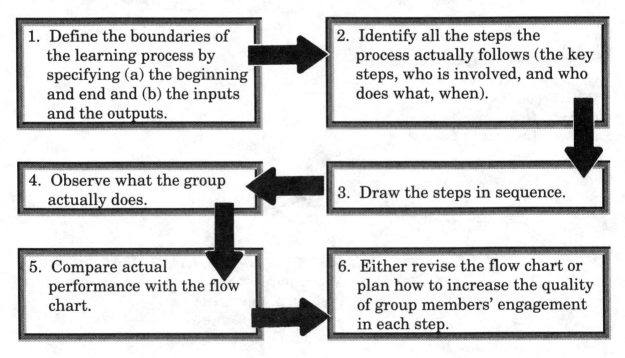

1. Define the boundaries of the learning process by specifying (a) the beginning and end and (b) the inputs and the outputs.

2. Identify all the steps the process actually follows (the key steps, who is involved, and who does what, when).

3. Draw the steps in sequence.

4. Observe what the group actually does.

5. Compare actual performance with the flow chart.

6. Either revise the flow chart or plan how to increase the quality of group members' engagement in each step.

Cooperation In The Classroom, Interaction Book Company, 7208 Cornelia Drive, Edina, MN 55435, (612) 831-9500, FAX (612) 831-9332

Deciding on the Size of the Group

There is a folk saying about snowflakes. Each snowflake is so fragile and small. But when they stick together, it is amazing what they can do. The same is true for people. When we work together, there is no limit to human ingenuity and potential. For students to work together, they must be assigned to groups. To assign students to groups, you must decide (a) how large a group should be, (b) how students should be assigned to a group, (c) how long the groups will exist, and (d) what combination of groups will be used in the lesson.

While cooperative learning groups typically range in size from two to four, **the basic rule of thumb is: "*The smaller the better*."** There is, however, no ideal size for a cooperative learning group. A common mistake is to have students work in groups of four, five, and six members before the students have the skills to do so competently. In selecting the size of a cooperative learning group, remember this advice:

> **Group Size Depends On "Team"**
>
> **T** = Time Limits
>
> **E** = Students' Experience In Working In Groups
>
> **A** = Students' Age
>
> **M** = Materials And Equipment Available

1. **With the addition of each group member, the resources to help the group succeed increase.** As the size of the learning group increases, so does (a) the range of abilities, expertise, skills, (b) the number of minds available for acquiring and processing information, and (c) the diversity of viewpoints.

2. **The shorter the period of time available, the smaller the learning group should be.** If there is only a brief period of time available for the lesson, then smaller groups such as pairs will be more effective because they take less time to get organized, they operate faster, and there is more "air time" per member.

3. **The smaller the group, the more difficult it is for students to hide and not contribute their share of the work.** Small groups increase the visibility of students' efforts and thereby make them more accountable.

4. **The larger the group, the more skillful group members must be.** In a pair, students have to manage two interactions. In a group of three, there are six interactions to manage. In a group of four, there are twelve interactions to manage. As the size of the group increases, the interpersonal and small group skills required to manage the interactions among group members become far more complex and sophisticated.

5. **The larger the group, the less the interaction among members.** What results is less group cohesion, fewer friendships, and less personal support.

Cooperation In The Classroom, Interaction Book Company, 7208 Cornelia Drive, Edina, MN 55435, (612) 831-9500, FAX (612) 831-9332

6. **The materials available or the specific nature of the task may dictate a group size.** When you have ten computers and thirty students, you may wish to assign students to groups of three. When the task is practice tennis, group size of two seems natural.

7. **The smaller the group, the easier it is to identify any difficulties students have in working together.** Problems in leadership, unresolved conflicts among group members, issues over power and control, tendencies such as sitting back and waiting for others to do the work, and other problems students have in working together are more visible and apparent when groups are small. Groups need to be small enough to ensure all students are actively involved and participating equally.

THE GROUP SIZE WHEEL

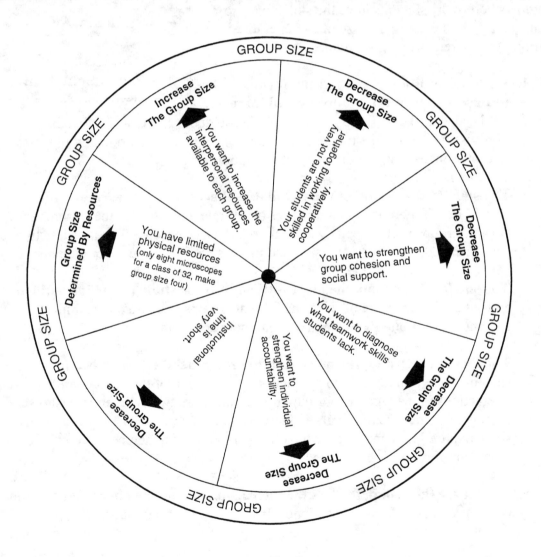

2 : 6

Cooperation In The Classroom, Interaction Book Company, 7208 Cornelia Drive, Edina, MN 55435, (612) 831-9500, FAX (612) 831-9332

Assigning Students to Groups

Sic parvis magna (Great things have small beginnings).

Sir Francis Drake's Motto

There is no ideal group membership. What determines a group's productivity is not who its members are, but rather how well the members work together. There may be times when you may use cooperative learning groups that are homogeneous in ability to teach specific skills or to achieve certain instructional objectives. Generally, however, there are advantages to heterogeneous groups in which students come from diverse backgrounds and have different abilities, experiences, and interests:

1. Students are exposed to a variety of ideas, multiple perspectives, and different problem-solving methods.

2. Students generate more cognitive disequilibrium, which stimulates learning, creativity, and cognitive and social development.

3. Students engage in more elaborative thinking, give and receive more explanations, and engage in more frequent perspective-taking in discussing material, all of which increase the depth of understanding, the quality of reasoning, and the accuracy of long-term retention.

To make groups heterogeneous, you assign students to groups using a random or stratified random procedure. Teacher selected groups can be either homogeneous or heterogeneous. When students select their own groups they usually form homogeneous ones. Each of these methods is explained below.

Random Assignment

The easiest and most effective way to assign students to group is randomly. You divide the number of students in your class by the size of the group desired. If you wish to have groups of three and you have thirty students in your class, you divide thirty by three. You have students number off by the result (e.g., ten). Students with the same number find each other (all one's get together, all two's get together, and so forth). David's favorite variation is to have students count off in a different language (e.g., English, Spanish, French, Hungarian) each time they are assigned to groups.

2 : 7

Cooperation In The Classroom, Interaction Book Company, 7208 Cornelia Drive, Edina, MN 55435, (612) 831-9500, FAX (612) 831-9332

Literature Characters

Give students cards with the names of characters in the literature they recently have read. Ask them to group with characters from the same story, play, or poem. Examples are Romeo and Juliet; Captain Hook, Peter Pan and Wendy; and Hansel, Gretel, Witch, and Step-Mother.

Geographical Areas

List a number of countries or states and have students group themselves according to most preferred to visit. Variations include grouping according to least preferred to visit, similar in terms of climate, similar in geological features, having the same exports, and so forth.

Math Method

There are endless variations to the math method of assigning students to groups. The basic structure is to give each student a math problem and ask them to (a) solve their problem, (b) find the classmates whose problems have the same answer, and (c) form a group. This may vary from simple addition in the first grade to complex equations in high school classes. Thus, to form a group of three, you may distribute the following three equations throughout the class $(3 + 3 = \_)$, $(4 + 2 = \_)$, $(5 + 1 = \_)$.

States and Capitols

To assign students to groups of two or four, divide the number of students in the class by two (30 divided by 2 = 15). Pick a geographic area of the U.S. and write out on cards the names of 15 states. Then on another set of cards write out the names of their capitol cities. Shuffle the cards and pass them out to students. Then have the students find the classmate who has the matching state or capitol. To form groups of four, have two adjacent states and their capitols combine.

Stratified Random Assignment

A related procedure is stratified random assignment. This is the same as random assignment except that you choose one (or two) characteristics of students (such as reading level, learning style, task-orientation, or personal interest) and make sure that one or more students in each group have that characteristic. To assign students to learning groups randomly, stratifying for achievement level, use the following procedure.

1. Rank order students from highest to lowest in terms of a pretest on the unit, a recent past test, past grades, or your best guess as a teacher.

2. Select the first group by choosing the highest student, the lowest student, and the two middle achievers. Assign them to the group unless they are all of one sex, they do not reflect the ethnic composition of the class, they are worst enemies, or

Cooperation In The Classroom, Interaction Book Company, 7208 Cornelia Drive, Edina, MN 55435, (612) 831-9500, FAX (612) 831-9332

they are best friends. If any of these is true, move up or down one student from the middle to readjust. (You may modify the procedure to assign students to groups of three or two members.)

3. Select the remaining groups by repeating the above procedure with the reduced list. If there are students left over, make one or two groups of three members.

There is a danger in assigning students to groups on the basis of certain characteristics. If you form groups so that there is a white male, a white female, a black male, and a black female in every group, for example, you are giving the class a clear message that gender and ethnicity are important factors to you as a teacher. Making these categories salient may cue students' stereotypes and prejudices. **The general rule is: If you assign students to groups based on categories, make them unique categories needed to complete the group task** (such as summarizer, creative thinker, time keeper, and library expert). As a teacher, you tell students, "*In your groups there is a creative thinker, a person who is good at keeping track of time, someone who knows how to use the library, and someone who is good at summarizing all the ideas suggested in the group. To complete this assignment, you will need the resources of each member.*" By emphasizing the personal abilities and talents of students rather than their social categories, you focus students on the person, not the social group.

Preferences

Have students write their favorite sport to participate in on a slip of paper. Then have them find groupmates who like to participate in the same sport. Variations include favorite food, celebrity, skill, car, president, animal, vegetable, fairy tale character, and so forth.

Teacher Selected Groups

You, the teacher, can decide who is going to work with whom. You can ensure that nonachievement-oriented students are a minority in each group or that students who trigger disruptive behavior in each other are not together. **One of our favorite methods is creating support groups for each isolated student.** You ask students to list three classmates with whom they would like to work. From their lists, you tally for each student the number of times classmates chose the student. You can then identify the classroom isolates (students who are not chosen by any of their classmates). These are the "at-risk" students who need your help. You take the most socially isolated student and assign two of the most skillful, popular, supportive, and caring students in the class to work with him or her. Then you take the second most isolated student and do the same. In this way you optimize the likelihood that the isolated students will become involved in the learning activities and build positive relationships with classmates. You want to ensure that in your classes, no student is left out, rejected, or believes that he or she does not belong.

Cooperation In The Classroom, Interaction Book Company, 7208 Cornelia Drive, Edina, MN 55435, (612) 831-9500, FAX (612) 831-9332

Self-Selected Groups

The least recommended procedure is to have students select their own groups. Student-selected groups often are homogeneous with high-achieving students working with other high-achieving students, white students working with other white students, minority students working with other minority students, and males working with other males. Often there is more off-task behavior in student-selected than in teacher-selected groups. A useful modification of the "select your own group" method is to have students list whom they would like to work with and then place them in a learning group with one person they choose and one or two or more students that the teacher selects.

For additional methods for assigning students to groups as well as a variety of team-building and warm-up activities see R. Johnson and Johnson (1985).

Length Of Group Life

A common concern is, "*How long should cooperative learning groups stay together?*" The type of cooperative learning group you use determines one answer to this question. Base groups last for at least one and ideally for several years. Informal cooperative learning groups last for only a few minutes or at most one class period. For formal cooperative learning groups there is no formula or simple answer to this question. Groups usually stay together to complete a task, unit, or chapter. During a course every student should work with every other classmate. Groups should stay together long enough to be successful. Breaking up groups that are having trouble functioning effectively is often counterproductive; students do not have the opportunity to learn the skills they need to resolve problems in collaborating with each other.

Using Combinations Of Cooperative Learning Groups

In many lessons you will want to use a combination of formal and informal cooperative learning groups as well as base groups. You will use more than one size group in any one lesson. You will need ways to assign students to new groups quickly. You will need procedures for making transitions among groups, moving students from pairs to fours to pairs to threes and so forth. It sometimes helps to have timed drills on how fast students can move from a formal cooperative learning group to an informal pair and then back to their formal group.

Assigning Roles to Ensure Interdependence

In planning the lesson, you think through what are the actions that need to occur to maximize student learning. **Roles** prescribe what other group members expect from a student (and therefore what the student is obligated to do) and what that person has a

Cooperation In The Classroom, Interaction Book Company, 7208 Cornelia Drive, Edina, MN 55435, (612) 831-9500, FAX (612) 831-9332

right to expect from other group members who have complementary roles. There is a progression for using roles to structure cooperative efforts:

1. Do not assign roles to let students get used to working together.

2. Assign only very simple roles to students such as forming roles or the roles of reader, recorder, and encourager of participation. Rotate the roles so that each group member plays each one several times.

3. Add to the rotation a new role that is slightly more sophisticated, such as checker-for-understanding. You assign the functioning roles at this point.

5. Over time add formulating and fermenting roles that do not occur naturally in the group, such as elaborator. Students typically do not relate what they are learning to what they already know until you specifically train them to do so.

IDENTIFYING THE VARIOUS TYPES OF ROLES

Form a pair. For each type of skill there are two examples of the roles that may be assigned to ensure students work together effectively. In column one, write the letters of the two roles that teach the skill.

	SKILLS	ROLES
	Forming Skills	a. Encouraging everyone to participate
		b. Use quiet voices
	Functioning Skills	c. Relating new learning to previous learning
		d. Criticizing ideas, not people
	Formulating Skills	e. Stay with your group
		f. Changing mind only if logically persuaded
	Fermenting Skills	g. Explaining step-by-step one's reasoning
		h. Giving one's ideas and conclusions

Cooperation In The Classroom, Interaction Book Company, 7208 Cornelia Drive, Edina, MN 55435, (612) 831-9500, FAX (612) 831-9332

TABLE 2.1 EXAMPLES OF ROLES APPROPRIATE FOR EACH AGE LEVEL

Category	Role	Primary	Intermediate	Secondary
Forming	Turn-Taking Monitor	First You, Then Me	Take Turns	Contribute In Sequence
Functioning	Recorder	Writer	Recorder	Scribe
	Encourager Of Participation	Say Nice Things	Give Positive Comments	Compliment
	Clarifier, Paraphraser	Now You Say It	Say It In Your Own Words	Paraphrase
	Consensus Seeker	Everyone Agree	Reach Agreement	Reach Consensus
Formulating	Summarizer	Put Together	Combine	Summarize
	Generator	Give Another Answer	Give Additional Answers	Generate Alternative Answers
Fermenting	Asker For Justification	Ask Why	Ask For Reasons	Ask For Justification
	Rationale Giver	Say Why	Give Facts And Reasons	Explain

One of the challenges in using cooperative learning is to describe group roles in an age-appropriate way. How you describe a role to primary students obviously needs to be different from the way you describe the role to high school students. Examples of the ways roles are renamed to make them age appropriate may be found in Table 2.1.

Roles can be sequenced so that more and more complex and difficult roles are assigned to students each week, month, and year. Initially, students may need to be assigned roles that help them form the group. Second, roles may be assigned that help the group function well in achieving learning goals and maintaining good working relationships among members. Third, roles may be assigned that help students formulate what they

2 : 12

Cooperation In The Classroom, Interaction Book Company, 7208 Cornelia Drive, Edina, MN 55435, (612) 831-9500, FAX (612) 831-9332

are learning and create conceptual frameworks. Finally, roles may be assigned that help students ferment each other's thinking. It is at this point that cognitive and social roles merge. The social skills represented by the roles should be taught like a spiral curriculum with a more complex version of the skill taught every year.

Solving And Preventing Problems In Working Together

At times there are students who refuse to participate in a cooperative group or who do not understand how to help the group succeed. You can solve and prevent such problems when you give each group member a specific role to play in the group. Assigning appropriate roles may be used to:

1. Reduce problems such as one or more members' making no contribution to the group or one member dominating the group.

2. Ensure that vital group skills are enacted in the group and that group members learn targeted skills.

3. Create interdependence among group members. You structure **role interdependence** by assigning each member complementary and interconnected roles.

Arranging the Room

The design and arrangement of classroom space and furniture communicates what is appropriate behavior and what learning activities will take place. Desks in a row communicate a different message and expectation than desks grouped in small circles. Spatial design also defines the circulation patterns in the classroom. **Circulation** is the flow of movement into, out of, and within the classroom. It is movement through space. You determine what students see, when they see it, and with whom students interact by the way you design your classroom.

No single classroom arrangement will meet the requirements of all lessons. Reference points and well-defined boundaries of work spaces are needed to move students from rows to triads to pairs to fours to rows. Color, form, and lighting (a) focus students' visual attention on points of emphasis in the classroom (the learning group, you, instructional materials) and (b) define the territorial boundaries of workspaces. You define boundaries by:

1. **Using labels and signs** that designate areas.

2. **Using colors** to attract visual attention and define group and individual spaces as well as different storage areas and resource centers.

2 : 13

Cooperation In The Classroom, Interaction Book Company, 7208 Cornelia Drive, Edina, MN 55435, (612) 831-9500, FAX (612) 831-9332

IMPORTANCE OF CLASSROOM DESIGN

Form a pair. Rank order the following outcomes of classroom design from most important ("1") to least important ("9").

	Students' academic achievement. The way in which interior space is designed influences the amount of time students spend on task and other variables affecting achievement.
	Students' visual and auditory focus. The way in which interior space is designed creates overall visual order, focuses visual attention, and controls acoustics.
	Students' participation in learning groups and activities. Classroom design influences the patterns of student (and teacher) participation in instructional activities, the emergence of leadership in learning groups, and the patterns of communication among students and between students and teachers.
	Opportunities for social contact and friendships among students.
	Learning climate. The design of interior space affects students and teachers' feelings (such as comfort, enjoyment, well-being, anger, depression) and general morale. Good spatial definition helps students feel secure by delineating structured learning areas.
	Classroom management. Spatial definition prevents discipline problems by defining how and where students work, how to interact with others, and how to move through the classroom.
	Students ease of access to each other, teachers, learning materials.
	Students ability to make quick transitions from one grouping to another.
	Teachers movement from group to group to monitor student interaction carefully during the lesson.

3. **Taping lines** on the floor or wall to define the different work areas.

4. **Using mobiles and forms** (such as arrows) taped on the wall or hanging from the ceiling to direct attention. You can designate work areas by hanging mobiles from the ceiling.

5. **Using lighting** to define specific work areas. Directed light (illuminating part of the room while leaving other areas dim) intensifies and directs students' attention. Brightly lit areas can draw people toward the areas and suggest activity. More

Cooperation In The Classroom, Interaction Book Company, 7208 Cornelia Drive, Edina, MN 55435, (612) 831-9500, FAX (612) 831-9332

dimly lit areas surrounding the lighted ones become area boundaries. As the activity in the classroom changes, the lighting could also change.

6. **Moving furniture** to define work and resource areas. Even tall plants, when placed in pots with wheels, can be moved to provide spatial boundaries.

7. **Displaying group work** to designate work spaces. If a cooperative group is to remain together for a period of several days or weeks, members may wish to build a poster or collage that designates their work area.

You can use many of these same procedures to control acoustically levels of noise in the classroom.

Planning the Instructional Materials

The types of task students are required to complete determine what materials are needed for the lesson. You, the teacher, decide how materials are to be arranged and distributed among group members to maximize their participation and achievement. Usually, you will wish to distribute materials to communicate that the assignment is to be a joint (not an individual) effort. You create:

1. **Materials interdependence** by giving each group only one copy of the materials. The students will then have to work together in order to be successful. This is especially effective the first few times the group meets. After students are accustomed to working cooperatively, teachers can give a copy of the materials to each student.

2. **Information interdependence** by arranging materials like a jigsaw puzzle so that each student has part of the materials needed to complete the assignment. Each group member can receive different books or resource materials to be synthesized. Such procedures require that every member participate in order for the group to be successful.

3. **Interdependence from outside enemies** by structuring materials into an intergroup tournament format and having groups compete to see who has learned the most. Such a procedure was introduced by DeVries and Edwards (1973). In the Teams-Games-Tournament format, students are divided into heterogeneous cooperative learning teams to prepare members for a tournament in which they compete with the other teams. During the intergroup competition the students individually compete against members of about the same ability level from other teams. The team whose members do the best in the competition is pronounced the winner by the teacher.

Cooperation In The Classroom, Interaction Book Company, 7208 Cornelia Drive, Edina, MN 55435, (612) 831-9500, FAX (612) 831-9332

Explaining The Task: Flow chart

1. Explain the assignment. The assignment needs to be a clear, measurable task.

2. Explain lesson objectives to ensure transfer and retention. Objectives may be stated as outcomes--*"At the end of this lesson you will be able to explain the causes of the French and Indian War."*

4. Explain the procedures students are to follow in completing the assignment.

3. Explain the concepts, principles, and strategies students need to use during the lesson and relate them to students' past experience and learning.

5. Require a visible product that each student signs. This keeps students on task and helps ensure they will behave responsibly.

6. Ask class members specific questions to check their understanding of the assignment.

7. Ask students to answer in pairs or triads the questions the lesson will focus on to (a) establish expectations about what the lesson will cover and (b) organize in advance what they know about the topic.

2 : 16

Cooperation In The Classroom, Interaction Book Company, 7208 Cornelia Drive, Edina, MN 55435, (612) 831-9500, FAX (612) 831-9332

Structuring The Task And Cooperative Structure

Explaining the Academic Task

At this point you have planned your lesson by making the preinstructional decisions and preparations. The next step is to face your class and inform them of (a) what to do to complete the assignment and (b) how to do it. The steps are explained on the flow chart on the previous page.

Explaining Criteria for Success

While explaining to students the academic task they are to complete, you need to communicate the level of performance you expect of students. Cooperative learning requires criterion-based evaluation. **Criterion-referenced or categorical judgments** are made by adopting a fixed set of standards and judging the achievement of each student against these standards. A common version of criterion-referenced grading involves assigning letter grades on the

Grade	Percent Correct
A	95 – 100
B	85 – 94
C	75 – 84
D	65 – 74
F	Less Than 64

basis of the percentage of test items answered correctly. Or you might say, *"The group is not finished until every member has demonstrated mastery."* Sometimes improvement (doing better this week than one did last week) may be set as the criterion of excellence. To promote intergroup cooperation, you may also set criteria for the whole class to reach. *"If we as a class can score over 520 words correct on our vocabulary test, each student will receive two bonus points."*

Structuring Positive Interdependence

Positive goal interdependence exists when a mutually/joint goal is established so that individuals perceive they can attain their goals if and only if their groupmates attain their goals (see Johnson & Johnson, 1992b, 1992c). Members know that they cannot succeed unless all other members of their group succeed. Positive interdependence is the heart of cooperative learning. Without positive interdependence, cooperation does not exist. Students must believe that they are in a "sink or swim together" learning situation. Positive interdependence will be discussed in detail in Chapter Four.

First, you structure positive goal interdependence. Every cooperative lesson begins with positive goal interdependence. To ensure that students think "**We, not me**" you (the teacher) say to students, *"You have three responsibilities. You are responsible for learning the assigned material. You are responsible for making sure that all other members of your group learn the assigned material. And you are responsible for making sure that all other class members successfully learn the assigned material."*

Cooperation In The Classroom, Interaction Book Company, 7208 Cornelia Drive, Edina, MN 55435, (612) 831-9500, FAX (612) 831-9332

Second, you supplement positive goal interdependence with other types of positive interdependence (such as reward, role, resource, or identity). Positive reward interdependence, for example, may be structured through providing group rewards--*"If all members of your group score above 90 percent on the test, each of you will receive five bonus points."* Usually, the more ways positive interdependence is structured in a lesson, the better.

Positive interdependence creates peer encouragement and support for learning. Such positive peer pressure influences underachieving students to become academically involved. Members of cooperative learning groups should give two interrelated messages, *"Do your work--we're counting on you!"* and *"How can I help you to do better?"*

Structuring Individual Accountability

In cooperative groups, everyone has to do his or her fair share of the work. **An underlying purpose of cooperative learning is to make each group member a stronger individual in his or her own right.** This is accomplished by holding all members accountable to learn the assigned material and help other group members learn. You do this by:

1. Assessing the performance of each individual member.

2. Giving the results back to the individual and the group to compare to preset criteria. The feedback enables members to (a) recognize and celebrate efforts to learn and contributions to groupmates' learning, (b) provide immediate remediation and any needed assistance or encouragement, and (c) reassign responsibilities to avoid any redundant efforts by members.

Individual accountability results in group members knowing they cannot "hitch-hike" on the work of others, loaf, or get a free ride. **Ways of ensuring individual accountability** include keeping group size small, giving an individual test to each student, giving random individual oral examinations, observing and recording the frequency with which each member contributes to the group's work, having students teach what they know to someone else, and having students use what they have learned on different problems.

Structuring Intergroup Cooperation

You can extend the positive outcomes resulting from cooperative learning throughout a whole class by structuring intergroup cooperation. You establish class goals as well as group and individual goals. When a group finishes its work, you encourage members to find other groups (a) who are not finished and help them understand how to complete the assignment successfully or (b) who are finished and compare answers and strategies.

Cooperation In The Classroom, Interaction Book Company, 7208 Cornelia Drive, Edina, MN 55435, (612) 831-9500, FAX (612) 831-9332

Specifying Desired Behaviors

When you use cooperative learning you must teach students the small group and interpersonal skills they need to work effectively with each other. In cooperative learning groups, students must learn both academic subject matter (**taskwork**) and the interpersonal and small group skills required to work as part of a group (**teamwork**). Cooperative learning is inherently more complex than competitive or individualistic learning because students have to simultaneously engage in taskwork and teamwork. If students do not learn the teamwork skills, then they cannot complete the taskwork. The greater the members' teamwork skills, the higher will be the quality and quantity of their learning. **You define the needed teamwork skills operationally by specifying the behaviors that are appropriate and desirable within learning groups.** How to do so is discussed at length in Chapter Five.

Three rules-of-thumb in specifying desired behaviors are as follows. **Be specific.** Operationally define each social skill through the use of a "T-Chart" (see Chapter 5). **Start small.** Do not overload your students with more social skills than they can learn at one time. One or two behaviors to emphasize for a few lessons is enough. Students need to know what behavior is appropriate and desirable within a cooperative learning group, but they should not be subjected to information overload. **Emphasize overlearning.** Having students practice skills once or twice is not enough. Keep emphasizing a skill until the students have integrated it into their behavioral repertoires and do it automatically and habitually.

The Cooperative Lesson

During the lesson students work together to complete the assignment. Their actions can be loosely or highly prescribed by explicit scripts (Johnson & Johnson, 1991). At the highest level of implementation you (the teacher) learn an **expert system** consisting of the five basic elements and the teacher's role and use it to create lessons uniquely tailored for your students, curriculum, needs, and teaching circumstances. Expertise in using cooperative learning is based on a conceptual, metacognitive understanding of its nature.

Besides implementing an expert system, there are other ways to implement cooperative lessons. **Group investigation** (Sharan & Hertz-Lazarowitz, 1980), in which students form cooperative groups according to common interests in a topic. All group members help plan how to research their topic. Then they divide the work. Each group member carries out his or her part of the investigation. The group synthesizes its work and presents these findings to the class.

You may use highly structured scripts, structures, and curriculum packages that are implemented in a prescribed lockstep manner. Dansereau (1985) and his colleagues have

Cooperation In The Classroom, Interaction Book Company, 7208 Cornelia Drive, Edina, MN 55435, (612) 831-9500, FAX (612) 831-9332

developed a number of **cooperative scripts** that structure student interaction as they work together. Kagan (1988) has identified a number of **cooperative learning structures**--ways of organizing the interaction of students by prescribing student behavior step-by-step to complete the assignment. **Cooperative curriculum packages** include Teams-Games-Tournament (TGT), a combination of ingroup cooperation, intergroup competition, and instructional games (DeVries & Edwards, 1974). Students then meet in cooperative learning teams of four or five members (a mixture of high, medium, and low achievers) to complete a set of worksheets on the lesson. Students then play academic games as representatives of their teams. Who competes with whom is modified each week to ensure that students compete with classmates who achieve at a similar level. The highest scoring teams are publicly recognized in a weekly class newsletter. Grades are given on the basis of individual performance. **Student Team Learning** (STAD) (Slavin, 1980) is a modification of TGT that has students take a weekly quiz instead of playing an academic game. **Team-Assisted-Individualization** (TAI) is a highly individualized math curriculum for grades 3 to 6 in which students work individualistically to complete math assignments using self-instructional (programmed learning) curriculum materials (Slavin, 1985). **Cooperative Integrated Reading And Composition** (CIRC) consists of a set of curriculum materials to supplement basal readers and ensure that cooperative learning is applied to reading, writing, spelling, and language mechanics (Stevens, Madden, Slavin, & Farnish, 1987).

During the lesson students work together to complete the assignment. Using cooperative learning effectively is an art based on engineering lessons so that they include the five basic elements. There are, however, standard procedures that can be used over and over again that provide a pattern and flow to classroom life. A class session, for example, can include the following cooperative procedures:

1. Checking homework.

2. Engaging in discussions.

3. Taking notes.

4. Reading assigned material (Read and Explain Pairs, Reading Comprehension Triads, Jigsaw).

5. Drilling and reviewing.

6. Writing compositions.

7. Resolving intellectual conflicts.

8. Conducting projects.

2 : 20

Cooperation In The Classroom, Interaction Book Company, 7208 Cornelia Drive, Edina, MN 55435, (612) 831-9500, FAX (612) 831-9332

CHECKING HOMEWORK

Task: Students are to bring their completed homework to class and understand how to do it correctly.

Cooperative: Students meet in their cooperative base groups that are heterogeneous in terms of math and reading ability to ensure that all group members understand how to complete all parts of the assignment correctly.

Procedure:

1. At the beginning of class students meet in cooperative base groups.

2. One member of each group, **the runner**, goes to the teacher's desk, picks up the group's folder, and hands out any materials in the folder to the appropriate members.

3. The group reviews the assignment step-by-step to determine how much of the assignment each member completed and how well each member understands how to complete the material covered. Two roles are utilized: **Explainer** (explains step-by-step how the homework is correctly completed) and **accuracy checker** (verifies that the explanation is accurate, encourages, and provides coaching if needed). The role of explainer is rotated so that each member takes turns explaining step-by-step how a portion of the homework is correctly completed. The other members are accuracy checkers. The base groups concentrate on clarifying the parts of the assignment that one or more members do not understand.

4. At the end of the review the runner records how much of the assignment each member completed, places members' homework in the group's folder, and returns the folder to the teacher's desk.

Expected Criteria For Success: All group members understand how to complete each part of the assignment correctly.

Individual Accountability: Regular examinations and daily randomly selecting group members to explain how to solve randomly selected problems from the homework.

Alternative Of Directed Homework Review: Students are assigned to pairs. Teacher randomly picks questions from the homework assignment. One student explains step-by-step the correct answer. The other student listens, checks for accuracy, and prompts the explainer if he or she does not know the answer. Roles are switched for each question.

Cooperation In The Classroom, Interaction Book Company, 7208 Cornelia Drive, Edina, MN 55435, (612) 831-9500, FAX (612) 831-9332

TURN TO YOUR NEIGHBOR SUMMARIES

A common practice in most classrooms is to hold a "whole-class discussion." You choose one student or a student volunteers to answer a question or provide a summary of what the lesson has covered so far. The student doing the explaining has an opportunity to clarify and extend what he or she knows through being actively involved in the learning process. The rest of the class is passive. You (the teacher) may ensure that all students are actively learning (and no one is passive) by requiring all students to explain their answers or to summarize simultaneously through the formulate, share, listen, and create procedure.

1. The task for students is to explain their answers and reasoning to a classmate and practice the skill of explaining. The cooperative goal is to create a joint answer that both members agree to and can explain.

2. **Students formulate an answer to a question** that requires them to summarize what the lesson has covered so far.

3. Students turn to a neighbor (classmate class by) and share their answers and reasoning.

4. **Students listen carefully to their partner's explanation.** They should take notes, nod their head, smile, and encourage their partner to explain the answer and reasoning in detail.

5. **The pair creates a new answer that is superior to their initial formulations** through the processes of association, building on each other's thoughts, and synthesizing.

6. The teacher monitors the pairs and assists students in following the procedure. To ensure individual accountability, you may wish to ask randomly selected students to explain the joint answer they created with their partner.

FORMULATE, SHARE, LISTEN, CREATE

2 : 22

Cooperation In The Classroom, Interaction Book Company, 7208 Cornelia Drive, Edina, MN 55435, (612) 831-9500, FAX (612) 831-9332

READ AND EXPLAIN PAIRS

Whenever you give material to students to read, students may read it more effectively in cooperative pairs than individually.

1. Assign students to pairs (one high reader and one low reader in each pair. Tell students what specific pages you wish them to read. The **expected criterion for success** is that both members are able to explain the meaning of the assigned material correctly.

2. The **task** is to learn the material being read by establishing the meaning of each paragraph and integrating the meaning of the paragraphs. The cooperative goal is for both members to agree on the meaning of each paragraph, formulate a joint summary, and be able to explain its meaning to the teacher.

3. The **procedure** the student pairs follow is:

   a. Read all the headings to get an overview.

   b. Both students silently read the first paragraph. Student A is initially the **summarizer** and Student Be is the **accuracy checker**. Students rotate the roles after each paragraph.

   c. The **summarizer** summarizes in his or her own words the content of the paragraph to his or her partner.

   d. The **accuracy checker** listens carefully, corrects any misstatements, and adds anything left out. Then he or she tells how the material relates to something they already know.

   e. The students move on to the next paragraph, switch roles, and repeat the procedure. They continue until they have read all the assignment. They summarize and agree on the overall meaning of the assigned material.

4. During the lesson you (the teacher) systematically (a) monitor each reading pair and assist students in following the procedure, (b) ensure **individual accountability** by randomly asking students to summarize what they have read so far, and (c) remind students that there is **intergroup cooperation** (whenever it is helpful they may check procedures, answers, and strategies with another group or compare answers with those of another group if they finish early).

2 : 23

Cooperation In The Classroom, Interaction Book Company, 7208 Cornelia Drive, Edina, MN 55435, (612) 831-9500, FAX (612) 831-9332

READING COMPREHENSION TRIADS

Tasks:

1. Read the (poem, chapter, story, handout) and answer the questions.
2. Practice the skill of checking.

Cooperative:

1. One set of answers from the group, everyone has to agree, everyone has to be able to explain each answer.
2. If all members score 90 percent or better on the test, each member will receive 5 bonus points.
3. To facilitate the group's work, each member is assigned a role: Reader, recorder, checker.

Expected Criteria For Success: Everyone must be able to answer each question correctly.

Individual Accountability:

1. One member from your group will be randomly chosen to explain the group's answers.
2. A test will be given on the assigned reading that each member takes individually.
3. Each group member will be required to explain the group's answers to a member of another group.

Expected Behaviors: Active participating, checking, encouraging, and elaborating by all members.

Intergroup Cooperation: Whenever it is helpful, check procedures, answers, and strategies with another group. When you are finished, compare your answers with those of another group and discuss.

Cooperation In The Classroom, Interaction Book Company, 7208 Cornelia Drive, Edina, MN 55435, (612) 831-9500, FAX (612) 831-9332

JIGSAW PROCEDURE

Whenever there is material you wish to present to a class or you wish students to read, the jigsaw method is an alternative to lecture and individual reading. You assign students to cooperative groups, give all groups the same topic, and take the material and divide it into parts like a jigsaw puzzle so that each student has part of the materials needed to complete the assignment. You give each member one unique section of the topic to learn and then teach to the other members of the group. Members study the topic and teach their part to the rest of the group. The group synthesizes the presentations of the members into the whole picture. In studying the life of Sojourner Truth (a black abolitionist and women's rights activist), for example, you give one student material on Truth's childhood, another material on her middle life, and another material on the final years of her life. Group members, therefore, cannot learn her total life unless all members teach their parts. In a jigsaw each student then has to participate actively in order for his or her group to be successful. The **task** for students is to learn all the assigned material. The **cooperative goal** is for each member to ensure that everyone in their group learn all the assigned material. The **Jigsaw Procedure** is as follows:

1. **Cooperative Groups:** Assign students to cooperative groups (you usually use groups of three, but you may jigsaw materials for groups of any size). Distribute a set of materials to each group so that each group gets one part of the materials. The set needs to be divisible into the number of members of the group. Number each part (Part 1, Part 2, Part 3).

2. **Preparation Pairs:** Ask students to form a preparation pair with a member of another group who has the same part they do (a pair of Part 1's, a pair of Part 2's, a pair of Part 3's). Students have two tasks:

   a. Learning and becoming an expert on their part of the lesson materials.

   b. Planning how to teach their part of the material to the other members of their groups.

   Students are to read their part of the material together, using the pair reading procedure of (a) both students silently read each paragraph (or "chunk"), (b) one student summarizes its meaning while the other student checks the summary for accuracy, and (c) the students reverse roles after each paragraph. In doing so pair members should list the major points they wish to teach, list practical advice related to major points, prepare a visual aid to help them teach the content, and prepare procedures to make the other members of their group active, not passive, learners. The **cooperative goal** is to create one teaching plan for the two members that both members are able to teach. Both members need their individual copy of the plan.

3. **Practice Pairs:** Ask students to form a practice pair with a member of another group who has the same part they do but who was in a different preparation pair. The **tasks** are for the members to practice teaching their part of the assigned material, listen carefully the their partner's practice, and incorporate the best ideas from the other's presentation into their own. The **cooperative goal** is to ensure that both members are practiced and ready to teach.

4. **Cooperative Groups:** Students return to their cooperative groups. Their tasks are to:

    a. Teach their area of expertise to the other group members.

    b. Learn the material being taught by the other members.

    The **cooperative goal** is to ensure that members master all parts of the assigned material.

5. **Monitoring:** While the pairs and the cooperative groups work, you systematically move from group to group and assist students in following the procedures.

6. **Evaluation:** Assess students' degree of mastery of all the material by giving a test on all the material that students take individually. You may wish to give members of groups whose members all score 90 percent or above five bonus points.

2 : 26

Cooperation In The Classroom, Interaction Book Company, 7208 Cornelia Drive, Edina, MN 55435, (612) 831-9500, FAX (612) 831-9332

DRILL-REVIEW PAIRS

There are times during a lesson that you may wish to have students review what they have previously learned and drill on certain procedures to ensure that they are overlearned. When you do so, cooperative learning is indispensable.

Task: Correctly solve the problems or engage in the procedures.

Cooperative: The mutual goal is to ensure that both pair members understand the strategies and procedures required to solve the problems correctly. The teacher assigns two roles: *Explainer* (explains step-by-step how to solve the problem) and *accuracy checker* (verifies that the explanation is accurate, encourages, and provides coaching if needed). Students rotate the two roles after each problem.

Individual Accountability: The teacher randomly chooses one member to explain how to solve a randomly selected problem.

Procedure: The teacher assigns (a) students to pairs and (b) assigns each pair to a foursome. The teacher then implements the following procedure:

1. Person A reads the problem and explains step-by-step the procedures and strategies required to solve it. Person B checks the accuracy of the solution and provides encouragement and coaching.

2. Person B solves the second problem, describing step-by-step the procedures and strategies required to solve it. Person A checks the accuracy of the solution and provides encouragement and coaching.

3. When the pair completes the problems, members check their answers with another pair. If they do not agree, they resolve the problem until there is consensus about the answer. If they do agree, they thank each other and continue work in their pairs.

4. The procedure continues until all problems are completed.

2 : 27

Cooperation In The Classroom, Interaction Book Company, 7208 Cornelia Drive, Edina, MN 55435, (612) 831-9500, FAX (612) 831-9332

COOPERATIVE WRITING AND EDITING PAIRS

When your lesson includes students writing an essay, report, poem, story, or review of what they have read, you should use cooperative writing and editing pairs.

Tasks: Write a composition and edit other students' compositions.

Criteria For Success: A well-written composition by each student. Depending on the instructional objectives, the compositions may be evaluated for grammar, punctuation, organization, content, or other criteria set by the teacher.

Cooperative Goal: All group members must verify that each member's composition is perfect according to the criteria set by the teacher. Students receive an individual score on the quality of their compositions. You can also give a group score based on the total number of errors made by the pair (the number of errors in their composition plus the number of errors in their partner's composition).

Individual Accountability: Each student writes his or her own composition.

Procedure:

1. The teacher assigns students to pairs with at least one good reader in each pair.

2. Student A describes to Student B what he or she is planning to write. Student B listens carefully, probes with a set of questions, and outlines Student A's composition. The written outline is given to Student A.

3. This procedure is reversed with Student B describing what he or she is going to write and Student A listening and completing an outline of Student B's composition, which is then given to Student B.

4. The students research individualistically the material they need to write their compositions, keeping an eye out for material useful to their partner.

5. The two students work together to write the first paragraph of each composition. This ensures that both have a clear start on their compositions.

Cooperation In The Classroom, Interaction Book Company, 7208 Cornelia Drive, Edina, MN 55435, (612) 831-9500, FAX (612) 831-9332

6. The students write their compositions individualistically.

7. When completed, the students proofread each other's compositions, making corrections in capitalization, punctuation, spelling, language usage, topic sentence usage, and other aspects of writing specified by the teacher. Students also give each other suggestions for revision.

8. The students revise their compositions, making all of the suggested revisions.

9. The two students then reread each other's compositions and sign their names (indicating that they guarantee that no errors exist in the composition).

While the students work, the teacher monitors the pairs, intervening where appropriate to help students master the needed writing and cooperative skills. When students complete their compositions, students discuss how effectively they worked together (listing the specific actions they engaged in to help each other), plan what behaviors they are going to emphasize in the next writing pair, and thank each other for the help and assistance received.

COOPERATIVE NOTE-TAKING PAIRS

The notes students take during a lesson are important in understanding what a student learns, both during the lesson and during reviews of the lesson. Most students, however, take notes very incompletely because of low working memory capacities, the information processing load required, and lack of skills in note taking. Students can benefit from learning how to take better notes and how to review notes more effectively.

1. You assign students to note-taking pairs. The **task** is to focus on increasing the quantity and quality of the notes taken during a lesson. The **cooperative goal** is for both students to generate a comprehensive set of accurate notes that will enable them to learn and review the material covered in the lesson.

2. Every ten minutes or so, you stop the lesson and have students hare their notes. Student A summarizes his or her notes to Student B. Student B summarizes his or her notes to Student A. Each pair member must take something from their partner's notes to improve his or her own notes.

Cooperation In The Classroom, Interaction Book Company, 7208 Cornelia Drive, Edina, MN 55435, (612) 831-9500, FAX (612) 831-9332

ACADEMIC CONTROVERSIES

Creating intellectual conflict (**controversy**) to improve academic learning is one of the most powerful and important instructional tools (Johnson & Johnson, 1995c). Academic controversies require a cooperative context and are actually an advanced form of cooperative learning. The basic format for structuring academic controversies is as follows.

1. Choose a topic that has content manageable by the students and on which at least two well-documented positions (pro and con) can be prepared. Organize the instructional materials into pro and con packets. Students need to know what their position is and where to find relevant information so they can build the rationale underlying the pro or con position on the issue.

2. Assign students to groups of four. Divide each group into two pairs. Assign pro and con positions to the pairs. A good reader or researcher should be in each pair.

3. Assign each pair the **tasks** of (a) learning its position and the supporting arguments and information, (b) researching all information relevant to its position (giving the opposing pair any information found supporting the opposing position), (c) preparing a series of persuasive arguments to support its position, and (d) preparing a persuasive presentation to be given to the opposing pair. Give students the following instructions:

   "Plan with your partner how to advocate your position effectively. Read the materials supporting your position. Find more information in the library reference books to support your position. Plan a persuasive presentation. Make sure you and your partner master the information supporting your assigned position and present it in a persuasive and complete way so that the other group members will comprehend and learn the information."

4. Highlight the **cooperative goals** of reaching a consensus on the issue, mastering all the information relevant to both sides of the issue (measure by a test taken individually), and writing a quality group report on which all members will be evaluated. Note that each group member will receive five bonus points if all members score 90 percent or better on the test covering both sides of the issue.

2 : 30

Cooperation In The Classroom, Interaction Book Company, 7208 Cornelia Drive, Edina, MN 55435, (612) 831-9500, FAX (612) 831-9332

5. Having each pair present its position to the other. Presentations should involve more than one media and persuasively advocate the "best case" for the position. There is no arguing during this time. Students should listen carefully to the opposing position and take notes. You tell students:

> *"As a pair, present your position forcefully and persuasively. Listen carefully and learn the opposing position. Take notes, and clarify anything you do not understand."*

6. Having students openly discuss the issue by freely exchanging their information and ideas. For higher-level reasoning and critical thinking to occur, it is necessary to probe and push each other's conclusions. Students ask for data to support each other's statements, clarify rationales, and show why their position is a rational one. Students evaluate critically the opposing position and its rationale, defend their own positions, and compare the strengths and weaknesses of the two positions. Students refute the claims being made by the opposing pair, and rebut the attacks on their own position. Students are to follow the specific rules for constructive controversy. Students should also take careful notes on and thoroughly learn the opposing position. Sometimes a *"time-out"* period needs to be provided so that pairs can caucus and prepare new arguments. Teachers encourage more spirited arguing, take sides when a pair is in trouble, play devil's advocate, ask one group to observe another group engaging in a spirited argument, and generally stir up the discussions.

> *"Argue forcefully and persuasively for your position, presenting as many facts as you can to support your point of view. Listen critically to the opposing pair's position, asking them for the facts that support their viewpoint, and then present counter-arguments. Remember this is a complex issue, and you need to know both sides to write a good report."*

7. Have the pairs reverse perspectives and positions by presenting the opposing position as sincerely and forcefully as they can. It helps to have the pairs change chairs. They can use their own notes, but may not see the materials developed by the opposing pair. Students' instructions are:

> *"Working as a pair, present the opposing pair's position as if you were they. Be as sincere and forceful as you can. Add any new facts you know. Elaborate their position by relating it to other information you have previously learned."*

8. Have the group members drop their advocacy and reach a decision by consensus. Then they:

Cooperation In The Classroom, Interaction Book Company, 7208 Cornelia Drive, Edina, MN 55435, (612) 831-9500, FAX (612) 831-9332

a. Write a group report that includes their joint position and the supporting evidence and rationale. Often the resulting position is a third perspective or synthesis that is more rational than the two assigned. All group members sign the report indicating that they agree with it, can explain its content, and consider it ready to be evaluated.

b. Take a test on both positions individually. If all group members score above the preset criteria of excellence (90 percent), each receives five bonus points.

You can find a more detailed description of conducting academic controversies in Johnson and Johnson (1995c). Peggy Tiffany, a 4th-grade teacher in Wilmington, Vermont, regularly conducts an academic controversy on whether the wolf should be a protected species. She gives students the cooperative assignment of writing a report on the wolf in which they summarize what they have learned about the wolf and recommend the procedures they think are best for regulating wolf populations and preserving wolves within the continental United States. She randomly assigns students to groups of four, ensuring that both male and female and high-, medium-, and low-achieving students are all in the same group. She divides the group into two pairs and assigns one pair the position of an environmental organization that believes wolves should be a protected species and assigns the other pair the position of farmers and ranchers who believe that wolves should not be a protected species.

Ms. Tiffany gives each side a packet of articles, stories, and information that supports their position. During the first class period each pair develops their position and plans how to present the best case possible to the other pair. Near the end of the period pairs are encouraged to compare notes with pairs from other groups who represent the same position. During the second class period each pair makes their presentation. Each member of the pair has to participate in the presentation. Members of the opposing pair take notes and listen carefully. During the third class period the group discusses the issue following a set of rules to help them criticize ideas without criticizing people, differentiate the two positions, and assess the degree of evidence and logic supporting each position. During the first half of the fourth hour the pairs reverse perspectives and present each other's positions. Students drop their advocacy positions, clarify their understanding of each other's information and rationale and begin work on their group report. Students spend the first half of the fifth period finalizing their report. You evaluate the report on the quality of the writing, the evaluation of opinion and evidence, and the oral presentation of the report to the class. The students then take an individual test on the wolf and, if every member of the group achieves up to criterion, they all receive the bonus points. Finally, during the sixth class period each group makes a 10-minute presentation to the entire class summarizing their report. All four members of the group need to participate orally in the presentation.

Within this lesson you structure positive interdependence by (a) having each group arrive at a consensus, submit one written report, and make one presentation; (b) jigsawing the materials to the pairs within the group; and (c) giving bonus points if all group members score well on the test. You structure individual accountability by having (a) each member of the pair orally participate in each step of the controversy procedure, (b) each member of the group orally participate in the group presentation, and (c) each member take an individual test on the material. The social skills emphasized are those involved in systematically advocating an intellectual position and evaluating and criticizing the position advocated by others, as well as the skills involved in synthesis and consensual decision making. Students derive numerous academic and social benefits from participating in such structured controversies (Johnson & Johnson, 1995c).

2 : 33

JOINT PROJECT

Task: Complete a project.

Cooperative: Each group completes one project. Members sign the project to indicate that they have contributed their share of the work, agree with the content, and can present/explain it. When a variety of materials are used (such as scissors, paper, glue, markers), assign each team member a responsibility for one of the materials. If appropriate, assign each group member a specific role.

Criteria For Success: A completed project that each group member can explain/present.

Individual Accountability:

1. Each group member may be given different color pens, markers, or pencils.

2. Each group member presents the group project to a member of another group.

3. Each student takes a test individually on the content covered by the project.

Expected Social Skills: Presenting ideas, eliciting ideas, and organizing work.

Intergroup Cooperation: Whenever it is helpful, check procedures, information, and progress with other groups.

Examples:

1. Using compass readings, draw a treasure map for another group to follow.

2. Make a list of the reasons for not growing up (Peter Pan by J. M. Barrie).

Cooperation In The Classroom, Interaction Book Company, 7208 Cornelia Drive, Edina, MN 55435, (612) 831-9500, FAX (612) 831-9332

Monitoring And Intervening

The only thing that endures over time is the law of the farm: I must prepare the ground, put in the seed, cultivate it, water it, then gradually nurture growth and development to full maturity...there is no quick fix.

Stephen Covey

Once the students begin working in cooperative learning groups, the teacher's role is to monitor students' interaction and intervene to help students learn and interact more skillfully.

Monitoring Students' Behavior

Your job begins in earnest when the cooperative learning groups start working. Resist that urge to get a cup of coffee or to grade papers. You observe the interaction among group members to assess students' (a) academic progress and (b) appropriate use of interpersonal and small group skills. Monitoring is covered in depth in Chapter Six.

Observations can be formal (with an observation schedule on which frequencies are tallied) or anecdotal (informal descriptions of students' statements and actions). Based on your observations, you can then intervene to improve students' academic learning and/or interpersonal and small group skills. Remember, **students respect what we inspect**. To **monitor** means to check continuously. **Monitoring has four stages:**

1. **Preparing for observing** the learning groups by deciding who will be the observers, what observation forms to use, and training the observers.

2. **Observing** to assess the quality of cooperative efforts in the learning groups.

3. **Intervening when it is necessary** to improve a group's taskwork or teamwork.

4. **Having students assess the quality of their own individual participation** in the learning groups to encourage self-monitoring, having groups assess the level of their effectiveness, and having both individuals and groups set growth goals.

In monitoring cooperative learning groups, there are a number of guidelines for teachers to follow.

1. Plan a route through the classroom and the length of time spent observing each group so that all groups are observed during a lesson.

Cooperation In The Classroom, Interaction Book Company, 7208 Cornelia Drive, Edina, MN 55435, (612) 831-9500, FAX (612) 831-9332

2. Use a formal observation sheet to count the number of times they observe appropriate behaviors being used by students. The more concrete the data, the more useful it is to you (the teacher) and to students.

3. Initially, do not try to count too many different behaviors. At first you may wish simply to keep track of who talks. Your observations should focus on positive behaviors.

4. Supplement and extend the frequency data with notes on specific student actions. Especially useful are descriptions of skillful interchanges that can be shared with students later and with parents in conferences or telephone conversations.

5. Train and utilize student observers. Student observers can obtain more complete data on each group's functioning and may learn important lessons about appropriate and inappropriate behavior. We can remember one first grade teacher who had a student who talked all the time (even to himself while working alone). He tended to dominate any group he was in. When she introduced student observers to the class, she made him an observer. One important rule for observers was not to interfere in the task but to gather data without talking. He was gathering data on who talks and he did a good job, noticing that one student had done quite a bit of talking in the group whereas another had talked very little. The next day when he was a group member, and there was another observer, he was seen starting to talk, clamping his hand over his mouth and glancing at the observer. He knew what was being observed and he didn't want to be the only one with marks. The teacher said he may have listened for the first time in the year. So the observer often benefits in learning about group skills.

6. Allocate sufficient time at the end of each group session for discussion of the data gathered by the observers.

Providing Task Assistance

Cooperative learning groups provide teachers with a "window" into students' minds. Through working cooperatively students make hidden thinking processes overt and subject to observation and commentary. From carefully listening to students explain to each other what they are learning, teachers can determine what students do and do not understand. Consequently, you may wish to intervene to clarify instructions, review important procedures and strategies for completing the assignment, answer questions, and teach both task skills as necessary. In discussing the concepts and information to be learned, you should make specific statements, such as *"Yes, that is one way to find the main idea of a paragraph,"* not *"Yes, that is right."* The more specific statement reinforces the desired learning and promotes positive transfer by helping the students associate a term with their learning. Metacognitive thought may be encouraged by

2 : 36

Cooperation In The Classroom, Interaction Book Company, 7208 Cornelia Drive, Edina, MN 55435, (612) 831-9500, FAX (612) 831-9332

asking students (a) *"What are you doing?"* (b) *"Why are you doing it?"* and (c) *"How will it help you?"*

Intervening to Teach Social Skills

Cooperative learning groups provide teachers with a picture of students' social skills. The social skills required for productive group work are discussed in detail in Chapter Five. They, along with activities that may be used in teaching them, are covered in even more depth in Johnson and F. Johnson (1997) and Johnson (1991, 1997). While monitoring the learning groups, you may intervene to suggest more effective procedures for working together or reinforce particularly effective and skillful behaviors. Choosing when to intervene is part of the art of teaching. In intervening, ask group members to:

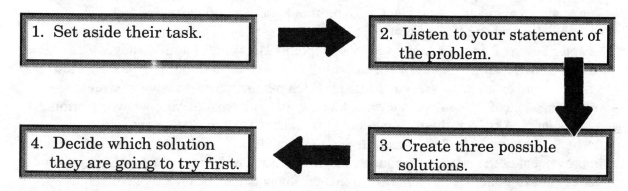

1. Set aside their task.
2. Listen to your statement of the problem.
3. Create three possible solutions.
4. Decide which solution they are going to try first.

In one third grade class, the teacher noticed when distributing papers that one student was sitting back from the other three group members. A moment later the teacher glanced over and only three students were sitting where four were a moment before. As she watched, the three students came marching over to her and complained that Johnny was under the table and wouldn't come out. *"Make him come out!"* they insisted (the teacher's role: police officer, judge, and executioner). The teacher told them that Johnny was a member of their group and asked what they had tried to solve their problem. *"Tried?"* the puzzled reply. *"Yes, have you asked him to come out?"* the teacher suggested. The group marched back and the teacher continued distributing papers to groups. A moment later the teacher glanced over to their table and saw no heads above the table (which is one way to solve the problem). After a few more minutes, four heads came struggling out from under the table and the group (including Johnny) went back to work with great energy. We don't know what happened under that table, but whatever it was, it was effective. What makes this story even more interesting is that the group received a 100 percent on the paper and later, when the teacher was standing by Johnny's desk, she noticed he had the paper clutched in his hand. The group had given Johnny the paper and he was taking it home. He confided to the teacher that this was the first time he could ever remember earning a 100 on anything in school. (If that was your record, you might slip under a few tables yourself.)

Cooperation In The Classroom, Interaction Book Company, 7208 Cornelia Drive, Edina, MN 55435, (612) 831-9500, FAX (612) 831-9332

Evaluating Learning And Processing Interaction

Providing Closure to the Lesson

You provide closure to lessons by having students summarize the major points in the lesson, recall ideas, and identify final questions for the teacher (see Johnson, Johnson, & Holubec, 1992). At the end of the lesson students should be able to summarize what they have learned and to understand where they will use it in future lessons.

Assessing the Quality and Quantity of Learning

The quality and quantity of student learning should be regularly assessed and occasionally evaluated using a criterion-referenced system. This is covered in depth in Chapter Seven. It is covered in even more depth in **Meaningful and Manageable Assessment Through Cooperative Learning** (Johnson & Johnson, 1996). Cooperative learning, furthermore, provides an arena in which **performance-based assessment** (requiring students to demonstrate what they can do with what they know by performing a procedure or skill), **authentic assessment** (requiring students to demonstrate the desired procedure or skill in a "real life" context), and **total quality learning** (continuous improvement of the process of students helping teammates learn) can take place. A wide variety of assessment formats may be used and students may be directly involved in assessing each other's level of learning and then providing immediate remediation to ensure all group members' learning is maximized.

Form a pair. Rank order each of the following columns from most important to you ("1") to least important to you.

What Is Assessed	Procedures	Ways CL Helps
_____ Academic Learning	_____ Goal Setting	_____ Additional Sources Of Labor
_____ Reasoning Strategies	_____ Testing	_____ More Modalities In Assessment
_____ Skills, Competencies	_____ Compositions	_____ More Diverse Outcomes
_____ Attitudes	_____ Presentations	_____ More Sources Of Information
_____ Work Habits	_____ Projects	_____ Reduction Of Bias
	_____ Portfolios	_____ Development Of Rubrics
	_____ Logs, Journals	_____ Implement Improvement Plan

Cooperation In The Classroom, Interaction Book Company, 7208 Cornelia Drive, Edina, MN 55435, (612) 831-9500, FAX (612) 831-9332

Processing How Well the Group Functioned

When students have completed the assignment, or at the end of each class session, students describe what member actions were helpful (and unhelpful) in completing the group's work and make decisions about what behaviors to continue or change. This is discussed in detail in Chapter Six. Group processing occurs at two levels--in each learning group and in the class as a whole. In **small group processing,** in each group members discuss how effectively they worked together and what could be improved. In **whole-class processing** teachers give the class feedback and have students share incidents that occurred in their groups. There are four parts to processing:

1. **Feedback:** You ensure that each student and each group and the class receives (and gives) feedback on the effectiveness of taskwork and teamwork. Feedback given to students should be descriptive and specific, not evaluative and general (see Johnson, 1997).

2. **Reflection:** You ensure that students analyze and reflect on the feedback they receive. You avoid questions that can be answered "yes" or "no." Instead of saying, *"Did everyone help each other learn?"* you should ask, *"How frequently did each member (a) explain how to solve a problem and (b) correct or clarify other member's explanations?"*

3. **Improvement Goals:** You help individuals and groups set goals for improving the quality of their work.

4. **Celebration:** You encourage the celebration of members' hard work and the group's success.

Summary And Conclusions

At this point you know what cooperative learning is and how it is different from competitive and individualistic learning. You know that there are three types of cooperative learning groups--formal cooperative learning groups, informal cooperative learning groups, and cooperative base groups. You know that the essence of cooperative learning is positive interdependence where students recognize that *"we are in this together, sink or swim."* Other essential components include individual accountability (where every student is accountable for both learning the assigned material and helping other group members learn), face-to-face interaction among students within which students promote each other's success, students appropriately using interpersonal and group skills, and students processing how effectively their learning group has functioned. These five essential components of cooperation form the conceptual basis for constructing cooperative procedures. You know that the research supports the

Cooperation In The Classroom, Interaction Book Company, 7208 Cornelia Drive, Edina, MN 55435, (612) 831-9500, FAX (612) 831-9332

proposition that cooperation results in greater effort to achieve, more positive interpersonal relationships, and greater psychological health and self-esteem than do competitive or individualistic efforts. You know the teacher's role in implementing formal cooperative learning. Any assignment in any subject area may be structured cooperatively. In using formal cooperative learning, the teacher decides on the objectives of the lesson, makes a number of preinstructional decisions about the size of the group and the materials required to conduct the lesson, explains to students the task and the cooperative goalstructure, monitors the groups as they work, intervenes when it is necessary, and then evaluates.

One of the things we have been told many times by teachers who have mastered the use of cooperative learning is, *"Don't say it is easy!"* We know it's not. It can take years to become an expert. There is a lot of pressure to teach like everyone else, to have students learn alone, and not to let students look at each other's papers. Students will not be accustomed to working together and are likely to have a competitive orientation. You may wish to start small by using cooperative learning for one topic or in one class until you feel comfortable, and then expand into other topics or classes. **Implementing formal cooperative learning in your classroom is not easy, but it is worth the effort.**

The next chapter will focus on the research evidence. Conviction springs from an accurate assessment of reality. The theory and research contrasting cooperative, competitive, and individualistic efforts provides the window into reality that results in the conviction that cooperative efforts must dominate instructional situations.

Implementation Assignment

1. Read Chapter Three.

2. Plan at least one cooperative lesson to implement in your classroom. Use the lesson plan forms from this chapter. Keep track of the successes and problems encountered so they can be discussed next session. Bring to class the lesson plans and the written comments on successes and problems.

3. Choose the student who will be the subject of your case study.

Cooperation In The Classroom, Interaction Book Company, 7208 Cornelia Drive, Edina, MN 55435, (612) 831-9500, FAX (612) 831-9332

COOPERATIVE LEARNING CONTRACT

Write down your major learnings from reading this chapter and participating in training session one. Then write down how you plan to implement each learning. Share what you learned and your implementation plans with your base group. Listen carefully to their major learnings and implementation plans. You may modify your own plans on the basis of what you have learned from your groupmates. Volunteer one thing you can do to help each groupmate with his or her implementation plans. Utilize the help groupmates offer to you. Sign each member's plans to seal the contract.

MAJOR LEARNINGS	IMPLEMENTATION PLANS

Date: _____ Participant's Signature: _____

Signatures Of Group Members: _____

_____

Cooperation In The Classroom, Interaction Book Company, 7208 Cornelia Drive, Edina, MN 55435, (612) 831-9500, FAX (612) 831-9332

COOPERATIVE LEARNING PROGRESS REPORT

Name: _____ School: _____

Subject Area: _____ Grade: _____

Date	Lesson	Successes	Problems

Describe Critical Or Interesting Incidents:

2 : 42

Cooperation In The Classroom, Interaction Book Company, 7208 Cornelia Drive, Edina, MN 55435, (612) 831-9500, FAX (612) 831-9332

EXERCISE

MATERIALS

Cooperation In The Classroom, Interaction Book Company, 7208 Cornelia Drive, Edina, MN 55435, (612) 831-9500, FAX (612) 831-9332

CHAPTER TWO QUIZ SHOW

Here Are The Answers, What Are The Questions

Given below are a set of answers. Work cooperatively in pairs to determine the question for each answer. Come to agreement as to which question should be paired with each answer and write the letter in the block.

ANSWERS

_____	1.	Two or three.
_____	2.	Start small and build.
_____	3.	Knee-to-knee, eye-to-eye.
_____	4.	Maximize heterogeneity.
_____	5.	Random, teacher assigned.
_____	6.	Group learning goal, jigsaw, roles, one book, bonus points.
_____	7.	Random checking, tests, homework completed, jigsaw, roles.
_____	8.	"Everyone participate, listen with care, check everyone's learning."
_____	9.	Provide task assistance and encourage cooperative skills.
_____	10.	Observation sheet.
_____	11.	Turn problems back to the group to solve.
_____	12.	Name 3 things members did well and 1 thing they could improve.

QUESTIONS

1. What is a way to formally observe the groups?
2. What is usually the best group composition?
3. What is the first strategy for solving group problems?
4. What are ways to structure positive interdependence?
5. What are some group expected behaviors?
6. What is the best group size?
7. How should students be seated?
8. What are questions to help groups process their interactions?
9. What does the teacher do while the groups are working?
10. How should students be assigned to groups?
11. What are ways to structure individual accountability?
12. How should you start using cooperative learning?

2 : 44

Cooperation In The Classroom, Interaction Book Company, 7208 Cornelia Drive, Edina, MN 55435, (612) 831-9500, FAX (612) 831-9332

The Teacher's Role in Cooperative Learning

Make Pre-Instructional Decisions

Specify Academic and Social Skills Objectives: Every lesson has both (a) academic and (b) interpersonal and small group skills objectives.

Decide on Group Size: Learning groups should be small (groups of two or three members, four at the most).

Decide on Group Composition (Assign Students to Groups): Assign students to groups randomly or select groups yourself. Usually you will wish to maximize the heterogeneity in each group.

Assign Roles: Structure student-student interaction by assigning roles such as Reader, Recorder, Encourager of Participation and Checker for Understanding.

Arrange the Room: Group members should be "knee to knee and eye to eye" but arranged so they all can see the instructor at the front of the room.

Plan Materials: Arrange materials to give a "sink or swim together" message. Give only one paper to the group or give each member part of the material to be learned.

Explain Task And Cooperative Structure

Explain the Academic Task: Explain the task, the objectives of the lesson, the concepts and principles students need to know to complete the assignment, and the procedures they are to follow.

Explain the Criteria for Success: Student work should be evaluated on a criteria-referenced basis. Make clear your criteria for evaluating students' work.

Structure Positive Interdependence: Students must believe they "sink or swim together." Always establish mutual goals (students are responsible for their own learning and the learning of all other group members). Supplement, goal interdependence with celebration/reward, resource, role, and identity interdependence.

Structure Intergroup Cooperation: Have groups check with and help other groups. Extend the benefits of cooperation to the whole class.

Cooperation In The Classroom, Interaction Book Company, 7208 Cornelia Drive, Edina, MN 55435, (612) 831-9500, FAX (612) 831-9332

Structure Individual Accountability: Each student must feel responsible for doing his or her share of the work and helping the other group members. Ways to ensure accountability are frequent oral quizzes of group members picked at random, individual tests, and assigning a member the role of Checker for Understanding.

Specify Expected Behaviors: The more specific you are about the behaviors you want to see in the groups, the more likely students will do them. Social skills may be classified as **forming** (staying with the group, using quiet voices), **functioning** (contributing, encouraging others to participate), **formulating** (summarizing, elaborating), and **fermenting** (criticizing ideas, asking for justification). Regularly teach the interpersonal and small group skills you wish to see used in the learning groups.

Monitor and Intervene

Arrange Face-to-Face Promotive Interaction: Conduct the lesson in ways that ensure that students promote each other's success face-to-face.

Monitor Students' Behavior: This is the fun part! While students are working, you circulate to see whether they understand the assignment and the material, give immediate feedback and reinforcement, and praise good use of group skills. Collect observation data on each group and student.

Intervene to Improve Taskwork and Teamwork: Provide **taskwork assistance** (clarify, reteach) if students do not understand the assignment. Provide **teamwork assistance** if students are having difficulties in working together productively.

Assess and Process

Evaluate Student Learning: Assess and evaluate the quality and quantity of student learning. Involve students in the assessment process.

Process Group Functioning: Ensure each student receives feedback, analyzes the data on group functioning, sets an improvement goal, and participates in a team celebration. Have groups routinely list three things they did well in working together and one thing they will do better tomorrow. Summarize as a whole class. Have groups celebrate their success and hard work.

Cooperation In The Classroom, Interaction Book Company, 7208 Cornelia Drive, Edina, MN 55435, (612) 831-9500, FAX (612) 831-9332

COOPERATIVE LESSON PLANNING FORM

Grade Level: _____ Subject Area: _____ Date: _____

Lesson: _____

Making Preinstructional Decisions

Academic Objectives: _____

Social Skills Objectives: _____

Group Size: _____ Method Of Assigning Students: _____

Roles: _____

Room Arrangement: _____

Materials: _____

◊ One Copy Per Group ◊ One Copy Per Person

◊ Jigsaw ◊ Tournament

◊ Other: _____

Explaining Task And Cooperative Goal Structure

1. Task: _____

   _____

2. Criteria For Success: _____

   _____

3. Positive Interdependence: _____

   _____

4. Individual Accountability: _____

5. Intergroup Cooperation: _____

6. Expected Behaviors: _____

   _____

2 : 47

Cooperation In The Classroom, Interaction Book Company, 7208 Cornelia Drive, Edina, MN 55435, (612) 831-9500, FAX (612) 831-9332

Monitoring And Intervening

1. Observation Procedure: _____ Formal _____ Informal

2. Observation By: _____ Teacher _____ Students _____ Visitors

3. Intervening For Task Assistance: _____

   _____

4. Intervening For Teamwork Assistance: _____

   _____

5. Other: _____

Assessing And Processing

1. Assessment Of Members' Individual Learning: _____

   _____

2. Assessment Of Group Productivity: _____

   _____

3. Small Group Processing: _____

   _____

4. Whole Class Processing: _____

   _____

5. Charts And Graphs Used: _____

   _____

6. Positive Feedback To Each Student: _____

   _____

7. Goal Setting For Improvement: _____

   _____

8. Celebration: _____

9. Other: _____

2 : 48

Cooperation In The Classroom, Interaction Book Company, 7208 Cornelia Drive, Edina, MN 55435, (612) 831-9500, FAX (612) 831-9332

CL LESSON PLANNING SHORT FORM

Grade Level: _____ Subject Area: _____ Date: _____

Lesson: _____

Objectives: _____Academic _____Social Skills

Group Size: _____ Method Of Assigning Students: _____

Roles: _____ Materials: _____

Academic Task:	**Criteria For Success:**

Positive Interdependence:	**Individual Accountability:**	**Expected Behaviors:**

Montoring: _____ Teacher _____ Students _____ Visitors

Behaviors Observed: _____

Assessment Of Learning: _____

Small Group Processing:	**Goal Setting:**	**Whole Class Processing:**

Celebration: _____

Other: _____

Cooperation In The Classroom, Interaction Book Company, 7208 Cornelia Drive, Edina, MN 55435, (612) 831-9500, FAX (612) 831-9332

Working Story Problems in Math Cooperatively

David W. Johnson and Roger T. Johnson

Subject Area: Math

Grade Level: Any

Lesson Summary: Group members work cooperatively to solve math story problems and ensure all group members understand the strategies required to solve each one.

Instructional Objective: The **academic** objective is for students to gain expertise in solving math story problems. The **social skills** objective is for students to gain expertise in giving help and encouragement to groupmates.

Materials:

Item	Number Needed
Story Problem Worksheet	One Per Group
Observation Sheet	One Per Group
Role Cards	One Set Per Group
Computation Sheet	One Per Student

Time Required: From twenty to sixty minutes

Pre-Instructional Decisions

Group Size: 4

Assignment to Groups: Randomly assign students to groups to ensure the groups are heterogeneous in math achievement. If, for example, there are twenty-eight students in your class, you would have the class count off by seven. All the "1s" make up one group, the "2s" make up another group, and so forth.

Cooperation In The Classroom, Interaction Book Company, 7208 Cornelia Drive, Edina, MN 55435, (612) 831-9500, FAX (612) 831-9332

Roles:

Reader: Reads the problem aloud to the group.

Checker: Checks to make sure all group members understand how to solve each problem.

Encourager: Watches to make sure everyone is participating and invites reluctant or silent members to join in.

Observer: Records the actions of each group member on an observation sheet while the group is solving the problems.

Students shuffle the role cards and deal them out so that each member is randomly assigned a role. Students are to help each other fulfill the role; a non-reader who ends up with the role of Reader, for example, will receive help from the other group members.

Explaining The Task And Cooperation

Instructional Task: Students are to (1) solve each of the problems on the worksheet correctly, (2) understand the strategies required to do so, and (3) be able to explain how they got the answer.

Positive Interdependence: The **cooperative goal** is for group members to agree on answers, understand how to solve each problem, and be able to explain the strategies required for solving each problem.

*"To help you work cooperatively, each member will be assigned a role. The **Reader** reads each problem clearly to the group. The **Checker** ensures that each member can explain at least one (and preferably two) ways to solve the problem. The **Encourager** acts as a cheerleader to ensure that everyone participates in the group discussion. The **Observer** records the actions of each group member on an observation sheet."*

*"The **cooperative reward** is that if all members score 90 percent or better on the test, each member will receive three bonus points. In addition, group members will receive two bonus points for each additional way they find to solve a problem."*

Individual Accountability: *"While discussing the problem, each member is expected to write out the computations required for the solution. The*

Cooperation In The Classroom, Interaction Book Company, 7208 Cornelia Drive, Edina, MN 55435, (612) 831-9500, FAX (612) 831-9332

computation sheet from each member is to be handed in with the group worksheet. Then I will call on individuals at random to explain how they worked a particular problem. On Friday, I will give you a test with similar problems to be taken individually and I will expect you to be able to solve these problems."

Criteria for Success: *"All members must be able to explain (a) the answer and (b) how to solve each problem to a classmate. You will also be able to earn bonus points for this activity. There may be more than one way to solve a problem in order to arrive at the correct answer. Your group will receive two bonus points for each additional strategy if finds."*

Expected Behaviors: *"I expect to see the following things observing the groups:*
- ❏ *All group members explain step-by-step how to solve an equal number of problems.*
- ❏ *Group members asking for help when they do not understand how to solve a problem.*
- ❏ *Group members encouraging each other to participate by providing clear and accurate explanations and help."*

To clarify the skill of **Encouraging Participating**, present a T-Chart and have students practice the skill several times before the lesson begins.

Intergroup Cooperation: *"When your group finishes, compare your answers with the answers of the surrounding groups. Identify at least two different strategies for solving the problem."*

Monitoring And Intervening

Monitoring: While the students are working, systematically observe each group's taskwork (efforts to solve the problems) and teamwork (efforts to work together effectively). Occasionally, randomly select a student to explain one of the answers. Often, turn students' questions back to the group to solve, or ask students to check with a neighboring group.

Intervening: When a group is obviously struggling, watch for the right moment, then intervene. Point out the problem and ask the group what can be done about it. This establishes the teacher's role as one of consultant rather than answer giver. *"What are three ways the group can solve this problem?"* is a useful phrase. You can add to the students'

Cooperation In The Classroom, Interaction Book Company, 7208 Cornelia Drive, Edina, MN 55435, (612) 831-9500, FAX (612) 831-9332

suggestions, explain a skill, and help the group decide on an effective strategy. Then refocus the group on the task and move on.

Assessing And Processing

Assessing: Groups hand in the computation sheets from each member along with a listing of the different strategies used to solve each problem. On Friday, an individual test is given that all students should take individually.

Small Group Processing: At the end of the lesson, have the observers show the data on the observation sheet to their group. The group analyzes the data to:

❑ *Determine how effectively they worked together. You can have each group record the observation data on a chart to track over time members' improvement in working together effectively.*

❑ *Set an improvement goal for what they could do better next time.*

Whole Class Processing: Lead a discussion on how well the groups worked together. Be careful to model good processing techniques by sticking close to actual observations and stressing positive behaviors. You may wish to determine class totals on some of the behaviors observed and chart the results to illustrate the class's improvement in teamwork skills.

Celebrating: Have the groups celebrate their hard work and success.

2 : 53

Cooperation In The Classroom, Interaction Book Company, 7208 Cornelia Drive, Edina, MN 55435, (612) 831-9500, FAX (612) 831-9332

ROLE CARDS

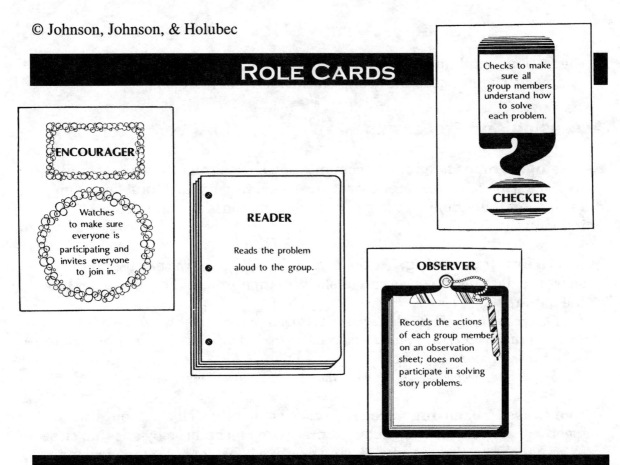

ENCOURAGER

Watches to make sure everyone is participating and invites everyone to join in.

READER

Reads the problem aloud to the group.

CHECKER

Checks to make sure all group members understand how to solve each problem.

OBSERVER

Records the actions of each group member on an observation sheet; does not participate in solving story problems.

OBSERVATION SHEET

Skill	Group Members		
Asks for Help			
Shares Ideas			
Gives Help			

Comments

2 : 54

Cooperation In The Classroom, Interaction Book Company, 7208 Cornelia Drive, Edina, MN 55435, (612) 831-9500, FAX (612) 831-9332

GUIDED PRACTICE IN STRUCTURING COOPERATIVE LEARNING

An important aspect of mastering cooperative learning is actually using it. A teacher may need to structure and teach 20 to 30 lessons cooperatively before gaining a rudimentary competence in doing so. During this training you will practice structuring several lessons cooperatively.

Task: Take the lesson you have just planned. Practice presenting the task and the positive interdependence components of the lesson.

Cooperative: Working in a pair, role play teaching the task and positive interdependence components of the lesson. Present the lesson as if the other person were your class. Use the following procedure:

1. Present your lesson:

   a. The **task** is...

   b. On this task I want you to work **cooperatively**. That means...

2. Listen carefully while your partner presents his or her lesson.

3. Help each other make the task and positive interdependence statements even more effective. After a cooperative goal, what other methods of positive interdependence could be added? How could the statements be more precise and specific next time?

Expected Criteria For Success: Both persons able to present the task and positive interdependence components of a cooperative lesson.

Individual Accountability: One member from your group will be randomly chosen to present his or her task and positive interdependence statements.

Expected Behaviors: Presenting, listening, processing, and encouraging.

Intergroup Cooperation: Whenever it is helpful, check your task and positive interdependence statements with another group.

Cooperation In The Classroom, Interaction Book Company, 7208 Cornelia Drive, Edina, MN 55435, (612) 831-9500, FAX (612) 831-9332

TEACHER'S ROLE IN COOPERATION

Working in pairs, consider each aspect of the teacher's role in using formal cooperative learning groups. Decide whether it involves academic learning (A), positive interdependence (PI), individual accountability (IA), social skills (SS), or monitoring-intervening-processing (MIP). Write a "Y" in the appropriate box if the element is involved, place a "N" if it is not. If you answer "Y," give an example.

A	PI	IA	SS	MIP	Step 1: Making Preinstructional Decisions
					1. Specifying Objectives
					a. Academic
					b. Social
					2. Decide On Group Size
					3. Assign Students To Groups
					4. Decide On Roles
					5. Plan Materials
					6. Arrange Room
					7. Plan Monitoring Procedures And Forms
					Step 2: Setting The Lesson
					1. Explain Academic Task & Procedure
					2. Explain Criteria For Success
					3. Structure Positive Interdependence
					4. Structure Individual Accountability
					5. Specify Expected Social Skills
					6. Structure Intergroup Cooperation
					Step 3: Monitoring & Intervening
					1. Arrange Face-To-Face Interaction
					2. Monitor Students' Behavior
					3. Provide Task Assistance
					4. Provide Social Skills Prompting, Encouragement
					5. Provide Closure
					Step 4: Assessing & Processing
					1. Assess & Evaluate Student Learning
					2. Process Group Functioning
					3. Set Improvement Goals
					4. Groups Celebrate Hard Work & Success

Cooperation In The Classroom, Interaction Book Company, 7208 Cornelia Drive, Edina, MN 55435, (612) 831-9500, FAX (612) 831-9332

COOPERATION IN THE CLASSROOM: CHAPTER TWO SUMMARY

Complete this table by writing in four parts of the teacher's role, the decisions teachers make in preparing to conduct the lesson, the parts of explaining the task and positive interdependence to students, the generic cooperative procedures to use during a lesson, the components of monitoring student learning groups, and the parts of assessing student learning and processing group effectiveness. Form a pair and compare your answers. For any answers on which you disagree, look up the correct answer in the chapter.

Parts Of Teacher's Role	Pre-Instructional Decisions	Explaining Task And Cooperative Structure	Cooperative Scripts That May Be Used	Monitoring And Intervening	Assessing And Processing

2 : 57

Cooperation In The Classroom, Interaction Book Company, 7208 Cornelia Drive, Edina, MN 55435, (612) 831-9500, FAX (612) 831-9332

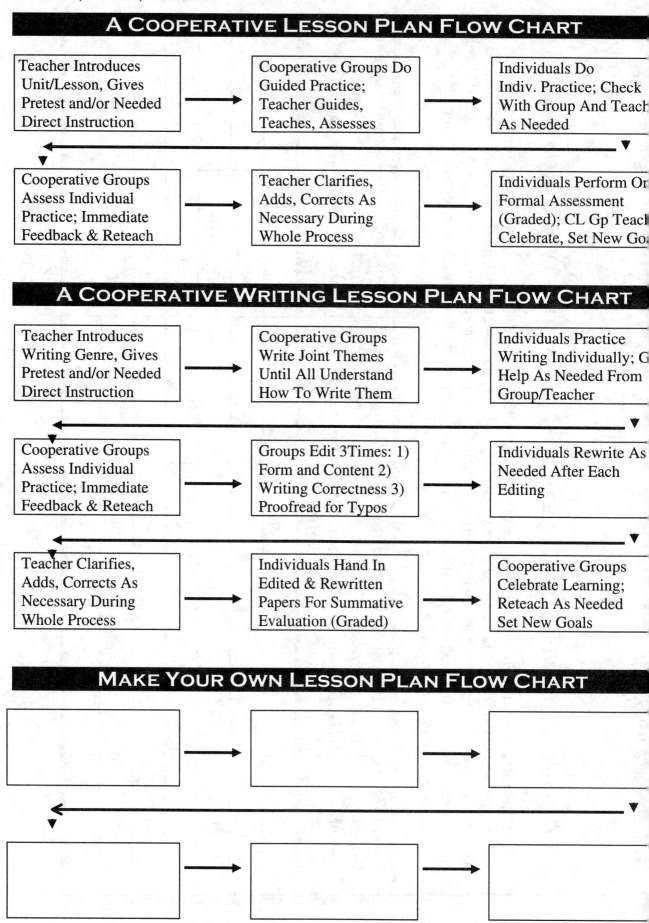

A COOPERATIVE LESSON PLAN FLOW CHART

| Teacher Introduces Unit/Lesson, Gives Pretest and/or Needed Direct Instruction | → | Cooperative Groups Do Guided Practice; Teacher Guides, Teaches, Assesses | → | Individuals Do Indiv. Practice; Check With Group And Teach As Needed |

| Cooperative Groups Assess Individual Practice; Immediate Feedback & Reteach | → | Teacher Clarifies, Adds, Corrects As Necessary During Whole Process | → | Individuals Perform Or Formal Assessment (Graded); CL Gp Teach Celebrate, Set New Goa |

A COOPERATIVE WRITING LESSON PLAN FLOW CHART

| Teacher Introduces Writing Genre, Gives Pretest and/or Needed Direct Instruction | → | Cooperative Groups Write Joint Themes Until All Understand How To Write Them | → | Individuals Practice Writing Individually; G Help As Needed From Group/Teacher |

| Cooperative Groups Assess Individual Practice; Immediate Feedback & Reteach | → | Groups Edit 3Times: 1) Form and Content 2) Writing Correctness 3) Proofread for Typos | → | Individuals Rewrite As Needed After Each Editing |

| Teacher Clarifies, Adds, Corrects As Necessary During Whole Process | → | Individuals Hand In Edited & Rewritten Papers For Summative Evaluation (Graded) | → | Cooperative Groups Celebrate Learning; Reteach As Needed Set New Goals |

MAKE YOUR OWN LESSON PLAN FLOW CHART

CHAPTER THREE:

RESEARCH ON COOPERATIVE LEARNING

Introduction

It is 12,896 B.C. A small group of hunters surround a band of reindeer as they ford an icy river. The hunters are armed with harpoons tipped with spearheads carved from reindeer antler. As the reindeer wallow in the water the hunters run in and slaughter them. It is the coordinated action of the group of Cro-Magnon hunters that makes them more successful than their Neantherthal cousins, who hunt as individuals.

Our origins are somehow linked with the fate of the Neanderthals. We have never been proud of our extinct predecessors, partly because of their looks. Nevertheless, the Neanderthals represent a high point in the human story. Their lineage goes back to the earliest members of the genus *Homo*. They were the original pioneers. Over thousands of years, Neanderthals moved out of Africa by way of the Near East into India and China and Malaysia, and into southern Europe. In recent times, 150,000 or so years ago, they pioneered glacial landscapes. The Neanderthals were the first to cope with climates hospitable only to woolly mammoths and reindeer.

There is no anatomical evidence that the Neanderthals were inferior to us (the Cro-Magnons) cerebrally, and no doubt whatever that they were our physical superiors. Their strongest individuals could probably lift weights of half a ton or so. Physically, we are quite puny in comparison. But we gradually replaced the Neanderthals during an overlapping period of a few thousand years. As the glaciers from Scandinavia advanced, northern populations of Neanderthals moved south while our ancestors were moving north out of Africa. We met in Europe. They vanished about 30,000 years ago.

There are numerous explanations for the disappearance of the Neanderthals. Perhaps they evolved into us. Perhaps we merged. It may have mainly been a matter of attrition and population pressure. Perhaps there was an intergroup competition for food, with the Neanderthals unable to meet our challenge and dying off in marginal areas. Perhaps the Neanderthals were too set in their ways and were unable to evolve and refine better ways to cooperate, whereas we were continually organizing better cooperative efforts to cope with changing climatic conditions. There seems to be little doubt that we were more able to form and maintain cooperative efforts within small groups.

Cooperation In The Classroom, Interaction Book Company, 7208 Cornelia Drive, Edina, MN 55435, (612) 831-9500, FAX (612) 831-9332

TIME-LINE: HISTORY OF COOPERATIVE LEARNING

Given below is a partial time-line on the history of cooperative learning. Please excuse the absence of anyone or any event that should be listed—the absences are unintended. In limited space it is not possible to list all the people and events important to the history of cooperative learning.

Date	Event
BC	Talmud
First Century	Quintillion, Seneca (Qui Docet Discet)
1600s	Johann Amos Comenius of Moravia
1700s	Joseph Lancaster, Andrew Bell
1806	Lancaster School Established In United States
Early 1800s	Common School Movement In United States
Late 1800s	Colonel Frances Parker
Early 1900s	John Dewey, Kurt Lewin, Jean Piaget, Lev Vygotsky
1929 - 1930s	Books on Cooperation & Competition by Maller, Mead, May & Dobb Liberty League & Nat. Ass. Manufacturers promoted competition
1940s	
1940s	WWII, Office of Strategic Services, Military Related Research
1949	Morton Deutsch, Theory & Research On Cooperation & Competition
1950s	
1950s	Applied Group Dynamics Movement, National Training Laboratories Deutsch Research On Trust, Individualistic Situations Naturalistic Studies
1960s	
1960s	Stuart Cook (1969) Research On Cooperation Madsen (Kagan) Research On Cooperation & Competition in Children Inquiry (Discovery) Learning Movement: Bruner, Suchman B. F. Skinner, Programmed Learning, Behavior Modification
1962	Morton Deutsch Nebraska Symposium, Cooperation & Trust, Conflict

Cooperation In The Classroom, Interaction Book Company, 7208 Cornelia Drive, Edina, MN 55435, (612) 831-9500, FAX (612) 831-9332

	Robert Blake & Jane Mouton, Research On Intergroup Competition
1966	David Johnson, U of MN, Began Training Teachers In Coop. Learning
1969	Roger Johnson Joined David At University of Minnesota
1970s	
1970	David W. Johnson, **Social Psychology of Education**
1971	Robert Hamblin: Behavioral Research On Cooperation/Competition
1973	David DeVries & Keith Edwards, Combined Instructional Games Approach With Intergroup Competition, Teams-Games-Tournament
1974 - 1975	David & Roger Johnson Research Review On Cooperation/Competition, David & Roger Johnson, **Learning Together And Alone**
Mid 1970s	Annual Symposium At APA Began (David DeVries & Keith Edwards, David & Roger Johnson, Stuart Cook, Elliot Aronson, Elizabeth Cohen, Others) Robert Slavin Began Development Of Cooperative Curricula Spencer Kagan Continued Research On Cooperation Among Children
1976	Shlomo & Yael Sharan, **Small Group Teaching** (Group Investigation)
1978	Elliot Aronson, **Jigsaw Classroom** **Journal of Research & Development In Education**, Cooperation Issue Jeanne Gibbs, **Tribes**
1979	First IASCE Conference in Tel Aviv, Israel
1980s	
1981, 1983	David & Roger Johnson, Meta-Analyses Of Research On Cooperation
1985	Elizabeth Cohen, **Designing Groupwork**
	Spencer Kagan Developed Structures Approach To Cooperative Learning
	AERA and ASCD Special Interest Groups Founded
1989	David & Roger Johnson, **Cooperation & Competition: Theory & Research**
1990s	
Early 1990s	Cooperative Learning Gains Popularity Among Educators
1996	First Annual Cooperative Learning Leadership Conference, Minneapolis

Cooperation In The Classroom, Interaction Book Company, 7208 Cornelia Drive, Edina, MN 55435, (612) 831-9500, FAX (612) 831-9332

During the time we (the Cro-Magnons) overlapped with the Neanderthals, our ancestors developed highly sophisticated cooperative effects characterized by social organization, group-hunting procedures, creative experimentation with a variety of materials, sharing of knowledge, divisions of labor, trade, and transportation systems. We sent out scouts to monitor the movements of herds of animals we preyed on. The Neanderthals probably did not. We cached supplies and first aid materials to aid hunting parties far away from our home bases. The Neanderthals did not. Neanderthals apparently engaged their prey chiefly in direct combat. We learned more efficient ways of hunting, such as driving animals over cliffs, that fundamentally changed our relationship with the rest of the animal kingdom (i.e., instead of behaving like lions and other carnivores, going after young and old and sick animals to weed out the less fit, large-scale game drives wiped out entire herds and perhaps entire species). We developed more sophisticated tools and weapons to kill from a distance, such as the spear-thrower and the bow and arrow. The Neanderthals probably did not. The Neanderthals used local materials to develop tools. We were more selective, often obtaining special fine-grained and colorful flints from quarries as far as 250 miles away. This took a level of intergroup cooperation and social organization that the Neanderthals did not develop. We improved the tool-making process through experimentation and sharing knowledge. The Neanderthals did not. The Neanderthals used stone almost exclusively for tools. We used bone and ivory to make needles and other tools. We "*tailored*" our clothes and made ropes and nets. Our ability to obtain more food than we needed resulted in trading and the formation of far-ranging social networks. Status hierarchies, the accumulation of wealth, artistic efforts, laws, and story telling to preserve traditions followed, as more complex forms of cooperation were developed. Whether we replaced or evolved from the Neanderthals, our ingenuity was especially evident in organizing cooperative efforts to increase our standard of living and the quality of our lives. We excelled at organizing effective small group efforts.

In spite of the fact that small group efforts are the hallmark of our species, there is a myth that competition is more effective. In this chapter we shall address that myth. The history of the theorizing, research, and practice in cooperative learning is then discussed. Finally, the research directly comparing the relative effects of competitive, individualistic, and cooperative efforts is reviewed.

The Myth Of Competition

Despite our history of cooperation, there is a myth that the world is based on the competitive principle of "*survival of the fittest*" and that "*only the strongest survive*." Believing that it is a "*dog-eat-dog*" world, many individuals compete fiercely with their peers. Yet if you ask individuals who have made remarkable achievements during their lifetimes, they typically say their success came from cooperative efforts (Kouses & Posner, 1967). Not only is cooperation connected with success, competitiveness has been found to be detrimental to career success (Kohn, 1986). The more competitive a person is, the less chance he or she has of being successful. Perhaps the most definitive

Cooperation In The Classroom, Interaction Book Company, 7208 Cornelia Drive, Edina, MN 55435, (612) 831-9500, FAX (612) 831-9332

research on this issue has been conducted by Robert L. Helmreich and his colleagues (Helmreich, 1982; Helmreich, Beane, Lucker, & Spence, 1978; Helmreich, Sawin, & Carsrud, 1986; Helmreich Spence, et al., 1980). They first determined that high achievers, such as scientists, MBA's, and pilots, tend not to be very competitive individuals. Then Helmreich and his associates examined the relationship between the competitive drive within individuals and career success. They conceptualized the **desire to achieve** as consisting of **competitiveness** (desire to win in interpersonal situations, where one tends to see that success depends on another's failure), **mastery** (desire to take on challenging tasks), and **work** (positive attitudes toward hard work). A sample of 103 male Ph.D. scientists was rated on the three factors based on a questionnaire. Achievement was defined as the number of times their work was cited by colleagues. The result was that the most citations were obtained by those high on the Work and Mastery scales but low on the Competitiveness scale. Startled by these results, Helmreich and his associates conducted follow-up studies with academic psychologists, businessmen working in "cut-throat" big business (measuring achievement by their salaries), undergraduate male and female students (using grade-point average as the achievement measure), fifth- and sixth-grade students (measuring achievement by performance on standardized achievement tests), airline pilots (measuring achievement by performance ratings), airline reservation agents (measuring achievement by performance ratings), and supertanker crews. In all cases they found a negative correlation between achievement and competitiveness. With regard to the faculty members, the researchers proposed that competitive individuals focused so heavily on outshining others and putting themselves forward that they lose track of the scientific issues and produce research that is more superficial and less sustained in direction. As yet Helmreich and his colleagues have not been able to identify a single professional arena where highly competitive individuals tended to be more successful.

Given that competitiveness seems to be detrimental to career success, why has it been so prevalent in classrooms? One answer may be that the preceding evidence is too new. No one knows about it yet. Next, therefore, the history of the theorizing, research, and practice in cooperative learning is discussed. Another answer may be that the above evidence is not enough. Interesting, but not conclusive. The research directly comparing the relative effects of competitive, individualistic, and cooperative efforts, therefore, is reviewed.

History Of Cooperative Learning

Two are better than one, because they have a good reward for toil. For if they fall, one will lift up his fellow; but woe to him who is alone when he falls and has not another to lift him up...And though a man might prevail against one who is alone, two will withstand him. A threefold cord is not quickly broken.

Ecclesiastes 4:9-12

Cooperation In The Classroom, Interaction Book Company, 7208 Cornelia Drive, Edina, MN 55435, (612) 831-9500, FAX (612) 831-9332

Cooperative learning has been around a long time. It will probably never go away. Its rich history of theory, research, and actual use in the classroom makes it one of the most distinguished of all instructional practices.

Where We Have Been: Theoretical Roots

There are at least three general theoretical perspectives that have guided research on cooperative learning--social interdependence, cognitive-developmental, and behavioral (see Figure 2.1). The **social interdependence perspective** began in the early 1900s, when one of the founders of the Gestalt School of Psychology, Kurt Kafka, proposed that groups were dynamic wholes in which the interdependence among members could vary. One of his colleagues, Kurt Lewin (1935, 1948) refined Kafka's notions in the 1920s and 1930s while stating that (a) the essence of a group is the interdependence among members (created by common goals) that results in the group's being a "dynamic whole" so that a change in the state of any member or subgroup changes the state of any other member or subgroup, and (b) an intrinsic state of tension within group members motivates movement toward the accomplishment of the desired common goals. One of Lewin's graduate students, Morton Deutsch, formulated a theory of cooperation and competition in the late 1940s (Deutsch, 1949, 1962). One of Deutsch's graduate students, David Johnson (working with his brother Roger Johnson), extended Deutsch's work into social interdependence theory (Johnson, 1970; Johnson & Johnson, 1974, 1989a).

The social interdependence perspective assumes that the way social interdependence is structured determines how individuals interact which, in turn, determines outcomes. Positive interdependence (cooperation) results in **promotive interaction** as individuals encourage and facilitate each other's efforts to learn. Negative interdependence (competition) typically results in **oppositional interaction** as individuals discourage and obstruct each other's efforts to achieve. In the absence of interdependence (individualistic efforts) there is **no interaction** as individuals work independently without any interchange with each other.

The **cognitive developmental perspective** is largely based on the theories of Jean Piaget and Lev Semenovich Vygotsky. From Piaget and related theories comes the premise that when individuals co-operate on the environment, socio-cognitive conflict occurs that creates cognitive disequilibrium, which in turn stimulates perspective-taking ability and cognitive development. Piagetians argue that during cooperative efforts participants will engage in discussions in which cognitive conflicts will occur and be resolved, and inadequate reasoning will be exposed and modified. The work of Vygotsky and related theorists is based on the premise that knowledge is social, constructed from cooperative efforts to learn, understand, and solve problems. Group members exchange information and insights, discover weak points in each other's reasoning strategies, correct one another, and adjust their understanding on the basis of others' understanding.

3 : 6

Cooperation In The Classroom, Interaction Book Company, 7208 Cornelia Drive, Edina, MN 55435, (612) 831-9500, FAX (612) 831-9332

Figure 3.2 A General Theoretical Framework

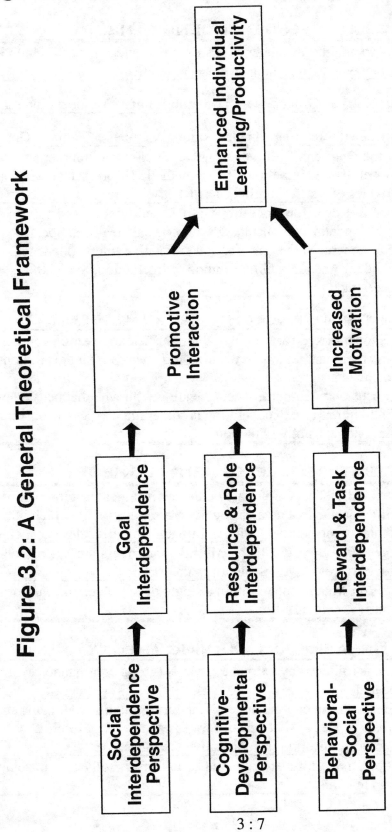

Figure 3.2: A General Theoretical Framework

3 : 7

Cooperation In The Classroom, Interaction Book Company, 7208 Cornelia Drive, Edina, MN 55435, (612) 831-9500, FAX (612) 831-9332

HISTORY OF THEORY AND RESEARCH

SOCIAL INTERDEPENDENCE THEORY

Premise:	Way social interdependence is structured determines who individuals interact which, in turn, determines outcomes.
Early 1900s	Kurt Koffka: Groups Were Dynamic Wholes, Members Interdependent
1920 - 1940	Kurt Lewin: Interdependence Among Members, Common Goals
1940s - 1970s	Morton Deutsch: Positive, Negative, & No Goal Interdependence (Cooperative, Competitive, Individualistic Efforts), Two Mediating Variables (Trust & Conflict), Distributive Justice
1960s -	David & Roger Johnson: Impact of Social Interdependence on Achievement, Relationships, Psychological Health & Social Development, Mediating Variables (Positive Interdependence, Individual Accountability, Promotive Interaction, Social Skills, Group Processing)
1970s -	Dean Tjosvold: Research in Business & Industry Setting
Assumptions:	1. Cooperative efforts are based on intrinsic motivation generated by interpersonal factors in working together and joint aspirations to achieve a significant goal. 2. Focus on relational concepts dealing with what happens among individuals (e.g., cooperation is something that exists only among individuals, not within them).

COGNITIVE DEVELOPMENTAL THEORY

Premise:	When individuals co-operate on the environment, socio-cognitive conflict occurs that creates cognitive disequilibrium, which in turn stimulates perspective-taking ability and cognitive development.
Contributors:	Piaget, Vygotsky, Kohlberg, Murray, controversy theorists (Johnsons & Tjosvold), cognitive restructuring theorists
Assumptions:	Focus on what happens within a single person (e.g., disequilibrium, cognitive reorganization).

BEHAVIORAL LEARNING THEORY

Premise:	Actions followed by extrinsic rewards (group contingencies) are repeated.
Contributors:	Skinner (group contingencies), Bandura (imitation), Homans and Thibaut & Kelley (balance of rewards and costs), Mesch-Lew-Nevin (specific application to cooperative learning)
Assumptions:	Cooperative efforts are powered by extrinsic motivation to achieve group rewards.

3 : 8

Cooperation In The Classroom, Interaction Book Company, 7208 Cornelia Drive, Edina, MN 55435, (612) 831-9500, FAX (612) 831-9332

Related to developmental theorists are the (a) **controversy** theorists (Johnson & Johnson, 1979, 1992) who posit that being confronted with opposing points of view creates uncertainty or conceptual conflict, which creates a reconceptualization and an information search, which results in a more refined and thoughtful conclusion, and (b) the **cognitive restructuring** theorists who state that in order for information to be retained in memory and incorporated into existing cognitive structures, the learner must cognitively rehearse and restructure the material (Wittrock, 1978). An effective way of doing so is explaining the material to a collaborator.

The **behavioral learning theory** perspective focuses on the impact of group reinforcers and rewards on learning. The assumption is that actions followed by extrinsic rewards are repeated. Skinner focused on group contingencies, Bandura focused on imitation, and Homans as well as Thibaut and Kelley focused on the balance of rewards and costs in social exchange among interdependence individuals. More recently, Slavin (1983) has emphasized the need for extrinsic group rewards to motivate efforts to learn in cooperative learning groups.

There are basic differences among the three theoretical perspectives. Social interdependence theory assumes that cooperative efforts are based on intrinsic motivation generated by interpersonal factors in working together and joint aspirations to achieve a significant goal. The behavioral-social perspective assumes that cooperative efforts are powered by extrinsic motivation to achieve group rewards. Social interdependence theory is made up of relational concepts dealing with what happens among individuals (e.g., cooperation is something that exists only among individuals, not within them), whereas the cognitive-developmental perspective is focused on what happens within a single person (e.g., disequilibrium, cognitive reorganization). The differences in basic assumptions among the three theoretical perspectives create theoretical conflicts and disagreements that have yet to be fully explored or resolved. These three theoretical perspectives have, however, generated a considerable body of research to confirm or disprove their predictions.

Where We Have Been: Research

We know a lot about cooperation and we have known it for some time. In the late 1800's Triplett (1898) in the United States, Turner (1889) in England, and Mayer (1903) in Germany conducted a series of studies on the factors associated with competitive performance. Since then we have learned a lot about cooperation. In 1929 Maller wrote a book about it (**Cooperation and Competition: An Experimental Study in Motivation**). In 1936 Margaret Mead (**Cooperation and Competition Among Primitive Peoples**) and in 1937 May and Doob (**Competition and Cooperation**) wrote research reviews on it. In 1949 Deutsch published a research study and a theory on it. In the 1950s Muzafer Sherif (Sherif & Hovland, 1961) conducted his famous studies on three summer camps in which he engineered intense intergroup competition and studied its resolution. Stuart Cook (1969), in collaboration with Shirley and Larry Wrightsman,

Cooperation In The Classroom, Interaction Book Company, 7208 Cornelia Drive, Edina, MN 55435, (612) 831-9500, FAX (612) 831-9332

conducted a study on the impact of cooperative interaction on relationships between black and white college students. James Coleman (1961) published an observational study of American schools in which a pervasive competitiveness was documented. In 1963 Miller and Hamblin reviewed twenty-four studies on cooperation and competition. From an anthropological perspective, Millard C. Madsen (1967) and his associates developed a series of dyadic games that allowed comparison of children's preferences for competitive and cooperative interaction, across ages and various cultures. One of Madsen's students, Spencer Kagan, began a series of studies on cooperation and competition in children. The research of Madsen and Kagan presents a consistent picture of rural children collaborating more than urban children, and middle-class urban Americans children being most strongly motivated to compete.

In the 1970s the authors of this book published comprehensive research reviews on cooperation and competition (**The Social Psychology of Education**), 1974, and 1975 (**Learning Together and Alone**, first edition). From then on the research review articles are too many to mention. Since 1898 over 550 experimental and 100 correlational research studies have been conducted on cooperative, competitive, and individualistic efforts (see Johnson & Johnson, 1989a for a complete review of these studies).

The effectiveness of cooperative learning has been confirmed by both theoretical and demonstration research. There is a "scientific" literature and a "professional" literature on cooperative learning. The scientific literature is made up of carefully controlled research studies conducted to validate or disconfirm theory. Most of the studies are either laboratory or field experimental studies. The vast majority of the research on cooperative learning was conducted to validate or disconfirm theory. The results of these theoretical studies are highly consistent in supporting the use of cooperative over competitive and individualistic learning. It is this combination of hundreds of studies producing validated theory that could be operationalized into practice that has created such interest in cooperative learning. The professional literature is made up of field quasi-experimental or correlational studies demonstrating that cooperative learning works in real classrooms for a prolonged period of time. The demonstration studies may be grouped into summative evaluations demonstrating that cooperative learning produces beneficial results, comparative summative evaluations demonstrating that one cooperative learning procedure works better than others, formative evaluations aimed at improving ongoing implementations of cooperative learning, and survey studies on the impact of cooperative learning on students (Johnson & Johnson, 1991d). Demonstration studies are case studies that simply indicate that a certain method worked at that time in those circumstances.

Cooperative learning can be used with some confidence at every grade level, in every subject area, and with any task. Research participants have varied as to economic class, age, sex, nationality, and cultural background. A wide variety of research tasks, ways of structuring cooperation, and measures of the dependent variables have been used. The research has been conducted by many different researchers with

Cooperation In The Classroom, Interaction Book Company, 7208 Cornelia Drive, Edina, MN 55435, (612) 831-9500, FAX (612) 831-9332

markedly different orientations working in different settings, countries, and decades. The research on cooperative learning has a validity and a generalizability rarely found in the educational literature.

Cooperation is a generic human endeavor that affects many different instructional outcomes simultaneously. Over the past 90 years researchers have focused on such diverse outcomes as achievement, higher-level reasoning, retention, achievement motivation, intrinsic motivation, transfer of learning, interpersonal attraction, social support, friendships, prejudice, valuing differences, social support, self-esteem, social competencies, psychological health, moral reasoning, and many others. These numerous outcomes may be subsumed within three broad categories (Johnson & Johnson, 1989a): effort to achieve, positive interpersonal relationships, and psychological health (see Figure 3.2 and Table 3.1).

History Of Practical Use Of Cooperative Learning

There is a rich and long history of practical use of cooperative learning. Thousands of years ago the **Talmud** stated that in order to understand the Talmud, one must have a learning partner. As early as the first century, **Quintillion** argued that students could benefit from teaching one another. The Roman philosopher, Seneca advocated cooperative learning through such statements as, "*Qui Docet Discet*" (when you teach, you learn twice). **Johann Amos Comenius** (1592-1679) believed that students would benefit both by teaching and by being taught by other students. In the late 1700's **Joseph Lancaster** and **Andrew Bell** made extensive use of cooperative learning groups in England, and the idea was brought to America when a Lancastrian school was opened in New York City in 1806. Within the **Common School Movement** in the United States in the early 1800s there was a strong emphasis on cooperative learning. Certainly, the use of cooperative learning is not new to American education. There have been periods in which cooperative learning had strong advocates and was widely used to promote the educational goals of that time.

One of the most successful advocates of cooperative learning in America was **Colonel Francis Parker**. In the last three decades of the 19th Century, Colonel Parker brought to his advocacy of cooperative learning enthusiasm, idealism, practicality, and an intense devotion to freedom, democracy, and individuality in the public schools. His fame and success rested on the vivid and regenerating spirit that he brought into the schoolroom and on his power to create a classroom atmosphere that was truly cooperative and democratic. When he was superintendent of the public schools at Quincy, Massachusetts (1875-1880), he averaged more than 30,000 visitors a year to examine his use of cooperative learning procedures (Campbell, 1965). Parker's instructional methods of structuring cooperation among students dominated American education through the turn of the century. Following Parker, **John Dewey** promoted the use of cooperative learning groups as part of his famous project method in instruction (Dewey, 1924). In the late

Cooperation In The Classroom, Interaction Book Company, 7208 Cornelia Drive, Edina, MN 55435, (612) 831-9500, FAX (612) 831-9332

1930s, however, interpersonal competition began to be emphasized in public schools (Pepitone, 1980).

In the mid 1960s the authors began training teachers how to use cooperative learning at the University of Minnesota. The **Cooperative Learning Center** resulted from our efforts to synthesize existing knowledge concerning cooperative, competitive, and individualistic efforts (Johnson, 1970; Johnson & Johnson, 1974, 1978, 1983, 1989a), to formulate theoretical models concerning the nature of cooperation and its essential components, to conduct a systematic program of research to test our theorizing, to translate the validated theory into a set of concrete strategies and procedures for using cooperation in classrooms, schools, and school districts (Johnson & Johnson, 1989b, 1992a, 1992b; Johnson, Johnson, & Holubec, 1984/1993), and to build and maintain a network of schools and colleges implementing cooperative strategies and procedures throughout North America and many other countries.

In the early 1970s David DeVries and Keith Edwards at Johns Hopkins University developed Teams-Games-Tournaments (TGT) and Sholmo and Yael Sharan in Israel developed the group investigation. In the late 1970s Robert Slavin extended DeVries and Edwards' work at Johns Hopkins University by modifying TGT into Student-Team-Achievement-Divisions (STAD) and modifying computer-assisted instruction into Team-Assisted Instruction (TAI). Spencer Kagan developed the Co-op Co-op procedure. In the 1980s Kagan and Donald Dansereau developed cooperative structures and scripts and many other individuals worked out further cooperative procedures.

Research On Social Interdependence

Learning together to complete assignments can have profound effects. Building on the theorizing of Kurt Lewin and Morton Deutsch, the premise may be made that the type of  interdependence structured among students determines how they interact with each other which, in turn, largely determines instructional outcomes. Structuring situations cooperatively results in promotive interaction, structuring situations competitively results in oppositional interaction, and structuring situations individualistically results in no interaction among students. These interaction patterns affect numerous variables, which may be subsumed within the three broad and interrelated outcomes of effort exerted to achieve, quality of relationships among participants, and participants' psychological adjustment and social competence (see Figure 3.3) (Johnson & Johnson, 1989a). In most cases, references to individual studies are not included in this chapter. Rather, the reader is referred to the reviews that contain the references to the specific studies that corroborate the point being made.

Cooperation In The Classroom, Interaction Book Company, 7208 Cornelia Drive, Edina, MN 55435, (612) 831-9500, FAX (612) 831-9332

Interaction Patterns

Two heads are better

than one.

Heywood

Simply placing students near each other and allowing interaction to take place does not mean that learning will be maximized, high quality peer relationships will result, or student psychological adjustment, self-esteem, and social competencies will be maximized. Students can obstruct as well as facilitate each other's learning. Or they can ignore each other. The way students interact depends on how interdependence is structured in the situation.

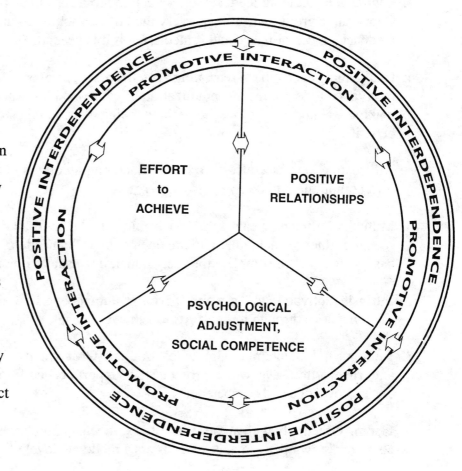

What makes cooperation work is students promoting each other's success and well-being. Positive interdependence creates promotive interaction. **Promotive interaction** occurs as individuals encourage and facilitate each other's efforts to reach the group's goals (such as maximizing each member's learning). Group members promote each other's success by (Johnson & Johnson, 1989a):

1. Giving and receiving help and assistance. Both academic and personal help and support is given and received in cooperative groups.

2. Exchanging resources and information. Group members seek information and other resources from each other, comprehend information given accurately and without bias, and make optimal use of the information provided. Orally explaining, elaborating, and summarizing information and teaching one's knowledge to others results in

3 : 13

cognitive organizing and processing information, higher-level reasoning, insights, and personal commitment to achieving the group's goals. Listening critically to the explanations of groupmates provides the opportunity to utilize other's resources.

3. Giving and receiving feedback on academic progress and responsible group behavior. Cooperative groups ensure that every member is monitored and given immediate feedback on performance and remediation if it is needed.

4. Challenging each other's reasoning. Intellectual controversy promotes curiosity, motivation to learn, reconceptualization of what one's knows, higher quality decision making, greater insight into the problem being considered, and many other important benefits.

5. Advocating increased efforts to learn. Encouraging others to learn increases one's own commitment to do so.

6. Mutually influencing each other's reasoning and behavior. Group members actively seek to influence each other and are open to be influenced. If another group member has a better way to complete the assignment, it is usually quickly adopted.

7. Intrinsic motivation to learn and strive for mutual benefit. Learning for learning's sake increases through joint efforts to achieve.

8. Building and maintaining high levels of trust. Group members tend to act in trusting and trustworthy ways, which provides the support needed for taking risks to increase one's knowledge and competencies.

9. Coping effectively with anxiety and stress. Focusing on joint success reduces anxiety about one's own performance and fosters a moderate level of arousal.

Negative interdependence typically results in students opposing and obstructing each other's learning. **Oppositional interaction** occurs as students discourage and obstruct each other's efforts to achieve. Students focus both on increasing their own achievement and on preventing any classmate from achieving higher than they do. **No interaction** exists when students work independently without any interaction or interchange with each other. Students focus only on increasing their own achievement and ignore as irrelevant the efforts of others.

Achievement

In **Look Homeward Angel** Thomas Wolfe records how in grammar school Eugene learned to write from a classmate, learning from a peer what *"all instruction failed"* to teach him. Is Eugene the only one? To find out several other questions have to be answered. The **first** is, *"What is the conclusion when all the available studies are*

Cooperation In The Classroom, Interaction Book Company, 7208 Cornelia Drive, Edina, MN 55435, (612) 831-9500, FAX (612) 831-9332

included in the analysis?" Over 375 experimental studies on achievement have been conducted over the past 90 years (Johnson & Johnson, 1989a). A meta-analysis of all studies indicates that cooperative learning results in significantly higher achievement and retention than do competitive and individualistic learning (see Table 3.1). The **second** question is, *"What is the conclusion when only the methodological high quality studies are included in the analysis?"* The superiority of cooperative over competitive or individualistic efforts was still pronounced (see Table 3.1).

The **third** question is, *"What is the conclusion when the results of studies that used 'pure' operationalizations of cooperation are compared with the results of studies that used 'mixed' operationalizations of cooperation?"* Some cooperative learning procedures contained a mixture of cooperative, competitive, and individualistic efforts while others contained pure cooperation. The original jigsaw procedure (Aronson, 1978), for example, is a combination of resource interdependence and an individualistic reward structure. Teams-Games-Tournaments (DeVries & Edwards, 1974) and Student-Teams-Achievement-Divisions (Slavin, 1980) are mixtures of cooperation and intergroup competition. Team-Assisted-Instruction (Slavin, Leavey, & Madden, 1982) is a mixture of individualistic and cooperative learning. When the results of "pure" and "mixed" operationalizations of cooperative learning were compared, the pure operationalizations produced higher achievement (effect sizes: cooperative vs. competitive, pure = 0.71, mixed = 0.40, cooperative vs. individualistic, pure = 65, mixed = 0.42).

Besides higher achievement and greater long-term retention of what is learned, cooperation, compared with competitive or individualistic efforts, tends to result in more (Johnson & Johnson, 1989):

1. **Higher-level reasoning** (critical thinking) and meta-cognitive thought. Cooperative efforts promotes a greater use of higher level reasoning strategies and critical thinking than do competitive or individualistic efforts (effect sizes = 0.93 and 0.97 respectively). Even writing assignments show more higher-level thought when they are done cooperatively.

2. **Process gain.** In cooperative groups, members more frequently generate new ideas, strategies, and solutions that they would think of on their own.

3. **Transfer of what is learned within one situation to another** (group to individual transfer). What students learn in a group today, they are able to do alone tomorrow.

4. **Positive attitudes toward the subject being studied.** Cooperative efforts result in more positive attitudes toward the subject area and greater continuing motivation to learn more about it. The positive attitudes extend to the instructional experience.

TABLE 2: SOCIAL INTERDEPENDENCE

Conditions	Achievement	Interpersonal Attraction	Social Support	Self-Esteem
TOTAL STUDIES				
Coop vs. Comp	0.67	0.67	0.62	0.58
Coop vs. Ind	0.64	0.60	0.70	0.44
Comp vs. Ind	0.30	0.08	-0.13	-0.23
HIGH QUALITY STUDIES				
Coop vs. Comp	0.88	0.82	0.83	0.67
Coop vs. Ind	0.61	0.62	0.72	0.45
Comp vs. Ind	0.07	0.27	-0.13	-0.25
MIXED OPERATIONALIZATIONS				
Coop vs. Comp	0.40	0.46	0.45	0.33
Coop vs. Ind	0.42	0.36	0.02	0.22
PURE OPERATIONALIZATIONS				
Coop vs. Comp	0.71	0.79	0.73	0.74
Coop vs. Ind	0.65	0.66	0.77	0.51

Notes: Coop = Cooperation, Comp = Competition, Ind = Individualistic Reprinted from Johnson, D. W., & Johnson, R. (1989). **Cooperation and competition: Theory and research**. Edina, MN: Interaction Book Company.

   5. **Time on task.** Cooperators spend more time on task than do competitors (effect size = 0.76) or students working individualistically (effect size = 1.17).

Kurt Lewin often stated, *"I always found myself unable to think as a single person."* Learning is a personal but social process that results when individuals cooperate to construct shared understandings and knowledge. Both competitive and individualistic structures, by isolating students from each other, tend to depress achievement. When teachers want to maximize students' learning, increase their retention of what they are

Cooperation In The Classroom, Interaction Book Company, 7208 Cornelia Drive, Edina, MN 55435, (612) 831-9500, FAX (612) 831-9332

studying, and promote the use of higher-level reasoning strategies, they would be well advised to use cooperative rather than competitive or individualistic learning.

Positive Interpersonal Relationships

Vince Lombardi, the famous coach of the Green Bay Packers, once said, *"Heartpower is the strength of your corporation."* Learning communities are based as much on relationships as they are on intellectual discourse. Love of learning and love of each other are what inspire students to commit more and more of their energy to their studies. Long-term, hard, persistent efforts to achieve come from the heart, not the head. Within any classroom teachers must reach students' hearts if students are to exert extraordinary efforts to learn. The key to reaching students' hearts is through peer relationships. The more students care about each other and the more committed they are to each other's success, the harder each student will work and the more productive students will be. As relationships become more positive, absenteeism and dropping out of school decreases, student commitment to educational goals increases, feelings of personal responsibility to the school increase, willingness to take on difficult tasks increases, motivation and persistence in working toward goal achievement increase, satisfaction and morale increases, willingness to endure pain and frustration on behalf of learning increases, willingness to listen to and be influenced by classmates and teachers increases, commitment to each other's learning and success increases, and productivity increases (Johnson & F. Johnson, 1991; Johnson & Johnson, 1989). To maximize student learning, teachers need to promote caring and committed relationships among classmates.

Individuals care more about each other and are more committed to each other's success and well-being when they work together cooperatively than when they compete to see who is best or work independently from each other. The more students learn in cooperative groups, the more they like each other. Since 1940, over 180 studies have compared the impact of cooperative, competitive, and individualistic efforts on interpersonal attraction. Cooperative efforts, compared with competitive and individualistic experiences, promotes considerable more liking among individuals (effect sizes = 0.66 and 0.60, respectively). When only the high quality studies were included in the analysis the effects sizes were 0.82 (cooperative vs. competitive) and 0.62 (cooperative vs. individualistic). The effects sizes are higher for the studies using pure operationalizations of cooperative learning than for studies using mixed operationalizations (cooperative vs. competitive, pure = 0.79 and mixed = 0.46; cooperative vs. individualistic, pure = 0.66 and mixed = 0.36). These positive feelings extend to the teacher and the principal, both of whom tend to be liked better by cooperators than by students working competitively or individualistically.

Cooperators tend to like each other when they are homogeneous and also when they differ in intellectual ability, handicapping conditions, ethnic membership, social class, and gender (Johnson & Johnson, 1989). Heterogeneity is a great resource when individuals work cooperatively. The positive impact of heterogeneity results from

3 : 17

Cooperation In The Classroom, Interaction Book Company, 7208 Cornelia Drive, Edina, MN 55435, (612) 831-9500, FAX (612) 831-9332

frequent and accurate communication, accurate perspective taking, mutual inducibility, multi-dimensional views of each other, feelings of psychological acceptance and self-esteem, psychological success, and expectations of rewarding and productive future interaction (Johnson & Johnson, 1989). Cooperative learning has been demonstrated to be an essential prerequisite for managing diversity within the school.

Besides liking each other, cooperators give and receive considerable social support, both personally and academically. Since the 1940s there have been 106 studies comparing the relative impact of cooperative, competitive, and individualistic efforts on social support. Cooperative experience promoted greater social support than did competitive or individualistic experiences. This is important, as social support has been found to promote achievement and productivity, physical health, psychological health, and successful coping with stress and adversity.

Positive peer relationships influence the retention rate of schools and the social and cognitive development of students. It is from their interaction with peers that students adopt attitudes and values, become prosocial or antisocial oriented, learn to take multi-perspectives simultaneously, development autonomy, develop aspriations for posti-secondary education, and learn how to cope with adversity and stress.

Psychological Health

Cooperative experiences, compared with competitive and individualistic ones, affect psychological and social development in a number of ways. First, cooperation tends to promote psychological health. Asley Montagu was fond of saying, *"With few exceptions, the solitary animal is, in any species, an abnormal creature."* Karen Horney said, *"The neurotic individual is someone who is inappropriately competitive and, therefore, unable to cooperate with others."* Montagu and Horney recognized that the essence of psychological health is the ability to develop and maintain cooperative relationships. **Working cooperatively with peers, and valuing cooperation, results in greater psychological health (and greater social competencies and higher self-esteem) than does competing with peers or working independently.** Cooperativeness is positively related to a number of indices of psychological health such as emotiional maturity, well-adjusted social relations, strong personal identity, ability to cope with adversity, social competencies, and basic trust in and optimism about people. Personal ego-strength, self-confidence, independence, and autonomy are all promoted by being involved in cooperative efforts. Individualistic attitudes tend to be related to a number of indices of psychological pathology such as emotional immaturity, social maladjustment,

Cooperation In The Classroom, Interaction Book Company, 7208 Cornelia Drive, Edina, MN 55435, (612) 831-9500, FAX (612) 831-9332

delinquency, self-alienation, and self-rejection. Competitiveness is related to a mixture of healthy and unhealthy characteristics. Cooperative experiences are not a luxury. They are an absolute necessity for healthy development.

Second, cooperative experiences tend to promote positive self-esteem. Since the 1950s there have been over 80 studies comparing the relative impact of cooperative, competitive, and individualistic experiences on self-esteem. Cooperative experiences promoted higher self-esteem than did competitive or individualistic experiences. Our research demonstrated that cooperative experiences tended to be related to beliefs that one is intrinsically worthwhile, believing that others see one in positive ways, compares one's attributes favorably with those of one's peers, and judges that one is a capable, competent, and successful person. The reasons are that in cooperative efforts, students (a) realize that they are accurately known, accepted, and liked by one's peers, (b) know that they have contributed to own, others, and group success, and (c) perceive oneself and others in a differentiated and realistic way that allows for multidimensional comparisons based on complementarity of own and others' abilities. Competitive experiences tended to be related to conditional self-esteem based on whether one wins or loses. Individualistic experiences tended to be related to basic self- rejection.

Third, cooperative experiences tend to promote perspective-taking ability. An important aspect of psychological health is social perspective taking--the ability to understand how a situation appears to other people. The opposite of social perspective taking is egocentrism (being unaware of other perspectives other than your own). Cooperative experiences increase perspective taking ability while competitive and individualistic experiences tend to promote egocentrism. Fourth, cooperative experiences tend to promote the development of social skills. Individuals working cooperatively learn more social skills and become more socially competent than do persons competing or working individualistically. Finally, it is through cooperative efforts that many of the attitudes and values essential to psychological health and learned are adopted. Students need to develop a love of learning, a commitment to high quality work, respect for other people and their property, the value of diversity, a commitment to being a responsible citizen, and so forth. It is through interpersonal influences in cooperative endeavors that such attitudes are developed.

Everything Affects Everything Else

Each of the outcomes of cooperative efforts (to achieve, quality of relationships, and psychological health) influences the others and, therefore, they are likely to be found together (Johnson & Johnson, 1989). **First**, caring and committed friendships come from a sense of mutual accomplishment, mutual pride in joint work, and the bonding that results from joint efforts. The more students care about each other, on the other hand, the harder they will work to achieve mutual learning goals. **Second**, joint efforts to achieve mutual goals promote higher self-esteem, self-efficacy, personal control, and confidence in one's competencies. The healthier psychologically individuals are, on the other hand,

Cooperation In The Classroom, Interaction Book Company, 7208 Cornelia Drive, Edina, MN 55435, (612) 831-9500, FAX (612) 831-9332

the better able to they are to work with others to achieve mutual goals. **Third,** psychological health is built on the internalization of the caring and respect received from loved-ones. Friendships are developmental advantages that promote self-esteem, self-efficacy, and general psychological adjustment. The healthier people are psychologically (i.e., free of psychological pathology such as depression, paranoia, anxiety, fear of failure, repressed anger, hopelessness, and meaninglessness), on the other hand, the more caring and committed their relationships. Since each outcome can induce the others, they are likely to be found together. They are a package with each outcome a door into all three. And together they induce positive interdependence and promotive interaction.

Summary

Humans are small group beings. We always have been and we always will be. As John Donne said, *"No man is an island, entire of itself."* Throughout the history of our species we have lived in small groups. For 200,000 years humans lived in small hunting and gathering groups. For 10,000 years humans lived in small farming communities. It is only recently, the past 100 years or so, that large cities have become the rule rather than the exception. Despite our history as small group beings, there has been a myth that competition is the road to success. Actual studies of successful people, however, have found that they have a desire to achieve and master difficult tasks, but are surprisingly noncompetitive. What makes the myth all the more puzzling is that there is a rich history of theorizing, research, and practice on cooperative learning. At least three general theoretical perspectives have guided research on cooperative learning: social interdependence, cognitive-developmental, and behavioral. From 1898 to 1989 over 550 experimental and 100 correlational studies have been conducted. From these studies it is evident that cooperation, in comparision with competitive and individualistic efforts, promotes higher achievement (as well as retention, higher-level reasoning, creative generation of new ideas, and transfer of learning), more positive and supportive interpersonal relationships (even among heterogeneous individuals), and greater psychological health, social competencies, and self-esteem. Confidence in those results is increased by finding that (a) the results of the high-quality studies are similar and (b) studies using pure cooperation produced stronger results than did studies using mixtures of cooperative, competitive, and individualistic efforts.

Simply placing students in groups and telling them to work together does not in and of itself result in cooperative efforts. There are many ways in which group efforts may go wrong. You can have competition at close quarters or individualistic efforts with talking. Much of our research over the past 25 years has focused on identifying what makes cooperation work. If teachers are to be trained to implement cooperative learning successfully, they must understand the essential elements of cooperation. This is the focus of the next chapter.

Cooperation In The Classroom, Interaction Book Company, 7208 Cornelia Drive, Edina, MN 55435, (612) 831-9500, FAX (612) 831-9332

Implementation Assignment

1. Read Chapter 4.

2. Fill out Lesson Plan Log on lessons taught.

3. Share what you are doing with cooperative learning with colleagues.

4. Have a formal conversation with your principal explaining why you are using coopertive learning and asking for his or her assistance. Encourage questions and specify the kind of support you need.

5. Write down the highlights of your conversation to share with your base group.

Cooperation In The Classroom, Interaction Book Company, 7208 Cornelia Drive, Edina, MN 55435, (612) 831-9500, FAX (612) 831-9332

COOPERATIVE LEARNING CONTRACT

Write down your major learnings from reading this chapter and participating in training session one. Then write down how you plan to implement each learning. Share what you learned and your implementation plans with your base group. Listen carefully to their major learnings and implementation plans. You may modify your own plans on the basis of what you have learned from your groupmates. Volunteer one thing you can do to help each groupmate with his or her implementation plans. Utilize the help groupmates offer to you. Sign each member's plans to seal the contract.

MAJOR LEARNINGS	IMPLEMENTATION PLANS

Date: _____ Participant's Signature: _____

Signatures Of Group Members: _____

_____

Cooperation In The Classroom, Interaction Book Company, 7208 Cornelia Drive, Edina, MN 55435, (612) 831-9500, FAX (612) 831-9332

COOPERATIVE LEARNING PROGRESS REPORT

Name: _____ School: _____

Subject Area: _____ Grade: _____

Date	Lesson	Successes	Problems

Describe Critical Or Interesting Incidents:

Cooperation In The Classroom, Interaction Book Company, 7208 Cornelia Drive, Edina, MN 55435, (612) 831-9500, FAX (612) 831-9332

EXERCISE

MATERIALS

3 : 24

Cooperation In The Classroom, Interaction Book Company, 7208 Cornelia Drive, Edina, MN 55435, (612) 831-9500, FAX (612) 831-9332

 # Research Rationale Statement

Task: Write an explanation why you are using cooperative learning. The written rationale statement should include:

1. An introduction that includes these two statements:
   a. "Cooperative learning is not new, it is an American tradition."
   b. "In my classroom students learn in three ways: cooperatively, competitively, and individualistically."
2. A definition of cooperative learning that includes an example.
3. A summary of the more important consequences of cooperative learning. State that, "There is a great deal of research validating the use of cooperative learning." *Then include information about:*
   a. The importance of peer relationships.
   b. The interaction process promoted by cooperation.
   c. The outcomes resulting from cooperative efforts.
   Also include the research outcomes most important to you and to the person asking, "Why."
4. At least one classroom incident that illustrates the power of cooperative learning.
5. A summary or conclusion.

Cooperative: All members must sign each other's rationale statements indicating that they agree with the statement and verify its quality. The signature also means that they have followed the peer editing procedure.

Criteria For Success: A well-written research rationale statement by each participant that they can deliver orally.

Individual Accountability:

1. Each participant understands the breath and depth of the research on cooperative learning. This knowledge is reflected in his or her composition.
2. Each participant is able to explain why he or she is using cooperative learning to a member of another group.

Expected Behaviors: Explaining and listening.

Intergroup Cooperation: Whenever it is helpful to do so, check procedures and information with another group.

Cooperation In The Classroom, Interaction Book Company, 7208 Cornelia Drive, Edina, MN 55435, (612) 831-9500, FAX (612) 831-9332

Cooperative Learning Historical Search

Given below is a list of historical figures who in one way or another contributed to the development and use of cooperative learning. Interview other participants at the leadership conference and find out what they know about these historical figures. **Find out**:

1. **When the person lived.**

2. **The person's contribution to cooperative learning.**

3. **An interesting fact about the person.**

Person	Lived	Contribution	Interesting Fact
Morton Deutsch			
Seneca			
B. F. Skinner			
Francis Parker			
Kurt Koffka			
John Dewey			
Roger Johnson			
Joseph Lancaster			
Margaret Mead			
Kurt Lewin			
Jean Piaget			

3 : 26

Cooperation In The Classroom, Interaction Book Company, 7208 Cornelia Drive, Edina, MN 55435, (612) 831-9500, FAX (612) 831-9332

CHAPTER FOUR:

POSITIVE INTERDEPENDENCE AND INDIVIDUAL ACCOUNTABILITY

PRETEST

Objectives: Frequent exposure to new terms helps you learn them. After taking this pretest, you should be able to define and give examples of positive interdependence and individual accountability.

Instructions: Find a partner. Fold a sheet of paper and cover the answers on the right of the page. Read the first statement, agree on an answer, then uncover the answer and check. Continue through the pretest in this manner. The pretest should be easy at the beginning and become more difficult as you progress.

1. Not all groups are cooperative learning groups. In order for a group to be a cooperative learning group, there must be five essential elements. The most important essential element is positive interdependence. Thus, a cooperative learning group must have _____ interdependence.   **positive**

2. Positive interdependence ties the group members together in some way. A group in which the members are linked together has positive _____.   **interdependence**

3. Dick and Jane have an assignment which they are to complete together. Having to work together is an example of positive i_____.   **interdependence**

4. Jack and Jill will be successful only if they both pass the spelling test. This is also an example of _____ _____.   **positive interdependence**

4 : 1

Cooperation In The Classroom, Interaction Book Company, 7208 Cornelia Drive, Edina, MN 55435, (612) 831-9500, FAX (612) 831-9332

5. For positive interdependence to be present, group members must be linked together in some way. Toad and Mole are working at the same table on separate assignments. Is this positive interdependence? **No**

6. Tweedledum and Tweedledee are discussing their homework assignment. Is this positive interdependence? **No**

7. Mary, Colin, and Dickon are writing a paper together for their English assignment. Is this positive interdependence? **Yes**

8. Lucy and Edmund are studying for a vocabulary test where their score will be the number they both get correct. Is this positive interdependence? **Yes**

9. Tom and Huck will get bonus points only if they both turn in their homework on time. Is this an example of positive interdependence? **Yes**

10. Thus, for positive interdependence to be present, group members must be _____together in some way. **linked**

11. In addition to positive interdependence, a cooperative group must have individual accountability. Making sure that each individual is accountable for the learning and work of the group is individual _____. **accountability**

12. Even though students may have a group assignment, there is no guarantee that they will all learn it or help with it. Therefore, for cooperative learning groups to work, there must be i_____ accountability. **individual**

13. Individual accountability is making sure that each member of the group learns the material. Thus, quizzing all the group members over material learned in the group is an example of i_____ a_____. **Individual accountability**

14. Telling each member how well he or she contributed to the group is also an example of _____ _____. **Individual accountability**

Cooperation In The Classroom, Interaction Book Company, 7208 Cornelia Drive, Edina, MN 55435, (612) 831-9500, FAX (612) 831-9332

15. After the group finishes writing its paper, the teacher will pick one student at random to explain the material. Is this an example of individual accountability? **Yes**

16. Sherlock and Watson must give a report to the class on the material they researched. Both of them must participate in the report. Is this an example of individual accountability? **Yes**

17. A cooperative learning group must include positive interdependence and individual accountability in order to be a cooperative learning group. If a group is missing either one, then it is not a _____ _____ _____. **cooperative learning group**

18. Peter, Wendy, and Michael are to teach each other their vocabulary words. They will be tested individually and their grade will be their individual score plus a bonus based on how well the others do. Does this include both elements? **Yes**

19. Bilbo, Frodo, and Samwise are working on their geography maps at the same table. They will turn in their finished products. Does this include both elements? **No**

20. What essential element is missing from the group above? **Positive interdependence**

21. Fern, Wilbur, and Charlotte have been told to read the chapter and answer the questions together. Does this include both elements? **No**

22. What essential element is missing from the group above? **Individual accountability**

23. Flopsy, Mopsy, and Cottontail are each to investigate a different section of a report which they will then write together. Does this have both elements? **Yes**

24. Thus, two elements essential to a cooperative learning group are _____ _____ and _____ _____. **positive interdependence individual accountability**

4 : 3

Cooperation In The Classroom, Interaction Book Company, 7208 Cornelia Drive, Edina, MN 55435, (612) 831-9500, FAX (612) 831-9332

25. Which of the following situations correctly describes the two essential elements of a cooperative learning group?

   a. Athos, Porthos, and Aramis are sitting together while they write stories for a class assignment. Occasionally they ask each other how to spell certain words. Before turning in their papers, they read their stories to each other to get reactions and advice.

   b. Mary, Jane, and Michael are working on a group report in their history class. Since Mary is the most motivated, she takes over and does most of the work while Jane and Michael chat. When it is finished, they all sign their names to the report and hand it in.

   c. Christopher, Pooh, and Eeyore are working on a science lab experiment together. They argue over the procedure but finally get it written up. The teacher picks one of them at random to explain how the experiment is done before they can turn in their paper.

   Answer: _____   c

Extension Activity: When finished, see how many of the children's books you can identify from the names used in the examples.

CREATE A SLOGAN

Form a pair. Create a slogan, make it into a posture, and place it on your classroom wall. The slogan should capture the essence of positive interdependence. An example is, *"We Sink Or Swim Together."*

                    OUR SLOGAN IS:

Cooperation In The Classroom, Interaction Book Company, 7208 Cornelia Drive, Edina, MN 55435, (612) 831-9500, FAX (612) 831-9332

Introduction

The Killer Bees is a boys' high school basketball team from Bridgehampton, New York (a small, middle-class town on Long Island) (described in Katzenbach & Smith, 1993). Bridgehampton High School's total enrollment has declined since 1985 from 67 to 41, with less than 20 males attending the high school. There have never been more than 7 players on the team. Yet, since 1980 the Killer Bees have amassed a record of 164 wins and 32 losses, qualified for the state championship playoffs six times, won the state championship twice, and finished in the final four two other times. None of their players was ever really a star and the team players were never tall. Not one of the Killer Bees went on to play professional basketball. Although every Killer Bee was graduated and most went on to college, few had the talent to play basketball in college.

How did the Killer Bees become so successful with so few players and so little talent? There are at least three reasons why the Killer Bees consistently won against bigger supposedly more talented opponents. The first is that the Killer Bees' game was "team basketball." They won, not by superior talent, but through superior teamwork. The second reason is that team members adopted an incredible work ethic. They practiced 365 days a year on skill development and teamwork. The third reason was their versatility and flexibility in how they played their opponents. The source of the Killer Bee's focus on team work, hard work, and versatility was a richness and depth of purpose that eludes most teams. Their mission was more than winning basketball games. They were committed to bringing honor and recognition to their community and protecting and enhancing their legacy. They were also committed to each other. The commitment of team members was reciprocated by the community, whose members came to every game and relentlessly cheered the team on.

It is the potential for such performances that make cooperative groups the key to successful education. Teamwork can do for learning what it did for the Killer Bees' basketball performance. The truly committed cooperative learning group is probably the most productive instructional tool educators have. Creating and maintaining truly committed cooperative learning groups, however, is far from easy. In most classrooms they are rare. To implement cooperative learning, you must:

1. Understand (a) what is (and is not) a cooperative learning group and (b) the "basics" that make cooperative learning groups work.

2. Have the discipline to implement rigorously the basics of cooperative efforts.

This chapter defines positive interdependence and individual accountability and discusses the ways in which they may be structured in groups.

4 : 5

Cooperation In The Classroom, Interaction Book Company, 7208 Cornelia Drive, Edina, MN 55435, (612) 831-9500, FAX (612) 831-9332

TYPES OF POSITIVE INTERDEPENDENCE

Positive Goal Interdependence: Students perceive that they can achieve their learning goals if and only if all the members of their group also attain their goals. Members of a learning group have a mutual set of goals that they are all striving to accomplish.

Positive Celebration/Reward Interdependence: Group celebrates success. A joint reward is given for successful group work and members' efforts to achieve.

Positive Resource Interdependence: Each member has only a portion of the information, resources, or materials necessary for the task to be completed and the member's resources have to be combined in order for the group to achieve its goal.

Positive Role Interdependence: Each member is assigned complementary and interconnected roles that specify responsibilities that the group needs in order to complete a joint task.

Positive Identity Interdependence: The group establishes a mutual identity through a name, flag, motto, or song.

Environmental Interdependence: Group members are bound together by the physical environment in some way. An example is putting people in a specific area in which to work.

POSITIVE INTERDEPENDENCE

TASK
IDENTITY
RESOURCE
ENVIRONMENT
DUTY (ROLE)

FANTASY
REWARD
OUTSIDE ENEMY
GOAL

Positive Fantasy Interdependence: A task is given that requires members to imagine that they are in a life or death situation and must collaborate in order to survive.

Positive Task Interdependence: A division of labor is created so that the actions of one group member have to be completed if the next team member is to complete his or her responsibility.

Positive Outside Enemy Interdependence: Groups are placed in competition with each other. Group members then feel interdependent as they strive to beat the other groups and win the competition.

Cooperation In The Classroom, Interaction Book Company, 7208 Cornelia Drive, Edina, MN 55435, (612) 831-9500, FAX (612) 831-9332

Applying The Basics Of Cooperation

Educators fool themselves if they think well-meaning directives to "work together," "cooperate," and "be a team," will be enough to create cooperative efforts among students. There is a discipline to creating cooperation. The "basics" of structuring cooperation are not a series of elements that characterize good groups. They are a regimen that, if followed rigorously, will produce the conditions for effective cooperation. Cooperative learning groups are rare because educators (and students) seek shortcuts to quality groupwork and assume that "traditional classroom groups will do." Like persons who wish to lose weight without dieting, some educators seek easy alternatives to the disciplined application of the five basic elements of effective groups. Of the five basic elements, positive interdependence is the most important.

Positive Interdependence: We Instead Of Me

All for one and one for all.

Alexandre Dumas

Within a football game, the quarterback who throws the pass and the receiver who catches the pass are positively interdependent. The success of one depends on the success of the other. It takes two to complete a pass. One player cannot succeed without the other. Both have to perform competently if their mutual success is to be assured. If one fails, they both fail.

The discipline of using cooperative groups begins with structuring positive interdependence (see Johnson & Johnson, 1992b, 1992c). **Positive interdependence** is linking students together so one cannot succeed unless all group members succeed. Group members have to know that they "*sink or swim together*." It is positive interdependence that requires group members to roll up their sleeves and work together to accomplish something beyond individual success. When students clearly understand positive interdependence, they understand:

1. Each group member's efforts are required and indispensable for group success (i.e., there can be no "free-riders").

2. Each group member has a unique contribution to make to the joint effort because of his or her resources and/or role and task responsibilities (i.e., there can be no social loafing).

There are three steps in structuring positive interdependence:

Cooperation In The Classroom, Interaction Book Company, 7208 Cornelia Drive, Edina, MN 55435, (612) 831-9500, FAX (612) 831-9332

1. Assign the group a clear, measurable task. Members have to know what they are supposed to do.

2. Structure positive goal interdependence.

3. Supplement positive goal interdependence with other types of positive interdependence.

Positive Goal Interdependence

Positive goal interdependence exists when a mutual/joint goal is established so individuals perceive they can attain their goals if and only if their groupmates attain their goals. Members know that they cannot succeed unless all other members of their group succeed. In most cases, this means any single individual member cannot accomplish the goal; only the group can accomplish the goal. Increasing IBM's profits, for example, is a goal that can only be accomplished by the whole organization, not by any one member.

S = All Score Above Criteria

T = Task Improvement STOP

O = Overall Group Score

P = One Group Product

To ensure that students think "**We, not me**" you (the teacher) say to students, "*You have three responsibilities. You are responsible for learning the assigned material. You are responsible for making sure that all other members of your group learn the assigned material. And you are responsible for making sure that all other class members successfully learn the assigned material.*" Positive interdependence is the heart of cooperative learning. Without positive interdependence, cooperation does not exist. Students must believe that they are in a "sink or swim together" learning situation. **Teachers can create positive interdependence in several ways** (see Johnson & Johnson, 1992b, 1992c).

First, you structure positive goal interdependence. Every cooperative lesson begins with positive goal interdependence. Four ways to establish positive goal interdependence may be found in the table below.

Individuals will contribute more energy and effort to meaningful goals than to trivial ones. **Being responsible for others' success as well as for one's own gives cooperative efforts a meaning that is not found in competitive and individualistic situations.** The efforts of each group member, therefore, contribute not only to their own success, but also the success of groupmates. When there is meaning to what they do, ordinary people exert extraordinary effort. It is positive goal interdependence that gives meaning to the efforts of group members.

4 : 8

Cooperation In The Classroom, Interaction Book Company, 7208 Cornelia Drive, Edina, MN 55435, (612) 831-9500, FAX (612) 831-9332

Form a pair. Rank order the following procedures from "I would use most often" ("1") to "I would use least often" ("4"). Then write an additional teacher statement for implementing each procedure.

Rating	Procedure	Teacher Statement
4	1. The goal is for all members to score above the criteria specified when tested individually.	*"Make sure you score over 90 percent correct on the test and make sure everyone else in your group scores over 90 percent correct on the test."*
3	2. The goal is for all members to improve their performance over their previous scores.	*"Make sure each member of your group does better this week than he or she did last week."*
2	3. The goal is for the overall group score to reach the criterion specified when tested individually.	*"Each member of your triad can score up to 100. I will add your individual scores together to make a total group score. That score must be over 270 for you to be successful."*
1	4. The goal is for the group to produce one product (or set of answers) successfully.	*"Each group is to conduct one science experiment and turn in one report that each member has signed to indicate that he or she agrees with the report and can explain what was done, why, and how."*

Adding Other Types Of Positive Interdependence

When students first begin to work cooperatively, positive goal interdependence may not be enough to ensure cooperation will take place. **You often need to supplement positive goal interdependence with other types of positive interdependence, such as celebration/reward, role, resource, or identity interdependence.** Usually, the more ways you structure positive interdependence in a lesson, the better.

Celebration/Reward Interdependence

Students' efforts to learn and promote each other's learning need to be observed, recognized, and celebrated. You structure **celebration/reward interdependence** by:

1. Having group members celebrate their hard work and joint success.

Cooperation In The Classroom, Interaction Book Company, 7208 Cornelia Drive, Edina, MN 55435, (612) 831-9500, FAX (612) 831-9332

2. Giving each group member a tangible reward for successfully working together to complete a joint task.

Regular **celebrations** of group efforts and success enhance the quality of cooperation. Team celebrations highlight to members that (a) together they have accomplished something beyond what any one member could do, (b) each member's efforts have contributed to the common good (everyone's success, not just his or her own), (c) each member's efforts are appreciated, and (d) each member is respected as an individual. When group members' recognize and respect one's efforts, it builds long-term commitment to achieve.

You may use two types of **tangible rewards** to structure reward interdependence. When all group members achieve up to criterion or when the overall group score reaches criterion, group members may receive:

1. **Academic rewards** (bonus points added to their scores). *"If all group members score above 90 percent on the test, each of you will receive five bonus points."*

2. **Nonacademic rewards** (such as extra free time, extra recess time, stickers, stars, or food). *"If all members of your group score above 90 percent on the test, each of you will receive fifteen extra minutes of recess."*

Occasionally, there is a student who resists taking responsibility for groupmates' learning and behaves as if he or she did not care if the other group members learn or not. This may be time to use a group reward that is particularly attractive to the uncommitted student (as well as to the rest of the group). In one high school class in Los Angeles, we worked with a teacher who was unsuccessful motivating students with all the regular rewards (bonus points, free time, no homework, computer time, and so forth). When we problem-solved with her, she finally decided on offering students "minutes of their own music played in class on Friday" as a group reward. Using the cassette tape recorders from the foreign language lab with several sets of earphones, she was able to reward the groups that earned the reward through good work, while other groups watched as they did (or did not do) their homework. It worked! It is important to match rewards to students, especially the unmotivated students. It is also important to know that **extrinsic rewards should evolve to symbols for celebration and eventually become unnecessary as intrinsic motivation takes over.**

Role Interdependence

A basketball team is made up of guards, forwards, and a center. Team members are linked together by their complementary and interconnected roles. The division of labor specified by their roles structures players' actions during a game. Their best chance of success occurs when all members perform their specific role responsibilities reliably and

Cooperation In The Classroom, Interaction Book Company, 7208 Cornelia Drive, Edina, MN 55435, (612) 831-9500, FAX (612) 831-9332

accurately. The complementarity of their roles creates a social contract to interact with each other in prescribed ways.

You structure **role interdependence** by assigning each member complementary and interconnected roles (such as reader, recorder, checker of understanding, encourager of participation, and elaborator of knowledge) that specify responsibilities that the group needs in order to complete the joint task. The use of roles is described in Chapter Two. In cooperative groups, you divide responsibilities into roles that help the group to:

1. Form the group and organize it for work.

2. Function effectively (that is, achieve its goals and maintain effective working relationships among members).

3. Formulate what members know and integrate it with what they are learning.

4. Ferment members' thinking to enhance higher-level reasoning.

Such roles are vital to high-quality learning. The role of checker, for example, focuses on periodically asking each groupmate to explain what is being learned. Rosenshine and Stevens (1986) reviewed a large body of well-controlled research on teaching effectiveness and found "checking for comprehension" to be one specific teaching behavior that was significantly associated with higher levels of student learning and achievement. While the teacher cannot continually check the understanding of every student (especially if there are 30 or more students in the class), the teacher can engineer such checking by having students work in cooperative groups and assigning one member the role of checker.

Resource Interdependence

At Interaction Manufacturing a decision must be made whether to commit resources to manufacture and sell a new product. A team is constituted that includes members with markedly different expertise, such as engineering, manufacturing, marketing, and accounting. To make a sound decision the resources of all members must be utilized. Their dependence on each other's expertise binds them together.

Cooperation is enhanced when each member of a joint enterprise realizes that he or she does not personally have all the resources required to achieve the goal and, therefore, must solicit and utilize the varied resources of other members to succeed. You structure **resource interdependence** by giving each group member only a portion of the information, materials, or resources necessary for the task to be completed (given that members have to combine their resources to achieve their goals). Ways of structuring resource interdependence are listed in the table below.

4 : 11

Cooperation In The Classroom, Interaction Book Company, 7208 Cornelia Drive, Edina, MN 55435, (612) 831-9500, FAX (612) 831-9332

Form a pair. Rank order the following procedures from "I would use most often" ("1") to "I would use least often" ("4"). Then write a teacher statement for implementing each procedure.

Rating	Procedure	Example
_____	1. Limiting the resources given to the group.	You give only one pencil to a group of three students.
_____	2. Jigsawing information so that each member has part of the information required to complete the assignment.	You assign the task of writing a complete biography of Charles Dickens. Each group member receives information about a different part of Dickens' life. Members must learn each other's information to complete the assignment.
_____	3. Jigsawing materials so that each member has part of a set of materials.	One student can have crayons, another paper, another scissors, and another glue.
_____	4. Having each member make a separate contribution to a joint product.	You ask each group member to contribute a sentence to a paragraph, an article to a newsletter, or a chapter to a "book."

Identity Interdependence

The **Minnesota Vikings** represent a proud tradition of winning football. Each player thinks of himself as an individual, but also as "A Viking" bound together by a joint identity with every other member of the team. **Identity interdependence** is structured when the group establishes a mutual identity through a name or a group symbol such as a motto, flag, or song. English teachers may wish to give poets' names to groups, science teachers can give famous scientists' names to groups, or teachers may wish to have groups create their own subject relevant names.

Outside Enemy Interdependence

When two soccer teams meet, they see each other as opponents to beat. Competition creates outside enemies. Whether it is two teams, two companies, or two countries, striving to win creates internal positive interdependence at the same time it creates external negative interdependence. **Outside enemy interdependence** exists when groups are placed in competition with each other. Group members then feel interdependent as they strive to defeat the other groups. The further removed the competing groups are, the less likely is the occurrence of the negative behavior that often appears in competing with groups in the same class. Outside enemies can be the total score of last year's, the national average, the total score of another class, or the highest score of all the groups in one class.

Task Interdependence

Students are assigned the task of writing a report on the organisms found in swamp water. One student is responsible for obtaining swamp-water, another is responsible for making slides, another is responsible for viewing the slides through a microscope and describing what he or she sees, and the fourth member is responsible for writing down the organisms found in the swamp water.

Task interdependence exists when a division of labor or chain reaction is created so that the actions of one group member have to be completed if the next group member is to complete his or her responsibilities. Dividing an overall task into subunits that must be performed in a set order is an example of task interdependence. This factory-line model exists when groups are giving the assignment of baking a cake. Each group member is responsible for completing one step in the sequence. One member gathers the ingredients. The next member measures the exact quantities. The third member mixes the ingredients. The fourth group member bakes the cake. If the ingredients are not gathered, they cannot be measured, if they are not measured, they cannot be mixed. If they are not mixed, they cannot be baked.

TASK INTERDEPENDENCE: BAKING A CAKE

1. Gather the ingredients required by the recipe.

2. Measure the exact quantities.

4. Bake the cake.

3. Mix the ingredients and pour into pan.

Fantasy Interdependence

"You are the world's leading scientists. Your challenge is to save the world by creating three plans to save the ozone layer in our atmosphere. If you fail, life on Earth as we know it ends."

4 : 13

Cooperation In The Classroom, Interaction Book Company, 7208 Cornelia Drive, Edina, MN 55435, (612) 831-9500, FAX (612) 831-9332

Fantasy interdependence exists when group members strive to solve hypothetical problems such as how to deal with being shipwrecked on the moon. All group simulations involve fantasy interdependence as they require group members to deal with a hypothetical situation. A teacher may say:

> *"Imagine your plane has just crashed in the woods of Northern Minnesota in January. It is 30 degrees below zero. The four of you are the only survivors. Make a group plan as to how you will survive this situation. The plan must be based on the physics principles we have been studying the past semester."*

Environmental Interdependence

In a first grade classroom, the teacher makes a set of circles on the floor with masking tape.

> *"Look for your group symbol,"* she says, *"your group meets in that circle. While your group completes the assignment, all members must stay inside your circle."*

Environmental interdependence exists when group members are bound together by the physical environment in some way (such as a specific area to meet in). Groups may have a specific meeting space or "home base," meet under a mobile on the ceiling, or have the legs of their chairs touching in a circle.

Structuring Intergroup Cooperation

You can extend the positive outcomes resulting from cooperative learning throughout a whole class by structuring intergroup cooperation. You establish class goals as well as individual and group goals. You may give bonus points to each class member if everyone reaches a preset criterion of excellence. When a group finishes its work, the teacher should encourage the members to (a) find other groups who are finished and compare and explain answers and strategies or (b) find other groups who are not finished and help them understand how to complete the assignment successfully.

What We Know About Positive Interdependence

The authors have conducted a series of studies investigating the nature of positive interdependence and the relative power of the different types of positive interdependence (Frank, 1984; Hwong, Caswell, Johnson, & Johnson, 1993; Johnson, Johnson, Stanne, & Garibaldi, 1990; Johnson, Johnson, Ortiz, & Stanne, 1991; Lew, Mesch, Johnson, & Johnson, 1986a, 1986b; Mesch, Johnson, & Johnson, 1988; Mesch, Lew, Johnson, & Johnson, 1986). Six questions concerning positive interdependence have been addressed by our research. The **first** question is whether group membership in and of itself is

Cooperation In The Classroom, Interaction Book Company, 7208 Cornelia Drive, Edina, MN 55435, (612) 831-9500, FAX (612) 831-9332

sufficient to produce higher achievement and productivity or whether group membership and positive interdependence are required. The results of Hwong, Caswell, Johnson, and Johnson (1993) indicate that positive interdependence is necessary. Knowing that one's performance affects the success of groupmates seems to create "responsibility forces" that increase one's efforts to achieve.

POSITIVE INTERDEPENDENCE RESULTS IN STUDENTS REALIZING THAT ALL GROUP MEMBERS:
1. Share a common fate where they all gain or lose on the basis of the overall performance of group members. One result is a sense of personal responsibility (a) for the final outcome and (b) to do their share of the work.
2. Are striving for mutual benefit so that all members of the group will gain. There is recognition that what helps other group members benefits oneself and what promotes one's own productivity benefits the other group members.
3. Have a long-term time perspective so that long-term joint productivity is perceived to be of greater value than short-term personal advantage.
4. Have a shared identity based on group membership. Besides being a separate individual, one is a member of a team. The shared identity binds members together emotionally and creates an expectation for a joint celebration based on mutual respect and appreciation for the success of group members. The experience creates a positive cathexis so that group members like each other. Feelings of success are shared; pride is taken in other members' accomplishments as well as one's own.
5. The performance of group members is mutually caused. The efforts of each member are required for group success (i.e., there can be no "free- riders') and each member's contributions are unique (because of their role, resources, or task responsibilities). Each member shares responsibility for other members' productivity (mutual responsibility) and is obligated to other members for their support and assistance (mutual obligation). Each person views him- or herself as instrumental in the productivity of other group members and views other group members as being instrumental in his or her productivity. As a result of the mutual causation, cooperative efforts are characterized by positive inducibility (group members are open to being influenced by each other) and substitutability (if one member of the group has taken an action there is no need for other members to do so). There is a mutual investment in each other.

Cooperation In The Classroom, Interaction Book Company, 7208 Cornelia Drive, Edina, MN 55435, (612) 831-9500, FAX (612) 831-9332

The **second** question is whether interpersonal interaction is sufficient to increase productivity or whether positive interdependence is required. Debra Mesch and Marvin Lew conducted a series of studies investigating whether the relationship between cooperation and achievement was due to the opportunity to interact with peers or positive goal interdependence. Their results are quite consistent. Individuals achieved higher under positive goal interdependence than when they worked individualistically but had the opportunity to interact with classmates (Lew, Mesch, Johnson, & Johnson, 1985a, 1985b; Mesch, Johnson, & Johnson, 1988; Mesch, Lew, Johnson, & Johnson, 1985).

The **third** question is whether goal or reward interdependence is most important in promoting productivity and achievement. The results of the Mesch and Lew studies indicate that while positive goal interdependence is sufficient to produce higher achievement and productivity than an individualistic effort, the combination of goal and reward interdependence is even more effective. The impact of the two types of outcome interdependence seem to be additive.

The **fourth** question is whether different types of reward interdependence have differential effects on productivity. Michael Frank's (1984) study indicates not. Both working to achieve a reward and working to avoid the loss of a reward produced higher achievement than did individualistic efforts.

The **fifth** question is whether goal or resource interdependence is most important in enhancing productivity and achievement. Johnson and Johnson (in press) found goal interdependence promoted higher achievement than did resource interdependence. The study by Johnson, Johnson, Stanne, and Garibaldi indicated that while goal interdependence in and of itself increased achievement, the combination of goal and resource interdependence increased achievement even further. Compared with individualistic efforts, the use of resource interdependence alone seemed to decrease achievement and lower productivity.

Finally, there is a question as to whether positive interdependence simply motivates individuals to try harder or facilitates the development of new insights and discoveries through promotive interaction. The latter position is supported by the fact that some studies have found that members of cooperative groups use higher level reasoning strategies more frequently than do individuals working individualistically or competitively.

In summary, our research indicates that positive interdependence provides the context within which promotive interaction takes place, group membership and interpersonal interaction among students do not produce higher achievement unless positive interdependence is clearly structured, the combination of goal and reward interdependence increases achievement over goal interdependence alone, and resource interdependence does not increase achievement unless goal interdependence is present also.

Cooperation In The Classroom, Interaction Book Company, 7208 Cornelia Drive, Edina, MN 55435, (612) 831-9500, FAX (612) 831-9332

Individual Accountability/Personal Responsibility

What children can do together today, they can do alone tomorrow.

Vygotsky

Among the early settlers of Massachusetts there was a saying, "*If you do not work, you do not eat.*" Everyone had to do his or her fair share of the work. There is no free lunch in a cooperative learning group. A group is not truly cooperative if some members are "slackers" who let others do all the work. A group is not truly cooperative if members tell each other the answers without teaching each other how to get the answers. To be a cooperative group, each member must be held accountable to learn the assigned material and help other group members learn. Individual accountability results in group members knowing they cannot "hitch-hike" on the work of others, loaf, or get a free ride. As one group of middle-school students put it, *"In this chain there will be no weak links!"*

Using cooperative learning includes structuring group and individual accountability. You structure **group accountability** by assessing the overall performance of the group and giving the results back to group members to compare to a standard of performance. You structure **individual accountability** by:

1. Assessing the performance of each individual member.

2. Giving the results back to the individual and the group to compare to a preset standard of performance. The feedback enables members to (a) recognize and celebrate efforts to learn and contributions to groupmates' learning, (b) provide immediate remediation and any needed assistance or encouragement, and (c) reassign responsibilities to avoid any redundant efforts by members.

3. Ensuring group members hold each other responsible for contributing his or her fair share to the group's success.

Individual accountability is the key to ensuring that all group members are in fact strengthened by learning cooperatively. **The purpose of cooperative groups is to make each member a stronger individual in his or her own right.** After participating in a cooperative lesson, group members should be better prepared to complete similar tasks by themselves. There is a pattern to classroom learning. **First**, students learn knowledge, skills, strategies, or procedures in a cooperative group. **Second**, students apply the knowledge or perform the skill, strategy, or procedure alone to demonstrate their personal mastery of the material. Students learn it together and then perform it alone. Common ways to structure individual accountability include:

1. **Keeping the size of the group small.** The smaller the size of the group, the greater the individual accountability.

4 : 17

Cooperation In The Classroom, Interaction Book Company, 7208 Cornelia Drive, Edina, MN 55435, (612) 831-9500, FAX (612) 831-9332

2. **Giving an individual test to each student.** This includes practice tests to see who is and is not ready to take an examination.

3. **Giving random individual oral examinations.** You randomly select students to explain answers or present his or her group's work to you (in the presence of the group) or to the entire class.

4. **Observing each group and group member** and recording the frequency with which each member contributes to the group's work.

5. **Assigning one student in each group the role of checker of understanding.** The **checker** asks other group members to explain the reasoning and rationale underlying group answers.

6. **Having students teach what they learned to someone else.** When all students do this, it is called simultaneous explaining.

7. **Having group members edit each other's work.**

8. **Having students use what they have learned to solve a different problem.**

Positive interdependence and individual accountability are interrelated. In cooperative learning groups, members share responsibility for the joint outcome. Each group member takes **personal responsibility** for (a) contributing his or her efforts to accomplish the group's goals and (b) helping other group members do likewise. The greater the positive interdependence structured within a cooperative learning group, the more students will feel personally responsible for contributing their efforts to accomplish the group's goals. The shared responsibility adds the concept of ought to members' motivation--one **ough**t to do one's share, contribute, and pull one's weight. The shared responsibility also makes each group member personally accountable to the other group members. Students will realize that if they fail to do their fair share of the work, other members will be disappointed, hurt, and upset.

4 : 18

Cooperation In The Classroom, Interaction Book Company, 7208 Cornelia Drive, Edina, MN 55435, (612) 831-9500, FAX (612) 831-9332

Reducing Problem Behaviors

When students first start working in cooperative learning groups they sometimes engage in unhelpful behaviors. Whenever inappropriate student behavior occurs, your first move should be toward strengthening the perceived interdependence.

Student Is Not Participating Or Bringing Work Or Materials

Jigsaw Materials	Assign Student Role Essential For Group Success	Reward Group If All Members Achieve Up To Criterion To Increase Peer Pressure To Participate

A Student Is Talking About Everything But The Assignment

Give A Reward The Student Or Group Finds Especially Attractive	Structure Task So Steady Contributions Are Required For Group Success

A Student Is Working Alone And Ignoring The Group Discussion

Limit Resources In The Group (If There Is Only One Pencil, The Member Will Be Unable To Work Alone)	Jigsaw Materials So That The Students Cannot Complete The Assignment Without Other Members' Information

A Student Is Refusing To Let Other Members Participate

Jigsaw Resources	Assign Other Members Essential Roles (Such As Reader, Recorder, Summarizer)	Reward Group On Basis Of The Lowest Two Scores By Group Members

Cooperation In The Classroom, Interaction Book Company, 7208 Cornelia Drive, Edina, MN 55435, (612) 831-9500, FAX (612) 831-9332

Cooperative learning groups are characterized by members perceiving clear positive interdependence, holding each other personally and individually accountable to do his or her fair share of the work, promoting each other's learning and success, appropriately using the interpersonal and small group skills needed for successful cooperative efforts, and processing as a group how effectively members are working together. The most important is ensuring that students perceive positive interdependence in each lesson.

Creating cooperative learning groups is not easy. It takes daily, disciplined application of the basics of cooperative efforts. These basics are tough standards and present a difficult implementation challenge to teachers. At the same time, working hard to ensure that the basics are present in each learning group will accelerate teachers' efforts to ensure that all students are achieving up to their full potential.

Implementation Assignment

1. Read Chapter Five.

2. Take a sheet of paper and divide it into two columns. Label the first column "Procedures for structuring positive interdependence I have used," and label the second column "Procedures I would like to use." List at least ten procedures (two for each element) in the second column.

3. Repeat this procedure for individual accountability.

4. Try out the new procedures for structuring positive interdependence and individual accountability with your class. Interview students about the differences among the old and new ways. Find out which methods they perceive as being most effective. Bring back written notes on the interviews to share with your base group.

Cooperation In The Classroom, Interaction Book Company, 7208 Cornelia Drive, Edina, MN 55435, (612) 831-9500, FAX (612) 831-9332

COOPERATIVE LEARNING CONTRACT

Write down your major learnings from reading this chapter and participating in training session one. Then write down how you plan to implement each learning. Share what you learned and your implementation plans with your base group. Listen carefully to their major learnings and implementation plans. You may modify your own plans on the basis of what you have learned from your groupmates. Volunteer one thing you can do to help each groupmate with his or her implementation plans. Utilize the help groupmates offer to you. Sign each member's plans to seal the contract.

MAJOR LEARNINGS	IMPLEMENTATION PLANS

Date: _____ Participant's Signature: _____

Signatures Of Group Members: _____

_____

4 : 21

Cooperation In The Classroom, Interaction Book Company, 7208 Cornelia Drive, Edina, MN 55435, (612) 831-9500, FAX (612) 831-9332

COOPERATIVE LEARNING PROGRESS REPORT

Name: _____ School: _____

Subject Area: _____ Grade: _____

Date	Lesson	Successes	Problems

Describe Critical Or Interesting Incidents:

4 : 22

Cooperation In The Classroom, Interaction Book Company, 7208 Cornelia Drive, Edina, MN 55435, (612) 831-9500, FAX (612) 831-9332

EXERCISE

MATERIALS

4 : 23

Cooperation In The Classroom, Interaction Book Company, 7208 Cornelia Drive, Edina, MN 55435, (612) 831-9500, FAX (612) 831-9332

TYPES OF POSITIVE INTERDEPENDENCE

Form a pair. Match the correct definition with the type of interdependence.

TYPE OF INTERDEPENDENCE	DEFINITIONS
d Goal	a. Each member has only a portion of the information, materials, or resources necessary for the task to be completed.
g Celebration/Reward	b. The group establishes a mutual identity through a name or a group symbol such as a motto, flag, or song.
i Role	c. Group members are bound together by the physical environment.
a Resource	d. Individuals perceive they can attain their goals if and only if their groupmates attain their goals.
b Identity	e. Group members strive to solve hypothetical problems such as how to deal with being shipwrecked on the moon.
h Outside Enemy	f. A division of labor is created so that the actions of one group member have to be completed if the next group member is to complete his or her responsibilities.
f Task	g. Each group member receives the same tangible reward for successfully completing a joint task or group members celebrate their joint success.
e Fantasy	h. Groups are placed in competition with each other.
c Environmental	i. Each member is assigned complementary and interconnected roles that specify responsibilities the group needs in order to complete the joint task.

Cooperation In The Classroom, Interaction Book Company, 7208 Cornelia Drive, Edina, MN 55435, (612) 831-9500, FAX (612) 831-9332

REVIEWING TYPES OF POSITIVE INTERDEPENDENCE

Given below are a number of ways of structuring positive interdependence. Working as a pair, decide which type of positive interdependence each statement represents.

TYPE OF INTERDEPENDENCE	EXAMPLE
Fantasy	1. *"You are a group of diplomats working for the United Nations. You have been selected to create a plan to eliminate war throughout the world. Do so."*
Task	2. *"On this math assignment, one member will read the first problem aloud, another member will write out the equation, and the third member will solve the equation. Rotate the roles after each problem."*
Environmental	3. *"Yesterday you made a group mobile and hung it from the ceiling. Meet with your group and sit underneath your mobile."*
Outside Enemy	4. *"Students all over the country are doing this project. Their work will be evaluated on the same criteria as we are using. Let us see how many groups in this class can score above the national 75th percentile on this project."*
Identity	5. *"Using consensus, decide on a name for your team."*
Role	6. *"In your pair, one of you will be the summarizer and one will be the accuracy checker."*
Celebration/Reward	7. *"If everyone in your group scores 90 percent or better on the test, each of you will receive five bonus points."*
Resource	8. *"Each of you has information on Vietnamese culture. One of you has information on the Vietnamese economy, another information on communications within Vietnam, another on Vietnamese family and community, and another on Vietnamese folklore. As a group, write an overview of Vietnamese culture."*
Goal	9. *"I want one set of answers from the group, all members must agree with every answer, and each member must be able to explain each answer."*

4 : 25

Cooperation In The Classroom, Interaction Book Company, 7208 Cornelia Drive, Edina, MN 55435, (612) 831-9500, FAX (612) 831-9332

A VALEDICTION: ENCOURAGING COOPERATION

Thomas Morton, Vancouver, British Columbia

Subject Area:	English
Grade Level:	Secondary
Lesson Summary:	Groups must match paraphrases with stanzas of John Donne's **A Valediction: Forbidding Mourning** and learn the target vocabulary. They then brainstorm comparisons with which they write a group poem containing metaphors.
Instructional Objectives:	Students will gain practice in reading and interpreting poetry, will develop an awareness of metaphor, and will learn to write metaphors.
Time Required:	One and one-half hours

MATERIALS	NUMBER
A Valediction: Forbidding Mourning By John Donne	One Per Student
Set Of Role Cards	One Per Group
Set Of Task Cards	One Per Group
Instructions/Assessment Sheet	One Per Group

DECISIONS

Group Size:	Three (four if observer is used)
Assignment To Groups:	Either random or teacher assigned, with high, medium, and low achieving groups
Roles:	Reader Of Instructions, Recorder Of Answers
	Checker Of Understanding, Observer

4 : 26

Cooperation In The Classroom, Interaction Book Company, 7208 Cornelia Drive, Edina, MN 55435, (612) 831-9500, FAX (612) 831-9332

© Johnson, Johnson, & Holubec

THE LESSON: PART ONE

Instructional Tasks:
1. Discuss some of the background of John Donne and **A Valediction**.
2. Distribute a copy of **A Valediction** and read it to the class. Explain that in order to understand the poem fully, each group will be given a set of cards. On each card is a paraphrase of one of the stanzas of the poem. The cards are to be shuffled and dealt out to group members. Each group is to (a) arrange the cards in the correct order and (b) ensure all members understand the vocabulary used in the poem.

Biography: Born in 1572, Donne was a contemporary of Shakespeare. Passionate, charming, and intellectual, Donne sailed with Sir Walter Raleigh on a raid against the Spanish Azores and wrote love poetry. He fell out of favor with the ruling class for secretly marrying his noble patron's sixteen-year-old niece. Although his marriage was a happy one, Donne was imprisoned for a time, lost his job, and lived in poverty for many years. In 1615 he became an Anglican minister. He rose to prominence for his dramatic sermons and religious poetry (as passionate as his earlier love poems). Before visiting the Continent in 1612, Donne had a premonition of misfortune and wrote **A Valediction** to his wife. While he was away his wife gave birth to a still-born child.

Positive Interdependence: Group members must all agree on the order of the arrangement of the cards and verify that all members understand the vocabulary. Each member is assigned a role and is responsible for carrying out his or her assigned duties. Each member must sign the answer sheet, signifying that he or she agrees with the order and can explain both it and the vocabulary.

Individual Accountability: A member will be randomly selected to explain the group's answer to the whole class.

Expected Behaviors: Encouraging each other's participation, explaining the meaning of difficult words, summarizing the meaning of each stanza.

MONITORING AND PROCESSING: PART ONE

Monitoring: Observe each group to ascertain whether members can explain their ranking and whether they are using their group skills appropriately.

Intervening: Recognize the appropriate use of the expected behaviors and other social skills. If there is an opportunity to use a skill but members do

4 : 27

Cooperation In The Classroom, Interaction Book Company, 7208 Cornelia Drive, Edina, MN 55435, (612) 831-9500, FAX (612) 831-9332

not do so (for example, a worthwhile contribution that is not recognized), encourage members to do so. Occasionally randomly select a member to explain the group's ranking so far.

Processing: Once students have completed the task and signed their paper, ask them to discuss and write out group answers to the processing questions at the bottom of the sheet.

Closing Whole Class Discussion: Have students hand in their answers and processing. Discuss the poem as a class. Using a large compass, as randomly selected students to explain in detail Donne's extended metaphor in the last three stanzas.

THE LESSON: PART TWO

Instructional Tasks: A Valediction offers students the opportunity to use science and math to express tender and passionate feelings by means of mechanical, mathematical, and scientific analogies. Assign the tasks of:
1. Each group is brainstorm a list of at least twelve comparisons of a serious feeling like love or loneliness to things in science or math.
2. From their list, the group chooses the most interesting or exciting ones.
3. The group uses the selected metaphors to create a poem of at least six lines. The poem may have a comparison in each line or the group may devote the whole poem to one or two comparisons as Donne did with the compass metaphor.

Examples and questions that may help a class begin are *"What feeling do I have that is like magnetism? Electricity? What feelings and relationships can be compared to ordinary mechanical things like turning on a light switch, a bulb burning out, or an electric eye?"* Ask the class to give several other examples to launch their own list.

Positive Interdependence: Each group makes one list and writes one poem. All members must agree on the most interesting or exciting comparisons and the poem. All members must be able to explain the poem and the comparisons used.

Individual Accountability: Each member must contribute two comparisons to the overall list. Each member is responsible for fulfilling his or her assigned role.

Cooperation In The Classroom, Interaction Book Company, 7208 Cornelia Drive, Edina, MN 55435, (612) 831-9500, FAX (612) 831-9332

Criteria For Success: Evaluation will depend on the teacher's purpose and the level of the class. Criteria may include the completion of the minimum number of ideas, a poem with the minimum number of lines, and the use of the correct English. Originality and vividness of metaphors could also be assessed. This is a good opportunity to involve students in creating criteria and rubrics to be used in assessing the quality of the poems.

Expected Behaviors: Performing assigned roles, active participation, and encouraging other's participation.

MONITORING AND PROCESSING: PART TWO

Monitoring And Intervening: Observe each group to ensure roles are being performed, social skills are being used appropriately, and the tasks are being completed.

Closing: Randomly select a member of each group to read their poem to the class.

Assessing: Have groups trade poems and assess its quality using the criteria and rubrics generated to do so.

Processing: Have each group answer: *"What are three things your group did well? What is one thing your group could add to be even more effective tomorrow than you were today?"* Then conduct a whole-class processing session on the use of the skill, *Checking For Understanding*. Provide the total number of times you observed the skill being used.

Cooperation In The Classroom, Interaction Book Company, 7208 Cornelia Drive, Edina, MN 55435, (612) 831-9500, FAX (612) 831-9332

A VALEDICTION: INSTRUCTIONS

Shuffle the task cards. Deal them out equally to group members. Members are **not** to show their cards to each other. On each card is a number and one or two sentences that paraphrase one of the stanzas of **A Valediction: Forbidding Mourning**. They are not in the correct numbered order. Your group tasks are:

1. Understand the poem by arranging the cards in the order that reflects the sequence of stanzas in the poem.

2. Find out the meaning of the vocabulary used. Some of the words you must know are: **valediction, profanation, laity, trepidation, sublunary, breach, hearkens, obliquely**. Use the dictionary or the context of the word to define them.

Orally share what is written on your cards. Do not show your cards to anyone. You are to reach consensus on the order of the cards. Each member must be able to explain (a) why the group chose that order and (b) the meaning of any word in the poem.

OUR ORDER OF THE CARDS IS: ___ ___ ___ ___ ___ ___ ___ ___ ___

Signatures: Your signature means you agree with the group's order of the cards, understand the poem, and can explain the meaning of the poem's vocabulary.

_____   _____

_____   _____

PROCESSING OF GROUPS' WORK

1. List the cooperative skills members of your group used appropriately.
2. List a positive contribution by each member to the group's work.
3. List the cooperative skills that members find difficult to use.
4. List one skill your group should try to improve on next time.

Cooperation In The Classroom, Interaction Book Company, 7208 Cornelia Drive, Edina, MN 55435, (612) 831-9500, FAX (612) 831-9332

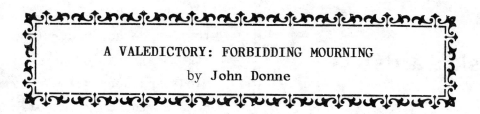

A VALEDICTORY: FORBIDDING MOURNING
by John Donne

As virtuous men pass mildly away,
  And whisper to their souls to go,
Wilst some of their sad friends so say,
  "The breath goes now," and some say, "No,"

So let us melt, and make no noise,
  No tear-floods, nor sigh-tempests move;
'Twere profanation of our joys
  To tell the laity our love.

Moving of the earth brings harms and fears,
  Men reckon what it did and meant;
But trepidation of the spheres,
  Though greater far, is innocent.

Dull sublunary lovers' love
  (Whose soul is sense) cannot admit
Absence, because it doth remove
  Those things which elemented it.

But we, by a love so much refined
  That our selves know not what it is,
Inter-assured of the mind,
  Care less, eyes, lips, and 'hands to miss.

Our two souls therefore, which are one,
  Though I must go, endure not yet
A breach, but an expansion.
  Like gold to airy thinness beat.

If they be two, they are two so
  As stiff twin compasses are two:
Thy soul, the fixed foot, makes no show
  To move, but doth, if the other do;

And though it in the center sit,
  Yet when the other far doth roam,
It leans, and hearkens after it,
  And grows erect, as the comes home.

Such wilt thou be to me, who must,
  Like the other foot, obliquely run;
Thy firmness makes my circle just,
  And makes me end where I began.

Cooperation In The Classroom, Interaction Book Company, 7208 Cornelia Drive, Edina, MN 55435,
  (612) 831-9500, FAX (612) 831-9332

Task Cards

1

Yet our love, so special that we do not understand it, is strong in our minds and does not need us to be together physically.

2

People fear and puzzle over earthquakes, but they do not even notice the wobbling of the earth on its axis.

3

When good men die quietly and say their last words, their friends are not even sure that they are dead.

4

And so we will be the same: Like the outside foot of a compass, I must move away, but your steadiness will make me return home, just as the compass completes the circle.

5

Let us too be quiet and not cry aloud. To do so would be an insult to our great happiness.

6

Everyday physical love cannot last if the lovers are separated, because the source of their love is removed.

7

The two of us are united spiritually. Though I must leave, the separation will not break us apart, but only stretch our union.

8

Though your compass foot is fixed in the centre, when mine moves away, you lean towards my foot and then straighten up as mine returns to you.

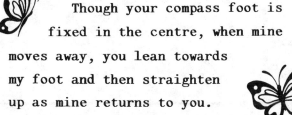

9

We are like the two feet of a compass used for drawing a circle. You are the foot in the circle's centre that turns only if the outside foot does.

CHAPTER FIVE:

TEACHING COOPERATIVE SKILLS

Why Teach Social Skills

"I will pay more for the ability to deal with people than any other ability under the sun."

John D. Rockefeller

What is your opinion? The interpersonal and group skills needed to work cooperatively with other individuals:

_____ Are inborn natural instincts.   _____ Must be taught and learned.

_____ Magically appear when they are needed.

If you answered that social skills are learned, then the next question is, *"Who teaches them to children, adolescents, and young adults?"*

_____ Parents, in the home.   _____ Teachers, in the classroom.

_____ Peers, on the playground.   _____ Have not the faintest idea!

Social skills are not a luxury, to be learned when time allows. They are a necessity to all aspects of living. The importance of social skills cannot be overstated (Johnson, 1997; Johnson & F. Johnson, 1997; Johnson & R. Johnson, 1989). Social skills are the connections among people. Any time you talk to, play with, interact with, or work with others, you are using social skills. Increasingly, however, large numbers of children, adolescents, and young adults do not possess the social skills necessary to establish and maintain positive relationships with their peers. Due to changes in the structure of family, neighborhood, and community life, many students are no longer taught how to interact effectively with others by parents and peers. The severity and persistence of social problems among children, adolescents, and young adults necessitate that schools become more involved in teaching social skills.

Cooperation In The Classroom, Interaction Book Company, 7208 Cornelia Drive, Edina, MN 55435, (612) 831-9500, FAX (612) 831-9332

Given below are six of the more important outcomes of being socially skilled. Form a pair. Rank order the outcomes from most important ("1") to the two of you to least important ("6").

RANK	OUTCOME OF SOCIAL SKILLS
	Personal development and identity: Our identity is created out of relationships with others. As we interact with others we note their responses to us, we seek feedback as to how they perceive us, and we learn how to view ourselves as others view us. Individuals who have few interpersonal skills have distorted relationships with others and tend to develop inaccurate and incomplete views of themselves.
	Employability, productivity and career success: Social skills may be even more important than education and technical skills to employability, productivity, and career success. Recent national surveys found that (a) when hiring new employees, employers value interpersonal and communication skills, responsibility, initiative, and decision-making skills and (b) 90 percent of the people fired from their jobs were fired for poor job attitudes, poor interpersonal relationships, inappropriate behavior, and inappropriate dress. In the real world of work, the heart of most jobs, especially the higher-paying, more interesting jobs, is getting others to cooperate, leading others, coping with complex power and influence issues, and helping solve people's problems in working with others.
	Quality of life: There is no simple recipe for creating a meaningful life, but the research indicates that for almost everyone a necessary ingredient for a high quality of life is some kind of satisfying, close, personal, intimate relationship.
	Physical health: Positive, supportive relationships have been found to be related to living longer lives, recovering from illness and injury faster and more completely, and experiencing less severe illnesses. Physical health improves when individuals learn the interpersonal skills necessary to take more initiative in their relationships and become more constructive in the way they deal with conflict. Loneliness and isolation kill. High quality relationships create and extend life.
	Psychological health: When individuals do not have the interpersonal skills to build and maintain positive relationships with others, psychological illness results. The inability to establish acceptable relationships often leads to anxiety, depression, frustration, alienation, inadequacy, helplessness, fear, and loneliness. The ability to build and maintain positive, supportive relationships, on the other hand, is related to psychological health and adjustment, lack of neuroticism and psychopathology, reduction of psychological distress, coping effectively with stress, resilience, self-reliance and autonomy, a coherent and integrated self-identity, high self-esteem, general happiness, and social competence.
	Ability to cope with stress: Positive and supportive relationships help individuals cope with stress by providing caring, information, resources, and feedback. Supportive relationships decrease the number and severity of stressful events, reduce anxiety, and help with the appraisal of the nature of the stress and one's ability to deal with it constructively. Discussions with supportive peers help individuals perceive the meaning of the stressful event, regain mastery over their lives, and enhance their self-esteem.

Cooperation In The Classroom, Interaction Book Company, 7208 Cornelia Drive, Edina, MN 55435, (612) 831-9500, FAX (612) 831-9332

Cooperative

SKILLS

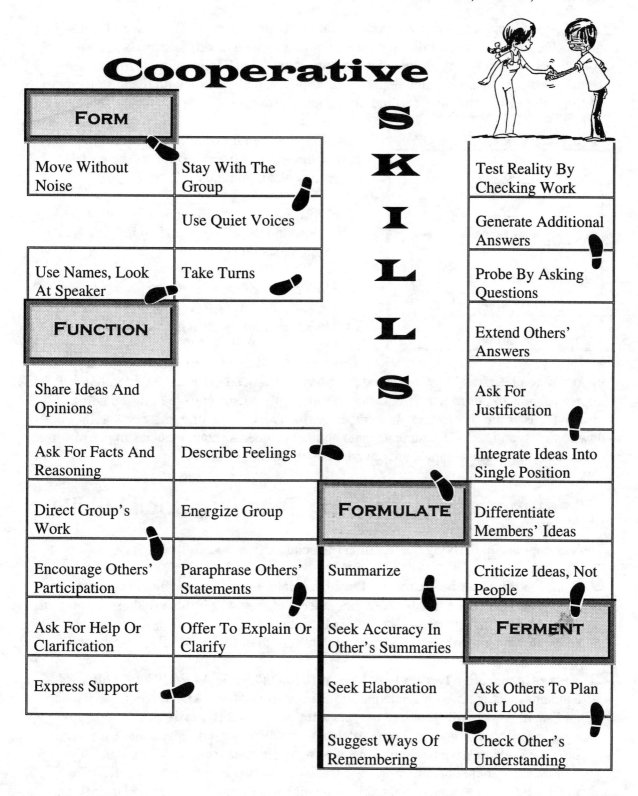

FORM

Move Without Noise	Stay With The Group
	Use Quiet Voices
Use Names, Look At Speaker	Take Turns

FUNCTION

Share Ideas And Opinions	
Ask For Facts And Reasoning	Describe Feelings
Direct Group's Work	Energize Group
Encourage Others' Participation	Paraphrase Others' Statements
Ask For Help Or Clarification	Offer To Explain Or Clarify
Express Support	

FORMULATE

Summarize
Seek Accuracy In Other's Summaries
Seek Elaboration
Suggest Ways Of Remembering

Test Reality By Checking Work
Generate Additional Answers
Probe By Asking Questions
Extend Others' Answers
Ask For Justification
Integrate Ideas Into Single Position
Differentiate Members' Ideas
Criticize Ideas, Not People

FERMENT

Ask Others To Plan Out Loud
Check Other's Understanding

5 : 3

Cooperation In The Classroom, Interaction Book Company, 7208 Cornelia Drive, Edina, MN 55435, (612) 831-9500, FAX (612) 831-9332

Overall, social science research indicates that life without a modicum of social skills is not much of a life. The inability to relate to other people leads to loneliness and isolation. **Loneliness and isolation** can stunt growth, spark failure, make life seem meaningless, create anxiety and depression, result in an obsession with the past, increase fragility, increase inhumaneness, and even shorten life.

When We Work In Groups We	
G	Give Encouragement
R	Respect Others
O	Stay On Task
U	Use Quiet Voices
P	Participate Actively
S	Stay In Our Group

Knowing that social skills should be taught is only part of the story. To teach students the social skills they need, you must:

❑ Know that social skills should be taught and understand the assumptions underlying teaching social skills.

❑ Understand what skills to teach.

❑ Understand how to teach social skills.

These topics are covered in this chapter. It is also important to understand how students' mastery of the social skills may be continuously improved, how to observe the frequency with which students engage in the social skills, how to focus group processing on members' effectiveness in using the social skills, and how to assess and report to interested stakeholders students' competencies in performing teamwork skills. These topics are covered in subsequent chapters.

Assumptions Underlying Teaching Social Skills

The assumptions underlying the teaching of social skills are as follows:

❑ **Social Skills Must Be Learned**: Placing socially unskilled students in a group and telling them to cooperate does not guarantee that they will be able to do so. You must teach students the social skills required for interacting effectively with others and motivate students to use the skills if students are to become socially competent.

❑ **Every Cooperative Lesson Is A Lesson In Social Skills As Well As Academics**: Students must learn both academic subject matter (**taskwork**) and the interpersonal and small group skills required to work with classmates (**teamwork**). Cooperative learning is inherently more complex than competitive or individualistic learning because students have to simultaneously engage in taskwork and teamwork. If group members are inept at teamwork, their taskwork will tend to be substandard. The greater the members' teamwork skills, the higher will be the quality and quantity of their learning. Ways of deciding which interpersonal and small group skills need to be emphasized include:

5 : 4

Cooperation In The Classroom, Interaction Book Company, 7208 Cornelia Drive, Edina, MN 55435, (612) 831-9500, FAX (612) 831-9332

© Johnson, Johnson, & Holubec

a. Observing students at work to determine which social skills they lack.

b. Asking students which social skills would increase their productivity.

c. Drawing a flow chart of how the group actually completes the assignment. On the basis of the process required, certain social (and cognitive) skills may be suggested or even required.

K	Keep On Task
I	Include Everyone
S	Six-Inch Voices
S	Stay With Your Group
E	Encourage Everyone
S	Share Ideas

❑ **Teachers Must Understand What Teamwork Skills To Teach And How To Teach Skills**: This is covered in the rest of this chapter.

❑ **Teachers Must Follow The Three Rules Of Teaching Teamwork Skills**:

a. **Be specific.** Operationally define each social skill by a T-Chart.

b. **Start small.** Do not overload your students with more social skills than they can learn at one time. One or two skills to emphasize for a few lessons is enough. Students should not be subjected to information overload.

c. **Emphasize overlearning.** Having students practice skills once or twice is not enough. Keep emphasizing a skill until the students have integrated it into their behavioral repertoires and do it automatically and habitually.

What Skills Need To Be Taught?

John Dougan, in his 11th-grade English class in Suffern, New York, begins a unit on grammar with teaching students a set of leadership skills. He structures **positive interdependence** by giving students the assignment of (1) mastering a leadership skill and (2) ensuring that all members of their group master the leadership skills. The leadership skills he teaches is **giving direction to the group's work** (reviewing the instructions and restating the purpose of the assignment, calling attention to the time limits, and offering procedures on how to complete the assignment most effectively).

The process he uses to teach the skills is as follows. **First**, he explains the skill. **Second**, he models/demonstrates the skill. **Third**, he asks the class to generate a series of phrases that could be used to engage in the skill. **Fourth**, he next selects three students to role play a group session in front of the class in which the leadership skill is used. After the role play the whole class discusses the skill again. **Fifth**, students are told to complete the first grammar assignment while using the leadership skill as frequently as possible. **Individual accountability** is structured by observing each group to verify that each

Cooperation In The Classroom, Interaction Book Company, 7208 Cornelia Drive, Edina, MN 55435, (612) 831-9500, FAX (612) 831-9332

group member engages in the leadership skill. John circulates throughout the room, systematically observing each group, and recording how frequently each leadership role is engaged in. Groups in which each member engages in the targeted skill at least twice receive five bonus points on the first grammar assignment (**positive reward interdependence**).

Numerous interpersonal and small group skills affect the success of cooperative efforts (Johnson, 1991, 1997; Johnson & F. Johnson, 1997; Johnson & R. Johnson, 1994). What cooperative skills teachers emphasize in their classes depends on what their students have and have not mastered. As teachers observe and monitor their students working in cooperative learning groups the teachers will notice where students lack important skills. Our list of required student behaviors may give teachers a starting point in examining how skillful their students are. There are four levels of cooperative skills:

1. **Forming**: The bottom-line skills needed to establish a functioning cooperative learning group.

2. **Functioning**: The skills needed to manage the group's activities in completing the task and in maintaining effective working relationships among members.

3. **Formulating**: The skills needed to build deeper-level understanding of the material being studied, to stimulate the use of higher quality reasoning strategies, and to maximize mastery and retention of the assigned material.

4. **Fermenting**: The skills needed to stimulate reconceptualization of the material being studied, cognitive conflict, the search for more information, and the communication of the rationale behind one's conclusions.

5 : 6

Cooperation In The Classroom, Interaction Book Company, 7208 Cornelia Drive, Edina, MN 55435, (612) 831-9500, FAX (612) 831-9332

SKILLS THAT HELP THE GROUP FORM

Forming skills are an initial set of management skills directed toward organizing the group and establishing minimum norms for appropriate behavior. Some of the more important behaviors in this category are:

☐ **Noise Monitor:** Ensures classmates move into cooperative learning groups quietly without bothering others. Students may need to practice the procedure for getting into groups several times before they become efficient in doing so.

☐ **Participation Monitor:** Ensures all group members stays with the group and participates in the group's work. Moving around the room during group time is nonproductive for the student doing it as well as for the other group members. Let students know that leaving the group is not acceptable behavior.

☐ **Voice Monitor**: Ensures all group members are using quiet voices. Cooperative learning groups do not need to be noisy. Students can learn to work very quietly using "12-inch" voices. The voice monitor can use a ruler to measure voice distance.

☐ **Turn Taking Monitor**: Ensures group members take turns in completing the assignment. All group members need to share in the learning and be part of the group's efforts to achieve. Taking turns is one way to formalize this.

☐ **Other forming skills** include keeping your hands (and feet) to yourself, looking at the paper, using names, looking at the speaker, and eliminating "put-downs."

Skills That Help The Group Function

The second level of cooperative skills are the **functioning skills** involved in managing the group's efforts to complete their tasks and maintain effective working relationships among members. Some of these skills are:

1. **Share Ideas And Opinions**: All group members need to share their ideas (and materials).

Cooperation In The Classroom, Interaction Book Company, 7208 Cornelia Drive, Edina, MN 55435, (612) 831-9500, FAX (612) 831-9332

© Johnson, Johnson, & Holubec

2. **Ask For Facts And Reasoning** (ask questions; seek ideas and opinions from others): Members need to ask questions to get others to share their ideas and thinking processes. Group members can then understand, discuss, and correct each other's thinking.

3. **Give Direction To The Group's Work**: Helping the group move ahead rather than staying stalled for lack of direction can be done by:

    a. Stating and restating the purpose of the assignment ("We are supposed to...").

    b. Setting or calling attention to time limits ("Can we do it this way in the time we have left?").

    c. Offering procedures on how to most effectively complete the assignment ("Why don't we try this?").

4. **Encourage Everyone To Participate**: Asking other members to share what they are thinking or what their ideas are is important for getting everyone's ideas as well as making others feel that their ideas are valued ("Nancy, what do you think?").

5. **Ask For Help Or Clarification**: Asking groupmates for help and assistance when it is needed is essential for group success ("I don't understand. I'm not sure what you mean.").

6. **Express Support And Acceptance**: Support can be expressed both verbally and nonverbally. Nonverbal support can be expressed through eye contact, nodding, and a look of interest. Verbal support includes praising and seeking others' ideas and conclusions.

7. **Offer To Explain Or Clarify**: When group members think that others may not understand, they should offer to explain or clarify ("Would you like me to go over this again?").

8. **Paraphrase**: Restating what other members have said in order to make certain that a message is understood or clarified. The purpose of paraphrasing is to negotiate for accurate understanding ("So you think that...?" "Do I understand you correctly to say...?").

9. **Energize The Group**: Members can energize the group to work hard to achieve their goals when motivation is low by suggesting new ideas, through humor, or by being enthusiastic ("Come on, let's get moving!").

5 : 8

Cooperation In The Classroom, Interaction Book Company, 7208 Cornelia Drive, Edina, MN 55435, (612) 831-9500, FAX (612) 831-9332

10. **Describe Feelings**: There are times when describing feelings will be helpful to the group ("I'm puzzled about why we didn't do better." "Everyone got an A! That makes me happy.").

SKILLS THAT HELP GROUPS FORMULATE KNOWLEDGE

Formulating skills are needed to provide the conceptual structures needed to build deeper level understanding, stimulate the use of higher quality reasoning strategies, and maximize mastery and retention. Since the purpose of learning groups is to maximize the learning of all members, there are skills specifically aimed at providing formal methods for processing the material being studied. They include:

❑ **Summarize Out Loud**: Summarizing out loud what has just been read or discussed as completely as possible without referring to notes or to the original material. All the important ideas and facts should be included in the summary. Every member of the group must summarize from memory often if their learning is to be maximized.

❑ **Seek Accuracy** (Correct): Seeking accuracy by correcting a member's summary, adding important information he or she did not include, and pointing out the ideas or facts that were summarized incorrectly is important ("I'm not sure that is right, I thought it was...").

❑ **Seek Elaboration**: Elaborating occurs when students relate material being learned to earlier learned material and to other things they know. Asking other group members to elaborate is an important learning skill ("This is like what we studied last week..." How does this relate to...?").

❑ **Help The Group Remember**: Members should seek clever ways of remembering the important ideas and facts by using drawings, mental pictures, and other memory aids ("Here is a way to remember this...").

❑ **Check For Understanding** (Demand Vocalization): Demanding vocalization to make the implicit reasoning process being used by other members overt and thus open to correction and discussion.

❑ **Ask For Others To Plan Out Loud**: Members should ask groupmates to plan out loud how they would teach or tell others about the material being studied. Planning how best to communicate the material can have important effects on quality of reasoning strategies and retention ("Here is how I would teach this material...").

5 : 9

Cooperation In The Classroom, Interaction Book Company, 7208 Cornelia Drive, Edina, MN 55435, (612) 831-9500, FAX (612) 831-9332

Skills That Help Groups Ferment Thinking And Reasoning

Fermenting includes the skills needed to engage in **academic controversies** to stimulate reconceptualization of the material being studied, cognitive conflict, the search for more information, and the communication of the rationale behind one's conclusions. Some of the most important aspects of learning take place when group members skillfully challenge each other's conclusions and reasoning (Johnson & R. Johnson, 1979, 1987). Academic controversies cause group members to "dig deeper" into the material, to assemble a rationale for their conclusions, to think more divergently about the issue, to find more information to support their positions, and to argue constructively about alternative solutions or decisions. Some of the skills involved in academic controversies are:

❑ **Criticize Ideas Without Criticizing People**: An important skill is intellectually challenging groupmates by criticizing their ideas while communicating respect for other group members ("I respect you, but in this case I have to disagree with your thinking.").

❑ **Differentiate Ideas And Reasoning Of Group Members**: First find out how members' thinking differs ("How do our information and conclusions differ?").

❑ **Integrate Ideas Into Single Positions**: After differentiating members' ideas and reasoning, students should synthesize and integrate them ("Would this combine everyone's ideas into a single conclusion?").

❑ **Ask For Justification**: Members should ask other members to give the facts and reasoning that justify why the member's conclusion or answer is the correct or appropriate one ("Why do you think this answer is correct?").

❑ **Extend Answers**: Members should extend other members' answers or conclusions by adding further information or implications ("Here is something else to consider..." I also know...").

❑ **Probe By Asking Indepth Questions**: Members ask questions that lead to deeper understanding or analysis ("Would it work in this situation . . .?" "What else makes you believe . . .?").

❑ **Generate Further Answers**: Students should go beyond the first answer or conclusion by producing a number of plausible answers to choose from ("Would this also work...? Would this be another possibility?").

Cooperation In The Classroom, Interaction Book Company, 7208 Cornelia Drive, Edina, MN 55435, (612) 831-9500, FAX (612) 831-9332

❑ **Test Reality By Checking The Group's Work**: Members should check out the group's work with the instructions, available time, and other examples of reality ("Do we have enough time to do the work this way?").

These skills are among those that keep group members motivated to go beyond the quick answer to the highest quality one. They are aimed at stimulating the reasoning and intellectual curiosity of group members.

Summary

Typically, teachers begin with the forming skills to ensure that the group members are present and oriented toward working with each other. The functioning skills then assist the group in operating smoothly and building constructive relationships among members. The formulating skills ensure that high quality learning takes place within the group and that the members engage in the necessary cognitive processing. The fermenting skills are the most complex and the most difficult to master. They ensure that intellectual challenge and disagreement take place within the learning groups.

The above skills are discussed in terms of upper elementary, secondary, and post-secondary students. Primary and preschool students will need simplified versions of the skills. It is important that teachers translate cooperative skills into language and images that their students can understand and identify with. For example, the fermenting skills could be simplified to skills such as adding an idea, asking for proof, and seeing the idea from the other person's shoes.

Knowing that social skills should be taught and what skills to teach is the beginning. Neither do any good unless educators know how social skills are taught. And once learned, they need to be continuously improved.

5 : 11

Cooperation In The Classroom, Interaction Book Company, 7208 Cornelia Drive, Edina, MN 55435, (612) 831-9500, FAX (612) 831-9332

COACHING SOCIAL SKILLS

1. *Ensure that cooperative learning groups are being used.*

2. *Select the cooperative skill to be taught and make a T-Chart for the skill.*

3. *Take the target student from the regular classroom.*

4. *Explain the skill to the student.*

❑ *Ask the student to suggest a positive example of the skill and predict a possible consequence for engaging in the skill.*

❑ *Ask the student to suggest an opposite example of the skill and predict a possible consequence for his/her negative example.*

❑ *Acknowledge appropriate positive and negative examples and restate the skill.*

❑ *Practice the skill with the student (private guided practice):*

❑ *Ask the student to role play the skill.*

❑ *Praise the student while discussing how well the skill was performed.*

❑ *Repeat until the student no longer awkwardly engages in the skill.*

6. *Explain how to use the skill in the student's cooperative group. Inform the student that you will be observing for the number of times he or she uses the skill in the group each day.*

7. *Observe the group session and record the frequency with which the student engages in the skill (public guided practice). Prompt the use of the skill if it is appropriate to do so. Record the frequency on a chart.*

8. *Just before the beginning of the next cooperative group meeting show the student his/her chart with the number of time he/she performed each skill the day (session) before. Discuss with the student the skills in which progress is good and the skills in which progress is slow. Ask the student why he/she is having difficulty with the skill. Set up criteria to reach in the cooperative session that is about to start, "Yesterday you praised a member's contributions four times. Let's see if you can praise contributions in today's session six times."*

9. *Repeat this procedure until the skill is firmly integrated into the student's behavior repertoire.*

5 : 12

Cooperation In The Classroom, Interaction Book Company, 7208 Cornelia Drive, Edina, MN 55435, (612) 831-9500, FAX (612) 831-9332

How Do You Teach Cooperative Skills?

When police evaluate potential suspects, they look for the joint presence of three characteristics: opportunity, motive, and means. Engaging in an interpersonal action requires the contact opportunity with other people for the act to occur, a reason sufficient to motivate the act, and access to a method or procedure whereby the act can occur. For students to work as a team, they need (a) an opportunity to work together cooperatively (where teamwork skills can be manifested), (b) a motivation to engage in the teamwork skills (a reason to believe that such actions will be beneficial to them), and (c) some proficiency in using teamwork skills. After providing students with the opportunity to learn in cooperative groups, you must provide students with the motive and means for doing so.

The first step is to ensure that students see the need for the teamwork skill. To establish the need for the teamwork skill, you can:

1. Ask students to suggest the teamwork skills they need to work together more effectively. From the skills suggested, choose one or more to emphasize.

2. Present a case to students that they are better off knowing, than not knowing the chosen skills. You can display posters, tell students how important the skills are, complement students who use the skills.

3. Setting up a role play that provides a counter-example where the skill is obviously missing in a group is a fun way to illustrate the need for the skill.

The second step is to ensure that students understand what the skill is, how to engage in the skill, and when to use the skill. You:

1. Operationally define the skill as verbal and nonverbal behaviors so that students know specifically what to do. It is not enough to tell students what skills you wish to see them use during the lesson (*"Please encourage each other's participation and check each other's understanding of what is being learned."*). What is encouraging to one student may be

Encouraging Participation	
Looks Like	**Sounds Like**
Smiles	What Is Your Idea?
Eye Contact	Awesome!
Thumbs Up	Good Idea!
Pat On Back	That's Interesting

discouraging to another. You must explain exactly what they are to do. One way to explain a social skill is through a T-Chart. You list the skill (e.g., encouraging participation) and then ask the class, *"What would this skill look like (nonverbal*

Cooperation In The Classroom, Interaction Book Company, 7208 Cornelia Drive, Edina, MN 55435, (612) 831-9500, FAX (612) 831-9332

behaviors)?" After students generate several ideas, you ask the class, *"What would this skill sound like (phrases)?"* Students list several ideas. You then display the T-Chart prominently for students to refer to.

2. Demonstrate and model the skill in front of the class and explain it step-by-step until students have a clear idea of what the skill sounds and looks like.

3. Have students role play the skill by practicing the skill twice in their groups before the lesson begins.

The third step is to set up practice situations and encourage mastery of the skill. To master a skill, students need to practice it again and again. You can guide their practice by:

1. **Assigning the social skill** as either a specific role for certain members to fulfill or a general responsibility for all group members to engage in. You may wish to introduce one or two new skills each week, review previously taught skills, and repeat this sequence until all the skills are taught.

2. **Observing each group** and recording which members are engaging in the skill with what frequency and effectiveness. Utilize student observers as soon as possible. You may wish to begin with a simple observation form that only has two to four skills on it. When you become used to the observation process, you may expand to an intermediate observation form that has six to eight actions listed and then to an advanced observation form that has ten to twelve actions on it. Student observers are trained in the same sequence of simple to intermediate to advanced observation forms. The procedures for observing may be found in Chapter 8.

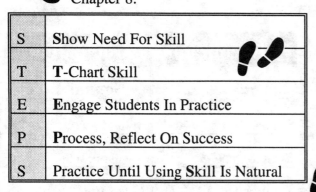

S	Show Need For Skill
T	T-Chart Skill
E	Engage Students In Practice
P	Process, Reflect On Success
S	Practice Until Using Skill Is Natural

3. **Cueing the use of the skill** periodically during the lesson by asking a group member to demonstrate the skill.

4. **Intervening in the learning groups** to clarify the nature of the social skill and how to engage in it.

5. **Coaching students** to improve their use of the skill.

The fourth step is to ensure that each student (a) receives feedback on his or her use of the skill and (b) reflects on how to engage in the skill more effectively next time. Practicing teamwork skills is not enough. Students must receive feedback on how frequently and how well they are using the skill. Organize the observation data into bar

5 : 14

Cooperation In The Classroom, Interaction Book Company, 7208 Cornelia Drive, Edina, MN 55435, (612) 831-9500, FAX (612) 831-9332

graphs and run charts and report the data to the class, groups, and individuals. Help students analyze and reflect on the data. The observer reports the information gathered to the group and group members report their impressions as to how they behaved. The observer shows the observation form to the group, holding it so every group member can see it. He or she then asks the group, *"What do you conclude about (a) your participation in the group and (b) the group functioning in general?"* The observer ensures that all group members receive positive feedback about their efforts to learn and help their groupmates learn. After small group processing, there is whole class processing in which the teacher shares his or her feedback to the class as a whole.

Reflection is needed in order to discover what helped and hindered them in completing the academic assignment and whether specific actions had a positive or negative effect. The observer helps group members process how well the group functioned, how frequently and well each member engaged in the targeted skill, and how the interaction among group members should be modified to make it more effective. On the basis of the feedback received and their own assessment of their skill used, the students reflect on how to use the skill more effectively in the future and set improvement goals. Finally, the groups should celebrate their hard work in learning and using the targeted social skills.

Mystery Person

1. Inform the class that you will be focusing on one student whose name will be kept secret.

2. Select a student randomly or select a student who will be a positive role model or who could benefit from some recognition.

3. Observe during the lesson without showing whom you are observing.

4. Describe to the whole class what the person did (frequency data) without naming the person.

5. Ask students to guess who the mystery person is.

Cooperation In The Classroom, Interaction Book Company, 7208 Cornelia Drive, Edina, MN 55435, (612) 831-9500, FAX (612) 831-9332

Teaching Social Skills

STEPS IN TEACHING A SKILL	TEACHER ACTIONS
Step 1: Establish The Need For The Skill	1. Students choose needed skills. 2. You choose and persuade. 3. Role play the absence of skill.
Step 2: Define The Skill	1. Define with T-chart. 2. Demonstrate, model, explain.
Step 3: Guide Practice Of The Skill	1. Assign the social skill as a role. 2. Record frequency & quality of use. 3. Periodically cue the skill. 4. Intervene to clarify. 5. Coach.
Step 4: Guide Feedback And Reflection	1. Report data to class, group, individuals. 2. Chart/graph the data. 3. Have students analyze the data. 4. Ensure every student receives positive feedback. 5. Have students set improvement goals. 6. Have groups celebrate their hard work.
Step 5: Repeat Steps 3 & 4 Repeatedly	Emphasize continuous improvement while proceeding through the stages of skill development over and over again.

The fifth step is to ensure that students persevere in practicing the skill until the skill seems a natural action. With most skills there is a period of slow learning, then a period of rapid improvement, then a period where performance remains about the same, then another period of rapid improvement, then another plateau, and so forth. Students have to practice teamwork skills long enough to make it through the first few plateaus and integrate the skills into their behavioral repertoires. There are stages most skill development goes through:

1. Self-conscious, awkward engaging in the skill.

2. Feelings of phoniness while engaging in the skill. After a while the awkwardness passes and enacting the skill becomes smoother. Many students, however, feel inauthentic or phony while using the skill. Students need teacher and peer encouragement to move through this stage.

> **SKILL DEVELOPMENT STAGES**
>
> *Awkard*
> *Phony*
> *Mechanical*
> *Integrated*

5 : 16

Cooperation In The Classroom, Interaction Book Company, 7208 Cornelia Drive, Edina, MN 55435, (612) 831-9500, FAX (612) 831-9332

3. Skilled but mechanical use of the skill.

4. Automatic, routine use where students have fully integrated the skill into their behavior repertoire and feel like the skill is a natural action to engage in.

Encourage students to improve continuously their teamwork skills by refining, modifying, and adapting them.

ENSURING EVERY GROUP MEMBER RECEIVES POSITIVE FEEDBACK

1. Each group focus on one member at a time. Members tell the target person one thing he/she did that helped them learn or work together effectively. The focus is rotated until all members have received positive feedback.

2. Members write a positive comment about each group member's participation on an index card. The students then give their written comments to each other so that every member will have, in writing, positive feedback from all the other group members.

3. Members comment on how well each other member used the social skills by writing an answer to one of the following statements and giving their written statements to each other.

   a. *I appreciated it when you..*   d. *I enjoy it when you...*

   b. *I liked it when you...*   e. *You really helped out the group when you...*

   c. *I admire your ability to...*

This procedure may also be done orally. In this case students look at the member they are complimenting, use his or her name, and give their comments. The person receiving the positive feedback makes eye contact and says "*thank you*." Positive feedback should be directly and clearly expressed and should **not** be brushed off or denied.

Using Bonus Points To Teach Social Skills

Many teachers may want to use a structured program to teach students the interpersonal and small group skills they need to cooperate effectively with classmates. Such a program will provide students with the opportunity to help earn bonus points for their groups as a result of their using targeted cooperative skills. These points can be accumulated for academic credit or for special rewards such as free time or minutes listening to one's own choice of music. The procedure for doing so is as follows:

Cooperation In The Classroom, Interaction Book Company, 7208 Cornelia Drive, Edina, MN 55435, (612) 831-9500, FAX (612) 831-9332

1. **Identify, define, and teach a social skill you want students to use in working cooperatively with each other.** This skill becomes a target for mastery. The skills may be forming skills of staying with your group and using quiet voices, functioning skills of giving direction to the group's work and encouraging participation, formulating skills of explaining answers, relating present learning to past learning, and fermenting skills of criticizing ideas without criticizing people, asking probing questions, and requesting further rationale (Johnson, Johnson, & Holubec, 1988).

2. **Use group points and group rewards to increase the use of the cooperative skill:**

   a. Each time a student engages in the targeted skill, the student's group receives a point.

   b. Points may only be awarded for positive behavior.

   c. Points are added and never taken away. All points are permanently earned.

3. **Summarize total points daily.** Emphasize daily progress toward the goal. Use a visual display such as a graph or chart.

4. **Develop an observational system that samples each group an equal amount of time.** In addition, utilize student observers to record the frequency of students using the targeted skills.

5. **Set a reasonable number of points for earning the reward.** Rewards are both social and tangible. The social rewards are having the teacher say, "That shows thought," "I like the way you explained it," "That's a good way of putting it," "Remarkably well done." The tangible reward is the points earned, which may be traded in for free time, computer time, library time, time to a play a game, extra recess time, and any other activity that students value.

6. In addition to group points, **class points may be awarded.** The teacher, for example, might say, "Eighteen people are ready to begin and helped the class earn a reward," or "I noticed 12 people worked the last 25 minutes." Class points may be recorded with a number line, beans in a jar, or checks on the chalk board.

7. In addition to social skills, **potential target behaviors can include task-oriented actions**, such as following directions, completing assigned tasks, handing in homework, behaving appropriately in out-of-class settings such as lunch or assemblies, or helping substitute teachers.

Cooperation In The Classroom, Interaction Book Company, 7208 Cornelia Drive, Edina, MN 55435, (612) 831-9500, FAX (612) 831-9332

Other T-Charts

CHECKING FOR UNDERSTANDING

Looks Like	Sounds Like
Eye contact	Explain that to me please.
Leaning forward	Can you show me?
Interested expression	Tell us how to do it.
Open gestures and posture	How do you get that answer?
	Give me an example please.
	How would you explain it to the teacher?

Contributing Ideas

Looks Like	Sounds Like
Leaning forward	My idea is...
Open gestures and posture	I suggest...
Taking turns	We could...
Member talking with others listening	I suggest we...
	This is what I would do.
	What if we...

SUMMARIZING

Looks Like	Sounds Like
Leaning forward	Our key ideas seem to be...
Pleasant expression	Let's review what we have said so far.
Open gestures and postures	At this point, we have...
	The points we have made so far are...
	Our thinking is …

5 : 19

Cooperation In The Classroom, Interaction Book Company, 7208 Cornelia Drive, Edina, MN 55435, (612) 831-9500, FAX (612) 831-9332

© Johnson, Johnson, & Holubec

Conclusion

If the potential of cooperative learning is to be realized, students must have the prerequisite interpersonal and small group skills and be motivated to use them. These skills need to be taught just as systematically as math and social studies. Doing so involves communicating to students the need for the social skills, defining and modeling the skills, having students practice the skills over and over again, processing how effectively the students are performing the skills, and ensuring that students persevere until the skills are fully integrated into their behavioral repertoires. Doing so will not only increase student achievement, it will also increase students' future employability, career success, quality of relationships, and psychological health.

The social skills students need to be taught are those involved in (a) forming cooperative learning groups, (b) providing the leadership needed to ensure the groups function effectively, (c) formulating conceptual understandings of the material being learned, and (d) fermenting each other's reasoning through intellectual arguments and challenges. For a more thorough and extensive coverage of social skills see **Reaching Out** (Johnson, 1997), **Joining Together** (Johnson & F. Johnson, 1997), **Human Relations and Your Career** (Johnson, 1991), and **Learning Together And Alone** (Johnson & R. Johnson, 1998).

Students have to learn social skills by seeing the need for the skill, understanding what the skill is and how to do it, practicing the skill until it is mastered, reflect on how well they are doing the skill, and persevere until the skill is overlearned at an automatic, routine-use level. Social skills have to be continuously improved.

Teachers have to know how to construct and use observation forms, use student observers, and structure group processing. That is the focus of the next chapter.

Implementation Assignment

1. Read Chapter Six.

2. Review the behaviors you have been encouraging during cooperative lessons. Ask your class what behaviors are needed to make their cooperative learning groups more effective. List their answers. Have the class star the three behaviors they think are the most important.

3. For each of the three skills identified have your students construct a T-Chart. Bring the charts to class to share with your base group.

4. Note in your journal the cooperative skills you wish to improve on.

Cooperation In The Classroom, Interaction Book Company, 7208 Cornelia Drive, Edina, MN 55435, (612) 831-9500, FAX (612) 831-9332

COOPERATIVE LEARNING CONTRACT

Write down your major learnings from reading this chapter and participating in training session one. Then write down how you plan to implement each learning. Share what you learned and your implementation plans with your base group. Listen carefully to their major learnings and implementation plans. You may modify your own plans on the basis of what you have learned from your groupmates. Volunteer one thing you can do to help each groupmate with his or her implementation plans. Utilize the help groupmates offer to you. Sign each member's plans to seal the contract.

MAJOR LEARNINGS	IMPLEMENTATION PLANS

Date: _____ Participant's Signature: _____

Signatures Of Group Members: _____

_____

5 : 21

Cooperation In The Classroom, Interaction Book Company, 7208 Cornelia Drive, Edina, MN 55435, (612) 831-9500, FAX (612) 831-9332

COOPERATIVE LEARNING PROGRESS REPORT

Name: _____ School: _____

Subject Area: _____ Grade: _____

Date	Lesson	Successes	Problems

Describe Critical Or Interesting Incidents:

5 : 22

Cooperation In The Classroom, Interaction Book Company, 7208 Cornelia Drive, Edina, MN 55435, (612) 831-9500, FAX (612) 831-9332

EXERCISE

MATERIALS

5 : 23

Cooperation In The Classroom, Interaction Book Company, 7208 Cornelia Drive, Edina, MN 55435, (612) 831-9500, FAX (612) 831-9332

© Johnson, Johnson, & Holubec

SOCIAL SKILL LESSON PLAN

☆ *What Social Skill Are You Going To Teach?* _____

Hint: *Start by choosing a social skill from the "Functioning" category: Share Ideas and Opinions, Give Direction To the Group's Work, Encourage Everyone To Participate, Ask for Help or Clarification, or Express Support and Acceptance.*

☆ Step 1: *How Will Students See The Need For The Skill?*

___ √ *Ask students to brainstorm what skills are needed to help the groups function more effectively.*

____ √ *Have a bulletin board display.*

___ √ *Tell the students why the skills are needed.*

_____ √ *Jigsaw materials on the need for the skill.*

I will_____

_____

_____

☆ Step 2: *How Will You Help Students Understand What The Skill Is and When It Should Be Used?*

___ ✓ *Have students help make a classroom T-Chart tp analyze the skill.*

____ ✓ *Have students discuss when it is appropriate to use the skill.*

_____ ✓ *Have students practice using the skill with a partner.*

Fill out this T-chart for the skill to prepare for having your students help you do it.

LOOKS LIKE	SOUNDS LIKE
Nonverbal, Body Language	Verbal Statements, Sentence Starters

5 : 24

Cooperation In The Classroom, Interaction Book Company, 7208 Cornelia Drive, Edina, MN 55435, (612) 831-9500, FAX (612) 831-9332

☆Step 3: *How Will You Ensure Students Practice The Skill?*

Hints:	
__Have practice sessions before each formal cooperative learning lesson,	__Give positive feedback to anyone who demonstrates the skill
__Announce that you will observe for the skill	__Assign the skill as a role.

I will_____

_____

_____

☆Step 4: *How Will You Ensure Students Receive Feedback and Process Their Skill Use?*

❑ **Teacher Monitoring:** How will you monitor students use of the skill and give them feedback?

___ ✓ *Formally observe* with a structured observation sheet and count how many times each student uses targeted skill and other needed behaviors

___ ✓ *Informally observe* each group; give verbal or written feedback on how well members are working together and using the targeted skill

I will_____

_____

_____

❑ **Teacher Intervening:** How will you prompt groups to use the skill?

___ ✓ *Noticeably give positive feedback to group using the skill to remind surrounding groups to use it.*

___ ✓ *Supplement positive feedback with a tangible reward to students or groups using the skill.*

___ ✓ *Give a "secret note" to a group member asking them to use the skill; praise the whole group when the group member does it.*

5 : 25

Cooperation In The Classroom, Interaction Book Company, 7208 Cornelia Drive, Edina, MN 55435, (612) 831-9500, FAX (612) 831-9332

I will_____

_____

_____

❑ **Training Student Observers:**

___ ✓ *Have one student in each group tally each time a member uses the skill while they continue to participate in the group work.*

___ ✓ *Teach students to observe using a formal observation sheet. Students take turns sitting outside of the group and observing members' use of the skill.*

❑ ***Processing:*** *Since students need to reflect on their skill use so they can congratulate themselves for progress and devise ways to continuously improve, how will you have students reflect on their use of the skill?*

___ ✓ *Ask them to analyze the feedback from you (the teacher), student observers, and their own memories.*

___ ✓ *Provide questions to help the groups engage in reflective thinking: "How well did each group member use the skill?" "How well did* **you** *use the skill?" "What are some things which helped group members use the skill?" "What are some things which helped* **you** *use the skill?"*

___ ✓ *Help them plan for continuous improvement with questions like "What are two ways to help group members become more skillful in using the skill?" "What are two ways to help* **you** *become more skillful in using the skill?" "Make a plan for improvement."*

Note: *Processing can be done by individual students, groups, and/or whole class.*

I will_____

_____

_____

_____

5 : 26

Cooperation In The Classroom, Interaction Book Company, 7208 Cornelia Drive, Edina, MN 55435, (612) 831-9500, FAX (612) 831-9332

☆Step 5: How Will You Ensure that Students Persevere In Practicing The Skill Until It Becomes Natural?

Daily:

___ ✓ Remind them that you will be listening for their use of the skill.

___ ✓ Give feedback on what you heard.

___ ✓ Have them process their use of the skill.

Periodically:

___ ✓ Discuss with the class the stages of learning a skill (awkward, phony, mechanical, and automatic).

___ ✓ Have students or groups rate their level of use and chart progress.

___ ✓ Give class reward if students use the skill a preset number of times.

___ ✓ Have the principal, an aide, a parent, or another teacher observe and give feedback on how frequently the skill is being used.

___ ✓ Tutor or coach target students on the use of the skill.

___ ✓ Have students think of places outside of class to use the skill, have them do so and report on how it went and what they noticed.

I will_____

_____

_____

_____

☆When most students have reached the automatic stage, plan and teach them another skill!

Cooperation In The Classroom, Interaction Book Company, 7208 Cornelia Drive, Edina, MN 55435, (612) 831-9500, FAX (612) 831-9332

REPORT FORM: SOCIAL SKILLS

Student: _____ Date: _____ Grade: _____

N = Needs Improvement   P = Making Progress   S = Satisfactory   E = Excellent

Shows Cooperative Attitude (Forming Skills)

_____ Moves Into Group Quietly

_____ Stays With Group; No Wandering

_____ Uses Quiet Voice In Group Work

_____ Takes Turns

_____ Uses Others' Names

_____ Respects Rights Of Others

_____ Positive About Working In Group

_____ Is Willing To Help Others

_____ Follows Directions

_____ Shows Courtesy Toward Others

Leadership (Functioning) Skills

_____ Clarifies Goals

_____ Gives Direction To Group's Work

_____ Contributes Ideas, Opinions

_____ Requests Others' Ideas, Opinions

_____ Summarizes, Integrates

_____ Encourages Others' Participation

_____ Supports; Gives Recognition, Praise

_____ Paraphrases

_____ Facilitates Communication

_____ Relieves Tension

Facilitates Understanding (Formulating) Skills

_____ Summarizes, Integrates

_____ Seeks Accuracy (Corrects)

_____ Relates New Learning To Old

_____ Helps Group Recall Knowledge

_____ Checks For Understanding

_____ Makes Covert Reasoning Overt

Intellectual Challenge (Fermenting) Skills

_____ Criticizes Ideas, Not People

_____ Differentiates Members' Ideas

_____ Integrates Members' Ideas

_____ Asks For Rationale, Justification

_____ Extends Others' Reasoning

_____ Probes, Asks Complex Questions

5 : 28

SKILL-TEACHING PLANNING FORM

Cooperative Skill: _____

Definition: _____

_____

LOOKS LIKE	SOUNDS LIKE

Help Students See Need For Skill By: _____

_____

Encourage The Use Of The Skill By: _____

_____

Process Use By: _____

_____

Refine Skill Later By: _____

_____

Notes on levels of use, problems, things learned for next time:

5 : 29

Cooperation In The Classroom, Interaction Book Company, 7208 Cornelia Drive, Edina, MN 55435, (612) 831-9500, FAX (612) 831-9332

GUIDED PRACTICE: TEACHING A SOCIAL SKILL

Task: Practice teaching social skills to your students.

Cooperative: Working in a pair, role play teaching the social skill as if the other person were your class. Use the following procedure:

1. Say to your class, "Stop working, close your books, look at me."

2. With the assistance of your students in a whole class discussion, construct a T-Chart for the skill.

3. State:

   a. *"Your task is to learn the skill of **summarizing**."*

   b. *"Work cooperatively. Make sure you can summarize, everyone in your group can summarize, and every group member can explain what the skill of summarizing is."*

4. Have the students practice the skill twice, using two different phrases.

5. Instruct students to resume work. Observe each group and note whether the skill of summarizing is being used by group members.

6. Repeat the above sequence with the following skills (each person teaches two social skills):

   a. Giving direction to the group's work.

   b. Asking for help or clarification.

   c. Criticizing ideas without criticizing people.

Expected Criteria For Success: Both persons able to teach a social skill.

Individual Accountability: Each person teaches two social skills to other.

Expected Behaviors: Presenting, listening, processing, and encouraging.

Intergroup Cooperation: Whenever it is helpful, check with other groups.

5 : 30

Cooperation In The Classroom, Interaction Book Company, 7208 Cornelia Drive, Edina, MN 55435, (612) 831-9500, FAX (612) 831-9332

COOPERATION IN THE CLASSROOM: CHAPTER FIVE SUMMARY

Complete this table by writing in six reasons for teaching social skills, the four types of social skills to teach, the five steps in teaching social skills, and the four stages of skill learning. Form a pair and compare your answers. For any answers on which you disagree, look up the correct answer in the chapter.

WHY TEACH SOCIAL SKILLS?	WHAT SOCIAL SKILLS TO TEACH	STEPS IN TEACHING SKILLS	STAGES OF SKILL LEARNING

5 : 31

Cooperation In The Classroom, Interaction Book Company, 7208 Cornelia Drive, Edina, MN 55435, (612) 831-9500, FAX (612) 831-9332

KNOW THAT SOCIAL SKILL

Given below are twelve specific social skills. Classify each skill into one of the following four categories by placing the number for the category in front of each skill. Form a pair and compare your answers. For any answers on which you disagree, look up the correct answer in the chapter.

	1 = Forming Skills		**3** = Formulating Skills
	2 = Functioning Skills		**4** = Fermenting Skills

	Criticize Ideas Without Criticizing People: Intellectually challenging groupmates by criticizing their ideas while communicating respect for other group members.
	Summarize Out Loud: Summarizing out loud what has just been read or discussed as completely as possible without referring to notes or to the original material.
	Give Direction To The Group's Work: Helping the group move ahead rather than staying stalled for lack of direction.
	Noise Monitor: Ensures classmates move into cooperative learning groups quietly without bothering others.
	Ask For Justification: Asking other members to give the facts and reasoning that justify why the member's conclusion is correct.
	Turn Taking Monitor: Ensures group members take turns in completing the assignment.
	Seek Elaboration: Asking other group members to relate material being learned to earlier learned material and to other things they know.
	Encourage Everyone To Participate: Asking other members to share what they are thinking or what their ideas.
	Voice Monitor: Ensures all group members use quiet voices.
	Share Ideas And Opinions: All group members need to share their ideas (and materials).
	Check For Understanding: Demanding vocalization to make the implicit reasoning process being used by other members overt and thus open to correction and discussion.
	Integrate Ideas Into Single Position: Synthesizing and integrating members' different and conflicting ideas and reasoning into one position that everyone can agree to.

Cooperation In The Classroom, Interaction Book Company, 7208 Cornelia Drive, Edina, MN 55435, (612) 831-9500, FAX (612) 831-9332

CHAPTER SIX:
MONITORING AND INTERVENING

Monitoring Learning Groups

Teachers are always observing and noticing what is going on around them. They look to see who is and who is not on task, which students are out of their seat, which students look puzzled, and which students are finished and waiting for their next assignment. Observation is a primary, yet often underutilized, tool of assessing learning and instruction. **Observation** is the recording and describing of behavior as it occurs. Its **purpose** is to provide objective data about:

P^2
P = Performances
P = Processes

1. **The quality of student performances**. Many student performances, such as giving a speech, playing tennis, providing leadership, helping a classmate, using higher-level reasoning, or drawing a picture can only be assessed through observational methods.

2. **The quality of the processes and procedures students use in completing assignments**. To improve continuously the process of learning, students must receive feedback concerning their actions in completing an assignment.

Bias In Observations

A major problem with observation is the potential lack of objectivity by the observers. An example of biased observing may be seen in a study conducted by Hastorf and Cantril (1954). They asked Dartmouth and Princeton students to watch a film of the football game between the two colleges. The game was an unusually rough one in which many penalties were called. The Princeton quarterback, an all-American, left the game in the second quarter with a broken nose and a mild concussion. The Dartmouth quarterback left the game in the third quarter with a broken leg. The Dartmouth and Princeton students were asked to watch the film and record the number and severity of the infractions committed by the two teams. Dartmouth won the game and its students saw the two teams committing an equal number of violations. The Princeton students saw the Dartmouth players as committing more than twice as many fouls as the Princeton team.

A solution to the problem of bias is the use of **structured coding systems**, which require observers to categorize each group behavior into an objectively definable category.

6 : 1

Cooperation In The Classroom, Interaction Book Company, 7208 Cornelia Drive, Edina, MN 55435, (612) 831-9500, FAX (612) 831-9332

FIGURE 6.1 MONITORING AND INTERVENING

Monitoring

Quality Of Student Performances

Quality Of Learning Processes

Observing

Preparing For Observation

Observing

Summarizing Results

Intervening

Improve Teamwork

Improve Taskwork

Structuring Self-Monitoring

Guides For Monitoring

Cooperation In The Classroom, Interaction Book Company, 7208 Cornelia Drive, Edina, MN 55435, (612) 831-9500, FAX (612) 831-9332

Observing

In using observation, you need to:

1. Prepare for observing by:

   a. Deciding which student behaviors, actions, and skills are to be observed.

   b. Deciding who will be the observers.

   c. Making a sampling plan.

   d. Constructing an observation form, checklist, or unstructured procedure to record the frequencies of targeted actions that are appropriate for the age of the students.

   e. Training the observers.

2. Observe and record how often each student performs the specified behaviors. Observation procedures may be formal or informal.

3. Intervene to increase students' teamwork and taskwork effectiveness.

4. Summarize the observations in a clear and useful manner.

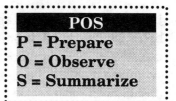

POS
P = Prepare
O = Observe
S = Summarize

SUMMARY OF OBSERVING			
ACTIONS OBSERVED	**WHO WILL OBSERVE**	**SAMPLING PLAN**	**OBSERVATION METHOD**
Academic Learning	Teacher (Always)		Formal
Reasoning	Students: Roving		Checklist
Skills	Students: One For Each Group		Informal
Attitudes	Visitors		
Work Habits			

Cooperation In The Classroom, Interaction Book Company, 7208 Cornelia Drive, Edina, MN 55435, (612) 831-9500, FAX (612) 831-9332

Preparing For Observing

In preparing for observing, you state your instructional objectives in the appropriate behavioral form. The objectives should describe student behavior that is observable and countable. Then you decide which actions to observe, who will observe, what the sampling plan will be, and how the observers will be trained. You then construct your observation form.

Which Actions Will We Observe?

The most thorough way to decide what to observe is to create a flow chart of the steps students will use in completing the assignment. The **flow chart** is created by:

1. Defining the boundaries: Clearly defining where the learning process begins and ends and what are its inputs and outputs.

2. Identifying all the steps the process actually follows (what are the key steps, who is involved, who does what, when).

3. Drawing the steps in a sequence.

The flow chart guides observation of what the group actually does. The results of the observation may then be compared with the flow chart. Either the flow chart is revised (to make it more realistic) or the quality with which group members engage in each step is improved. Included in the flow chart will be one of more of the following instructional outcomes.

1. **Academic learning and performance:** You observe students working in groups to determine (a) the extent to which students do or do not understand what they are studying and (b) if they are progressing in completing the assignment and to determine what students know, understand, and retain over time. This helps you pinpoint areas of learning that need to be focused on or retaught. There are many learning outcomes, such as oral and written communication skills, research skills, skills of organizing and analyzing information, and technology skills that can only be assessed through observing. There are many performances such as playing music, singing, dancing, dramatic enactments, or athletic skills that may be better assessed observing than by any other assessment procedure. Observing allows you to assess transfer and application of what is being learned. You can observe students' work to determine if they are on task completing their work or are off task engaging in some other activity than the prescribed academic learning.

2. **Cognitive reasoning:** You can assess many learning outcomes (such as depth of understanding, level of reasoning, mastery of scientific method and problem-solving

Cooperation In The Classroom, Interaction Book Company, 7208 Cornelia Drive, Edina, MN 55435, (612) 831-9500, FAX (612) 831-9332

procedures, construction of academic arguments, and meta-cognitive thinking) only by opening a *"window into students' minds"* and observing students *"thinking out loud."* The assessment issue is, *"How do you make covert cognitive reasoning overt and therefore open to correction and improvement?"* While paper-and-pencil tests and homework assignments indicate whether students can determine the "correct" answer, they usually do not reveal students' cognitive reasoning and depth of understanding. The only way to determine whether students really understand a procedure or concept is to listen to them explain it to someone else. Such oral explanations can be obtained either by (a) listening to students' explanations as they work in cooperative learning groups or (b) interviewing a student and requesting a detailed explanation of reasoning processes. The former is much more time efficient than the latter.

3. **Social skills**. One of the many advantages of cooperative learning is that it allows teachers, students, and other interested parties to assess students' mastery of the interpersonal and small group skills needed to work with others.

4. **Attitudes**: It is through observing that you assess the attitudes students develop, such as a love of learning, commitment to being a responsible citizen, desire to read, liking scientific reasoning, self-respect, liking of diversity, commitment to making the world a better place, and many others.

5. **Work Habits**: You observe to assess the work habits students develop, such as completing work on time, using time wisely, meeting responsibilities, striving for quality work, continuously improving one's work, striving to add value to each job one does, and so forth.

Who Will Observe?

1. **Teachers:** You, the teacher, are always an observer. In every lesson, you systematically roam from group to group. You gather specific information on the interaction of members in each group. When necessary, you intervene to improve students' efforts to learn and to help classmates learn.

2. **Students:** When students become experienced in working in cooperative learning groups, you should train them to be observers.

   a. Students may be roving observers who circulate throughout the classroom and monitor all learning groups. Similar to the teacher, student roving observers need a sampling plan to ensure that they observe all groups an approximately equal amount of time.

   b. Students may also observe their own groups (one observer per group). In this case, student observers remove themselves slightly from the group so they are

6 : 5

Cooperation In The Classroom, Interaction Book Company, 7208 Cornelia Drive, Edina, MN 55435, (612) 831-9500, FAX (612) 831-9332

close enough to see and hear the interaction among group members. Observers do not participate in the academic task or comment while the group is working. You set aside a time near the end of the class period for the learning groups to review the content of the lesson with the observer. The role of observer rotates so that each group member is an observer an equal amount of time.

3. **Visitors:** Visitors should not be allowed to sit and watch a lesson passively. When someone visits your classroom, hand them an observation form, explain the role of the observer, and put them to work. Visitors may be roving observers or they may observe one single group, depending on the purpose of their visit.

Making Sampling Plan For Roving Observers

FIVE MINUTE WALK

1. Select actions to observe.

2. Construct observation sheet.

3. Plan route through the classroom.

4. Gather data on every group.

5. Feedback the data to the groups and/or to the class as a whole.

6. Chart / graph the results.

Before the lesson begins you plan how much time you will spend observing each learning group (this is a **sampling plan**). You may observe one learning group for the entire class period, collecting information on every member. Or, if the class period lasts for 50 minutes and there are ten groups in the class, you may decide to observe each group for five minutes. Or, you may observe each group for two minutes and rotate through all the groups twice during one class period. If you decide you should intervene in a group or with a student, you temporarily suspend the sampling plan and then resume it after the intervention is over.

Constructing An Observation Procedure

There are three main procedures for observing: Using a formal observation form to record the frequency with which target actions are occurring, observation checklists for determining the quality with which target actions are occurring, and informal observing in which you record your impressions of what is taking place. These three procedures may be placed on a continuum from most subjective to most objective (see above).

OBSERVATION PROCEDURES CONTINUUM		
Subjective----------- To------------------------		Objective
Informal Observing	Checklist	Formal Form

Cooperation In The Classroom, Interaction Book Company, 7208 Cornelia Drive, Edina, MN 55435, (612) 831-9500, FAX (612) 831-9332

1. Constructing A Formal Observation Form

Observation forms are used to answer the question, "*How often are certain actions or events happening?*" **Observation forms** are used to tally and count the number of times a behavior, action, or event is observed in a specified time period. An example is given below. The form has to be designed so that all potential observers can use it (that is, age appropriate). **A structured (formal) observation form is created in the following way.**

1. Define exactly what behaviors, actions, skills, or events are being observed (such as contributes ideas, encourages participation, checks for understanding, gives group direction). All observers have to be looking for the same thing.

2. Determine time period during which data will be collected. One group may be observed for 50 minutes or each group may be observed for two minutes. Observations may be summarized after one class session or after several class sessions.

3. Entering the actions to be observed in the first column (each action or skill is placed in a separate row, the final row is reserved for the total of the columns).

4. Making an additional column for each member of the group and making a final column to record the total for each row on the form.

5. Making sure all columns are clearly labeled and wide enough to enter data.

OBSERVATION FORM

Observer: Date: Time Period:

Actions	Edythe	Keith	Dale	Total
Contributes Ideas				
Encourages Participation				
Checks For Understanding				
Gives Group Direction				
Other:				
Total				

Cooperation In The Classroom, Interaction Book Company, 7208 Cornelia Drive, Edina, MN 55435, (612) 831-9500, FAX (612) 831-9332

The simplest use of formal observation procedures is to observe whether students are engaged in academic learning or off-task. This type of observation can be used when students work individually by themselves or when students are working in cooperative learning groups. The observation form consists of a list of students in the class, two columns to indicate either on-task or off-task behavior, and a column for comments.

Observing On-Task Behavior

Class: **Group:**   **Date:**

Students	On-Task	Off-Task	Comments
Frank			
Helen			
Roger			
David			
Edythe			
Keith			
Dale			
Tai			
Roberta			
Phillip			
Juan			

2. Constructing An Observation Checklist

An **observation checklist** focuses on the quality with which each student has demonstrates a targeted action, skill, or procedure. Checklists include students' names, space for four to five targeted behaviors, a code or rating scale to signify the level of mastery (+ = frequently; 0 = sometimes; - = not yet), a space for comments or anecdotal notes, and a space to record the date so that developmental growth can be examined. Checklists may be used to observe students during lessons, on the playground, on field trips, in hallways. They can be used to observe students individually, in groups, with younger students, with older students, or with adults. An example is observing for student persistence.

Cooperation In The Classroom, Interaction Book Company, 7208 Cornelia Drive, Edina, MN 55435, (612) 831-9500, FAX (612) 831-9332

CHECKLIST FOR "PERSISTENCE"

Indicators	Not Yet Observed	Observed Sometimes	Observed Frequently
Accesses Information			
Does Not Give Up			
Tries Several Strategies			
Seeks Several Solutions			
Other:			

OBSERVATION CHECKLIST

BEHAVIOR	−	O	+	COMMENTS
1. Do students understand the task?				
2. Are students thinking out loud by explaining step-by-step how to complete the assignment?				
3. Are students challenging each other's reasoning and searching for new information and understandings?				
4. Are students engaging in the social and cognitive skills they are expected to practice in this lesson?				

3. Planning Unstructured Observations

As long as you are hearing or seeing the class, you are observing. Informal, off-the-cuff observation is always taking place; the challenge is to become aware of it and make it as accurate and helpful as possible. **Informal, unstructured observing** is the recording of only significant, specific events involving pupils. The emphasis is on significant,

6 : 9

Cooperation In The Classroom, Interaction Book Company, 7208 Cornelia Drive, Edina, MN 55435, (612) 831-9500, FAX (612) 831-9332

qualitative incidents that may occur somewhat infrequently. It is not necessary to record an observation for each pupil each day. Teachers make informal observations that are:

1. Specific (they don't degenerate into generalities).

2. Brief enough to write down quickly.

3. Capture an important aspect of the behavior of one or more pupils.

4. Answer questions about students' efforts to maximize own and other's learning.

To immediately record your informal observations you need a notebook, a few 3x5 inch index cards, or a form such as that given below. Such notes may be organized in a permanent way by placing them in a log. You may wish to write down positive incidents on cards and file them under the student's name (after they have been used to give the student feedback). You can then access the cards in parent conferences as examples of the student's competencies and positive qualities.

ANECDOTAL OBSERVATIONS

Observer:_____ Date:_____

Note 1:   Group:_____ Student(s):_____

Note 2:   Group:_____ Student(s):_____

Note 3:   Group:_____ Student(s):_____

Note 4:   Group:_____ Student(s):_____

6 : 10

Cooperation In The Classroom, Interaction Book Company, 7208 Cornelia Drive, Edina, MN 55435, (612) 831-9500, FAX (612) 831-9332

Training Observers

If students or visitors are to be used as observers, they must be trained to follow observation procedures, use the observation forms, and follow the sampling plan. Minimal training can make students quite proficient observers:

1. Explain the role of the observer.

2. Explain the observation procedure and the form or checklist to be used.

3. If possible, have observers practice using the form or checklist and then discuss any questions they may have.

4. Coach observers. Occasionally, sit side-by-side with a student observer and check your counts against his or hers. Discuss any discrepancy.

5. Process. Take a few minutes after an observation period to chat with students about what they learned in doing the observing.

6. Have all students observe a videotape of a group working and compare their observations with classmates. The videotape may be replayed and analyzed several times.

For very young students you may wish to keep the observer role very simple, perhaps only recording "*Who talks?*" Many teachers have had good success with student observers, even in kindergarten. One first grade teacher had a student who talked all the time (even to himself while working alone). The student tended to dominate. When the teacher introduced student observers to the class, she made this student an observer. One important rule for observers was not to gather data without talking. He was gathering data on who talks and he did a good job, noticing that one student had done quite a bit of talking in the group whereas another had talked very little. The next day when he was a group member, and there was another observer, he was seen starting to talk, clamping his hand over his mouth and glancing at the observer. He knew what was being observed and he didn't want to be the only one with marks. The observer often benefits in learning about how to behave more competently.

Observing

Cooperative learning groups offer a unique opportunity for immediate (a) diagnosis of level of understanding, (b) feedback from peers, and (c) remediation to correct misunderstandings and fill in gaps in students' understanding. Training students to observe facilitates the cycle of immediate diagnosis-feedback-remediation.

Cooperation In The Classroom, Interaction Book Company, 7208 Cornelia Drive, Edina, MN 55435, (612) 831-9500, FAX (612) 831-9332

BEING AN OBSERVER

1. Use one observation form for each group. Place a tally mark in the appropriate row and column when a student engages in one of the targeted actions. Look for patterns of behavior in the group. Do not worry about recording everything, but observe as accurately and rapidly as possible.

2. Initially, try not to count too many different behaviors at one time. You may wish to choose two to four behaviors from our observation sheet to record the first few times you observe. Once you have used the observation sheet several dozen times, you will be able to keep track of all the behaviors included.

3. Make notes on the back of the observation form if something takes place that should be shared with the group but does not fit into the actions being observed. Supplement and extend the frequency data with notes on specific student actions. Especially useful are skillful interchanges that you observe and can share with students later as objective praise. You can also share them with parents in conferences or telephone conversations.

4. Write down specific positive and important contributions by each group member (to ensure that every member will receive positive feedback).

5. When you use student observers, allocate several minutes at the end of the class for the group members to teach the observer what they have learned. Often important insights are made during this review.

6. After the learning session is over, have student observers total the columns and rows. Transfer the totals to long-term record sheets and the appropriate charts or graphs. The observation forms should be dated and kept to assess the growth of the students and groups. When you or a roving observer observes a group more than once during a class session, different colored ink may be used. This allows group members to assess their skill development at a glance.

7. Have observers give the information gathered to the group and help members deriving conclusions. The observer shows the observation form to the group, holding it so all members can see it. He or she asks the group, ***"What do you conclude about (a) your participation in the group and (b) the group functioning in general?"*** The observer ensures all group members receive positive feedback about their

Cooperation In The Classroom, Interaction Book Company, 7208 Cornelia Drive, Edina, MN 55435, (612) 831-9500, FAX (612) 831-9332

efforts to learn and help their groupmates learn. After small group processing, there is whole class processing.

8. Have observers help group members set goals for improving their competence in engaging in the social skills during the next group meeting by asking, **"What could you add to be even a better group tomorrow than you were today?"** The observer has members discuss the goals and publicly commit to achieving them. Emphasize the continuous improvement of students' competencies and group effectiveness.

9. You always observe during every lesson, even if you are using student observers.

10 Be open to discovering unexpected and unplanned outcomes. Unexpected outcomes can be the most interesting, and the next time you teach the same lesson you may wish to include them in the list of expected outcomes.

Intervening To Improve Taskwork And Teamwork

While monitoring a learning group you (the teacher) may see patterns of behavior that are dysfunctional to learning and teamwork. You may then wish to intervene. Reasons to intervene within a cooperative learning group include:

1. To correct misunderstandings or misconceptions about task instructions and the academic concepts and procedures being learned.

2. To correct the absence, incorrect use, or inappropriate use of interpersonal and small group skills or cognitive skills.

3. To reinforce the appropriate or competent use of social and cognitive skills.

While observing the learning groups you (the teacher) have to decide if you are going to intervene. If you decide to do so, you must know how to intervene effectively. Telling students how to be more effective is a very weak intervention. You do not want to solve the problem for the group. You want to highlight the problem for the group to solve and guide members to a solution that they themselves discover and implement. You join the group and follow the guidelines for intervening that appear below.

6 : 13

INTERVENING IN COOPERATIVE GROUPS

1. Join the group and have members set aside their task (*"Pencils down, close your books, look at me."*).

2. **Alternative One:** Point out the problem by showing the data you collected by observing (*"Here is what I observed."*). Ask students to identify the problem and plan how to correct it. Often just the awareness of the recorded information will get group members to take corrective action.

3. **Alternative Two:** Point out the problem by asking a question (*"Why has Roger make only two comments in the past 20 minutes?"*).

4. **Alternative Three:** Focus members on their reasoning processes by asking (a) *"What are you doing?"* (b) *"Why are you doing it?"* and (c) *"How will it help you?"*

5. **Alternative Four:** Have students role play the situation and practice new behaviors that would solve the problem.

6. Ask members to create three possible solutions (*"What are three plans for solving this problem?"*).

7. Ask members to decide which solution they are going to try first (*"Which plan will you implement first?"*)

8. If the group members cannot identify a clear procedure to correct the problem, guide them towards several alternative courses of action. Highlighting a problem may only create helplessness, demoralization, and frustration if students believe there is nothing they can do to solve it. Suggesting several strategies to choose from will empower students.

9. Tell students to go back to work (*"Open your books, read problem four, go back to work."*).

10. Use the language relevant to the learning. Instead of saying, *"Yes, that is right,"* say something more specific to the assignment, such as, *"Yes, that is one way to find the main idea of a paragraph."* The use of the more specific statement reinforces the desired learning and promotes positive transfer by helping the students associate a concept with their learning.

Cooperation In The Classroom, Interaction Book Company, 7208 Cornelia Drive, Edina, MN 55435, (612) 831-9500, FAX (612) 831-9332

There are a number of decisions teachers will have to make while observing students working cooperatively:

1. **Should I intervene now or wait for the processing time?** You may wish to stop the group's work and intervene immediately, or you may wish to wait until the processing time and then intervene.

2. **Should I intervene within this single group or should I intervene within the entire class?** Sometimes the problem is specific to a group and sometimes it is a generic problem that all groups may be experiencing.

3. **Should I tell students how to be more effective or structure a problem-solving process for them to discover the same point?** In a skillful intervention, you do not solve the problem for the group. You want students to learn how to diagnose and solve problems in group functioning. If you are too active in solving problems, students will not have the chance to do so. Guide students to a solution that they themselves discover and implement. It is only in the most extreme cases that you may wish to tell students how to behave more appropriately and skillfully.

4. **Should I have students talk about the issue or should I have them role play the situation and practice new behaviors?**

INTERVENING
O = Observe
IDQ = Intervene by sharing data or asking a question
SP = Have students process and plan how they will solve problem
BTW = Tell students to go back to work

5. **Does the problem identified have a clear procedure to correct it?** If not, highlighting the problem may only create helplessness, demoralization, and frustration. For every problem in group functioning identified, students should always believe that there is something they can do to correct it.

Ideas For Monitoring And Intervening

Check For	If Present	If Absent
Members seated closely together	Good seating.	Draw your chairs closer together
Group has right materials and are on right page	Good, you are all ready.	Get what you need--I will watch.
Students who are assigned roles are doing them	Good! You're doing your jobs.	Who is supposed to do what?
Groups have started task	Good! You've started.	Let me see you get started. Do you need any help?
Cooperative skills being used (in general)	Good group! Keep up the good work!	What skills would help here?
A specific cooperative skill being used	Good encouraging! Good paraphrasing!	Who can encourage Edye? Repeat in your own words what Edye just said.
Academic work being done well	You are following the procedure for this assignment. Good group!	You need more extensive answers. Let me explain how to do this again.
Members ensuring individual accountability	You're making sure everyone understands. Good work!	Roger, show me how to do #1. David, explain why the group chose this answer.
Reluctant students involved	I'm glad to see everyone participating.	I'm going to ask Helen to explain #4. Get her ready and I will be back.
Members explaining to each other what they are learning and their reasoning processes	Great explanations! Keep it up.	I want each of you to take a problem and explain to me step-by-step how to solve it.
Group cooperating with other groups.	I'm glad you're helping the other groups. Good citizenship!	Each of you go to another group and share your answer to #6.
One member dominating	Everyone is participating equally. Great group!	Helen, you are the first to answer every time. Could you be accuracy checker?
Groups that have finished	Your work looks good. Now do the activity written on the board.	You are being very thorough. But time is almost up. Let's speed up.
Group working effectively	Your group is working so well. What behaviors are helping you?	Tell me what is wrong in the way this group is working. Let's make three plans to solve the problem.

6 : 16

Cooperation In The Classroom, Interaction Book Company, 7208 Cornelia Drive, Edina, MN 55435, (612) 831-9500, FAX (612) 831-9332

NONVERBAL	VERBAL
S = Smiles	Close Your Books, Pencils Down, Look At Me
O = Open Gestures	I Have Noticed That...
F = Forward Learning	Explain What My Observation Form Shows
T = Touch	What Is Our Social Skills Goal?
T = Tonality	What Are Three Plans For Solving The Problem?
E = Eye Contact	I Will Come Back Later To See If The Plan Worked
N = Nodding Head	Open Your Books, Get Back To Work

Cooperative learning groups (a) give you a "window into students' minds" (revealing covert cognitive processes that have become overt) and (b) provide you with a picture of students' social skills. You intervene for two reasons.

1. To help students learn, improve, and refine their teamwork and taskwork skills when (a) they do not have the necessary skills to be effective or (b) there are disruptive and ineffective patterns of interaction among group members.

2. To catch students in the act of using the targeted skills in effective ways so their skillful actions can be recognized and celebrated.

A teacher noticed while distributing papers that one student was sitting back away from the other two members of his group. A moment later the teacher glanced over and only two students were sitting where three were a moment before. As she watched, the two students came marching over to her and complained that Johnny was under the table and wouldn't come out. *"Make him come out!"* they insisted. *"Johnny is a member of your group,"* the teacher said, *"what have you tried to solve their problem."* *"Tried?"* the puzzled reply. *"Yes, have you asked him to come out?"* the teacher suggested. The group marched back to their table and the teacher continued distributing papers to groups. A moment later the teacher glanced over and saw no heads above the table (which is one way to solve the problem). After a few more minutes, three heads came struggling out from under the table and the group (including Johnny) went back to work with great energy. We do not know what happened under that table; whatever it was, it was effective. What makes this story even more interesting is that the group received a 100 percent on the assignment and later, when the teacher was standing by Johnny's desk, she noticed he had the assignment clutched in his hand. The group had given Johnny the group's paper and he was taking it home. He confided to the teacher that this was the

Cooperation In The Classroom, Interaction Book Company, 7208 Cornelia Drive, Edina, MN 55435, (612) 831-9500, FAX (612) 831-9332

© Johnson, Johnson, & Holubec

first time he could ever remember earning a 100 on anything in school. (If that was your record, you might slip under a few tables yourself.)

TIPS	TRAPS
Intervene Only When Absolutely Needed	Jump In Frequently To Solve Problems
Intervene At Eye Level	Stand Over Group, Looking Down
Have Whole Group Focus On You	Have Only One Member Focus On You
Label Actions, Not Student	Embarrass, Insult By Labeling Student
Focus On "Here And Now"	Bring In The Past
Have Students Problem Solve	Tell Students What To Do
Have Students Generate Three Plans	Say "OK" To Students' Initial Plan

Summarizing Data

Reflection and analysis is assisted by plotting in a chart the data on members' interaction. To display the results of observations so that students, parents, and other interested parties may interpret them two charts are helpful: the bar chart and the run chart.

Constructing A Bar Chart

1. List the actions, conditions or causes you wish to monitor.

2. Collect the data on the number of times the actions conditions, or causes occurred in a predetermined period of time.

3. On the left-hand axis, list the measurement scale by recording the total number of actions, conditions, or causes on the left vertical axis.

4. Under the horizontal axis, write the actions, conditions, or causes observed. They may be placed in descending order (the most frequently occurring action to the left and the least occurring to the right):

   a. Identify the action, condition, or cause with the largest total. Working from left to right, (1) label the first bar on the horizontal axis of the chart with the action, condition, or cause, (2) record the total in the blank space, and (3) draw a vertical

6 : 18

Cooperation In The Classroom, Interaction Book Company, 7208 Cornelia Drive, Edina, MN 55435, (612) 831-9500, FAX (612) 831-9332

bar stretching from 0 to the total frequency of occurrence using the measurement scale on the left-hand axis as a guide.

b. Identify the action, condition, or cause with the second largest total. Label the second bar on the horizontal axis of the chart with the action, condition, or cause. Record the total in the blank space. Draw a vertical bar stretching from 0 to the total frequency of occurrence using the measurement scale on the left-hand axis as a guide.

c. Continue this procedure until every action, condition, or cause has been recorded on the chart in sequence from most to least frequently occurring.

5. Students and/or other audiences make an action plan by noting which actions are engaged in at an appropriate level and which should be increased or decreased.

Constructing A Run Chart

A **Run Chart** is used to monitor the process over time to see whether or not the long-range average is changing (see Figure 2.6). In a Run Chart data points are plotted on an x-y axis in chronological order. There are two guidelines for identifying meaningful trends or shifts in the average. First, when monitoring any process, an equal number of points should fall above and below the average. When nine points "run" on one side of the average, it indicates (a) a statistically unusual event and (b) the average has changed. Second, when six or more points steadily increase or decrease with no reversals, it indicates a statistically unusual event. Both cases point towards an important change the team needs to investigate. You create a run chart by:

1. Marking off the time period to be used along the horizontal axis.

2. Entering the unit of measurement along the left vertical axis.

3. Entering the data as it becomes available.

4. Analyzing the (historical) trend revealed by the position of the data points (each point can be compared to the overall average).

5. Making a plan as to how to either increase or decrease the frequency of occurrence of the targeted action, condition, or cause.

Cooperation In The Classroom, Interaction Book Company, 7208 Cornelia Drive, Edina, MN 55435, (612) 831-9500, FAX (612) 831-9332

BAR CHART AND RUN CHART

Long-Term Progress: Weekly Bar Chart

Group Members: _____

_____

Class: _____ Subject Area: _____

```
50
45
40
35
30
25
20
15
10
 5
```

Contributes   **Encourages**   **Integrates**   **Helps**
Ideas   **Others**   **Summarizes**   **Groupmates**

Long-Term Progress: Run Chart

Group Members: _____

_____

Class: _____ Subject Area: _____ Skill: **SUMMARIZES** ____

```
50
45
40
35
30
25
20
15
10
 5
```

Week 1   Week 2   Week 3   Week 4   Week 5

6 : 20

Cooperation In The Classroom, Interaction Book Company, 7208 Cornelia Drive, Edina, MN 55435, (612) 831-9500, FAX (612) 831-9332

Self-Monitoring

"No one remains quite what he was when he recognizes himself."

Thomas Mann (1875-1955), a German writer

Having students rate themselves and their groupmates is an important addition to most instructional units (Johnson & Johnson, 1996). In addition to observing students at work, and having students and visitors observe, students can also assess their own participation in cooperative learning groups and learning activities (i.e., **self-monitor**). The steps for self-assessment are (Johnson & Johnson, 1996):

1. **Involve students in developing a set of criteria to use in assessing their performances.** Students brainstorm a potential list of criteria (each cooperative group comes up with their list), you, the teacher, add potential criteria to the list, and the class rank orders the criteria from most important to least important.

ASSESSMENT CRITERIA			
Rank	**Student List**	**Teacher List**	**Final Negotiated List**

2. **Involve students in creating a rubric for each criterion.** Students begin with the criterion ranked most important and create the rubric by listing indicators of very poor, poor, middle, good, and very good levels of performance. You find exemplary and very poor student performances and have students analyze them to help develop a set of indicators that accurately measures students' strengths and weaknesses in using the targeted skills and actions. Rubrics are needed to assess the quality and quantity of each student's performance for each criterion.

Cooperation In The Classroom, Interaction Book Company, 7208 Cornelia Drive, Edina, MN 55435, (612) 831-9500, FAX (612) 831-9332

VERY POOR	POOR	MIDDLE	GOOD	VERY GOOD
Criterion Ranked One				
◆	◆	◆	◆	◆
◆	◆	◆	◆	◆
◆	◆	◆	◆	◆
Criterion Ranked Two				
◆	◆	◆	◆	◆
◆	◆	◆	◆	◆
◆	◆	◆	◆	◆
Criterion Ranked Three				
◆	◆	◆	◆	◆
◆	◆	◆	◆	◆
◆	◆	◆	◆	◆

3. **Train the students to use the criteria and rubrics** so that they are co-oriented, consistent, and reliable. Students have to be able to apply the criteria and rubrics in the same way at different times. Different students have to be able to apply the same criteria and rubrics in the same way. Give learning groups a student performance to score, discussing how the performance should be assessed on each criterion. Then have students (a) score a student performances separately and (b) compare their scoring with their groupmates to ensure all group members are using the criteria and rubrics in the same way.

My Scores	Groupmate Scores	Groupmate Scores	Consensus Scores

6 : 22

Cooperation In The Classroom, Interaction Book Company, 7208 Cornelia Drive, Edina, MN 55435, (612) 831-9500, FAX (612) 831-9332

4. **Conduct lesson and have each student assess his or her use of the targeted skills and actions.** It is sometimes helpful to have the other group members assess each member's use of the targeted skills, so that self-assessments can be compared with the assessments of groupmates. (See **My Checklist For Cooperative Groups.**)

5. **On the basis of the assessment, have students develop an action plan to improve their performance of the targeted skills and actions**. Students identify their strengths and weaknesses in using the targeted skills and actions, set improvement goals, and assess and chart their progress in achieving their goals.

Action Plan For Improving Skill:	
Strengths In Performing Skill:	
Weaknesses In Performing Skill:	
Improvement Goal:	
Ways I Will Assess Progress:	

6. **Have the class continuously improve the criteria, the rubrics, and students' skills in assessing the quality and quantity of their learning.** Periodically students need to recalibrate their use of the criteria and rubrics.

An alternative procedure is to have students complete a questionnaire in which the focus of the questions are what the member did (I, me), what other members did (you, they), or what all members did (we):

1. Students rate (self-assessments or "I" statements) how often and how well they individually performed the targeted social skills and other expected behaviors.

2. Students rate how often and how well each groupmate performed the targeted social skills and other expected behaviors. The "you" statements give students an opportunity to give other group members feedback about which actions were perceived as helpful or unhelpful.

3. Students rate the overall group. The "we" statements provide an opportunity for group members to reach consensus about which actions helped or hurt the group's work.

4. Students discuss and reflect on their learning experiences (under the guidance of an observant teacher), comparing their self-ratings with the ratings they receive from groupmates.

Cooperation In The Classroom, Interaction Book Company, 7208 Cornelia Drive, Edina, MN 55435, (612) 831-9500, FAX (612) 831-9332

Such self and other ratings allow students to see how the quality of their work has evolved. Then the results are used to help analyze how well group members worked together. For each question the frequencies can be summed and divided by the number of members in order to derive an average. Or, each group member can publicly share his or her answers in a whip--each group member has 30 seconds to share his or her answer to each question with no comment allowed from other group members (do one question at a time). A third procedure is having each group member name actions he or she performed that helped the group function more effectively, and then name one action the member to his/her right (or left) performed that also helped the group.

My Checklist For Cooperative Groups

Name: _____ **Date:** _____ **Class:** _____

1. When I knew an answer or had an idea, I shared it with the group.

    Never 1---2---3---4---5 All The Time

2. When my answer did not agree with someone else's, I tried to find out why.

    Never 1---2---3---4---5 All The Time

3. When I did not understand something, I asked others to explain.

    Never 1---2---3---4---5 All The Time

4. When someone else did not understand, I explained it until he or she did.

    Never 1---2---3---4---5 All The Time

5. I tried to make the people in the group feel appreciated and respected.

    Never 1---2---3---4---5 All The Time

6. Before I signed my name to our paper, I made sure that I understood everything, agreed with the answers, and was confident that all other members understood the answers.

    Never 1---2---3---4---5 All The Time

6 : 24

Cooperation In The Classroom, Interaction Book Company, 7208 Cornelia Drive, Edina, MN 55435, (612) 831-9500, FAX (612) 831-9332

STUDENT SELF AND PEER EVALUATION FORM

This form will be used to assess the members of your learning group. Fill one form out on yourself. Fill one form out on each member of your group. During the group discussion, give each member the form you have filled out on him or her. Compare the way you rated yourself with the ways your groupmates have rated you. Ask for clarification when your rating differs from the ratings given you by your groupmates. Each member should set a goal for increasing his or her contribution to academic learning of all group members.

Rating Your Self And Groupmates

Person Being Rated: _____ Date: _____ Group: _____

Write the number of points earned by the group member
(4 = Excellent, 3 = Good, 2 = Poor, 1 = Inadequate)

_____ *On time for class.*

_____ *Arrives prepared for class.*

_____ *Reliably completes all assigned work on time.*

_____ *Work is of high quality.*

_____ *Contributes to groupmates' learning daily.*

_____ *Asks for academic help and assistance when it is needed.*

_____ *Gives careful step-by-step explanations (not just tell answers).*

_____ *Builds on others' reasoning.*

_____ *Relates what is being learned to previous knowledge.*

_____ *Helps draw a visual representation of what is being learned.*

_____ *Voluntarily extends a project.*

6 : 25

Cooperation In The Classroom, Interaction Book Company, 7208 Cornelia Drive, Edina, MN 55435, (612) 831-9500, FAX (612) 831-9332

Guides For Monitoring

Your primary responsibility while monitoring is to watch, listen, and think about what you see. You decide when and if to intervene. Monitoring is the time to find out what your students do and do not understand and how skillful they are in working together. Things to look for may include:

Did heads come together in the group?	Who are my really skillful students?
Are all group members contributing verbally?	What strategies are groups using to accomplish the task?
What happens after an idea is shared? Is it paraphrased? Supported?	Who needs to improve on social skills? Which skills?

Effective monitoring of cooperative learning groups is part of your teaching. It can be your best time with your students. Do not neglect it! You now change from direct giver of information to teamwork and taskwork coach. Get your whistle, put on your track shoes, and get ready. As soon as you have given the cooperative group assignment, start watching the students and moving around the room. On the first round, look for obvious problems.

Round One: Check If Students Are Working Together

1. **Are group members seated close together (knee to knee, eye to eye)?** If not, help them move their chairs together. If students are left as loners because of absent group members, chose a group for them to join for the day and help them get included and welcomed by the members.

2. **Are groups on the right page?** Doing the right assignment? Doing it the way you asked? If not, clarify and get them on the right track.

3. **Have previously absent students been welcomed back and brought up to date?** Welcome them, make sure group members have welcomed them, and then have the groups go over what the absentees missed so they can get caught up and do appropriate make-up work.

4. **Are there students with obvious problems or concerns who need extra attention?** Bleary eyes or sullen looks often denote difficult days for students—a pat on the shoulder or a positive greeting by you and group members can go a long way toward putting them into a working mood or at least making their day more tolerable.

5. **If students were asked to bring work to the group, do they have it?** Ask to see such work and deal appropriately with students who did not meet their group

Cooperation In The Classroom, Interaction Book Company, 7208 Cornelia Drive, Edina, MN 55435, (612) 831-9500, FAX (612) 831-9332

responsibilities. This may include asking the group to problem solve positive ways to help a student meet his or her responsibilities (peer pressure with peer support) or removing the student from the group to do the required work while the group proceeds without him or her.

Round Two: Check If Students Are Doing The Work Well

1. **What is the quality and quantity of group work?** Give feedback on the work so far, clarify or reteach anything misunderstood, and praise good efforts and accomplishments. Helpful statements may be *"Better check number two again," "You have three right so far," "Excellent work on the first paragraph."*

2. **Is every student orally explaining?** Because this is so important for learning, watch for and encourage every student to explain the work. Make sure groups are including everyone in the explaining. Say, *"Listen to David," "Have you asked Edye?"*

3. **Can individual students explain the work or answers?** Give individual oral exams by randomly selecting one group member to explain the work so far. The other members encourage but do not give the answer. If the student can answer, the group gets praise. If the student can not answer, give the group more time and recheck the student later.

4. **Do you have a student for whom knowing all the answers is an unrealistic demand right now?** If so, pick one or two questions you will ask that student and alert the group by saying, *"I will ask Roger to explain the answer to number one today--get him ready."* Next week ask harder questions. Eventually, require the same amount and level of work. After the group has had ample time to prepare the student, go back and ask the student to explain. Praise the group for correct answers.

5. **How well are individual students doing?** Watch how individual students learn and how they interact with others. Take notes on positive behaviors to share with the class and with parents. Take notes on behaviors you want to change as the year progresses so you can plan for the skill teaching and processing.

6. **How well are students doing the assignment?** Do students need reteaching or more practice? Are they ready for individual work? Are they ready to move on to new material? Evaluate the learning pace and adjust accordingly. Also, you can adjust assignments for individuals. Students who do not need extra practice can be given challenge work. Students who can not do all the assignment can have it adjusted to an appropriate level.

7. **How well are students cooperating?** Praise skillful behaviors. Remind students of your expectations. Stay until they demonstrate the appropriate behaviors. Then praise their efforts. Describe what you saw to help groups gain awareness of their skillful or

Cooperation In The Classroom, Interaction Book Company, 7208 Cornelia Drive, Edina, MN 55435, (612) 831-9500, FAX (612) 831-9332

unskillful behaviors. Role playing sometimes helps students gain an awareness of their skillful and unskillful behaviors. Sometimes changing seating (putting a reluctant student in the middle) or roles (making a dominant student the encourager) helps. You may also wish to ask the group to suggest ideas for improving.

Remember to turn problems in working together effectively back to the group to solve. Help the group members define the problem carefully, have them think of several possible solutions, then have them pick one to try. Be aware that peer pressure coupled with peer support is a strong tool for handling problem students. Getting group members to say, "*We want you to help us; how can we help you do that?*" to a reluctant learner is powerful, although change may not be immediate. Your job is to encourage the group to persist and let the members know you support their efforts.

You may wish to take students with severe behavior problems aside, listen privately to their problems, have them describe what they are doing, have them look at how their actions are helping or not helping, and help them plan to improve their behavior. Practice with them to prepare them to return to the group. Coach the group members on helpful ways of responding. Be certain that you and group members encourage and acknowledge even small improvements.

Round Three: Formally Observe, Give Feedback, And Process

1. **Do I have time for formal observation?** Choose an observation sheet, pick a group, and gather specific data on several group skills such as "contributing ideas" and "asks for facts and reasoning." If you are teaching a skill or have assigned some specific roles, these can go on the observation sheet. Observe a group for five minutes, then interrupt and give positive feedback or give the group feedback during processing time later in the period. Keep the observation sheets so you can document progress (useful for parent conferences!).

2. **Are groups finishing the work and have nothing to do?** As groups finish, check over their work and quiz individual members. If their work is not satisfactory, have them revise it. When the work is satisfactory, give an extension activity related to the assignment (write a new problem and solve it; invent a new ending; think of another example), have them help other groups, or have them process extensively. Just letting them talk quietly for a short time is sometimes appropriate here because it can build group cohesiveness.

When the groups have finished the work, monitoring is over. Bring the lesson to a close by going over answers or summarizing the learning. Report the effective use of cooperative skills you saw while you monitored. Have group members give each other positive feedback, process their group's effectiveness, make plans for improving, and thank each other for the help.

Cooperation In The Classroom, Interaction Book Company, 7208 Cornelia Drive, Edina, MN 55435, (612) 831-9500, FAX (612) 831-9332

REVIEWING THE THREE ROUNDS

Devise key words and/or pictures for 3x5 cards to remind you what to do in each round.

ROUND ONE	ROUND TWO	ROUND THREE

Cooperation In The Classroom, Interaction Book Company, 7208 Cornelia Drive, Edina, MN 55435, (612) 831-9500, FAX (612) 831-9332

Summary

To improve the quality of learning in cooperative groups, the process of working together has to be carefully examined. The purposes of monitoring and intervening are to streamline the process to make it simpler (reduce complexity), eliminate unskilled and inappropriate actions (error-proofing the process), and improve continuously students' skills in working as part of a team. **Monitoring means to observe continuously. Observation** is aimed at recording and describing behavior as it occurs. Preparing for observing involves deciding what actions to observe, who will observe, what the sampling plan will be, constructing an observation form or checklist, and training observers. Conducting observations may focus on students' "on-task" behavior, academic efforts, or social skills. In summarizing observations, the data may be displayed in bar or run charts.

Students' social skills have to improve continuously. Teachers have to engineer a process through which students assess the current levels of their social skills and plan how to increase them. There are four steps in structuring group processing. The first is to decide what skills to emphasize. A social skills objective is made for the lesson. The second step is to explain the social skills to students. The social skill is operationally defined with a T-Chart and taught to students. The third step is monitoring the use of the skills in the cooperative learning groups. Teachers have to know how to construct a structured observation form and how to use student observers. The teacher prepares an observation form and observers use it to determine the frequency with which the social skills are used. The teacher intervenes in learning groups when help is needed and has students assess their use of the targeted skills. Students analyze the observation and self-assessment data and place it in Bar Charts or Run Charts to help draw conclusions and plan how to improve the quality of the group's work. The fourth step is analyzing and reflecting on the effectiveness of the group. Feedback is given. Goals for improvement are set. The group celebrates its hard work and success. These final activities are the focus of the next chapter.

Implementation Assignment

1. Read Chapter 7.

2. Review the monitoring forms in this chapter. Select those you will use with your class.

3. Implement the group monitoring and intervening procedures in your classroom. Train your students to be observers. Record the results to share with your base group.

4. Make a journal entry concerning the use of monitoring and intervening procedures.

Cooperation In The Classroom, Interaction Book Company, 7208 Cornelia Drive, Edina, MN 55435, (612) 831-9500, FAX (612) 831-9332

COOPERATIVE LEARNING CONTRACT

Write down your major learnings from reading this chapter and participating in training session one. Then write down how you plan to implement each learning. Share what you learned and your implementation plans with your base group. Listen carefully to their major learnings and implementation plans. You may modify your own plans on the basis of what you have learned from your groupmates. Volunteer one thing you can do to help each groupmate with his or her implementation plans. Utilize the help groupmates offer to you. Sign each member's plans to seal the contract.

MAJOR LEARNINGS	IMPLEMENTATION PLANS

Date: _____ Participant's Signature: _____

Signatures Of Group Members: _____

_____

6 : 31

Cooperation In The Classroom, Interaction Book Company, 7208 Cornelia Drive, Edina, MN 55435, (612) 831-9500, FAX (612) 831-9332

COOPERATIVE LEARNING PROGRESS REPORT

Name: _____ School: _____

Subject Area: _____ Grade: _____

Date	Lesson	Successes	Problems

Describe Critical Or Interesting Incidents:

6 : 32

Cooperation In The Classroom, Interaction Book Company, 7208 Cornelia Drive, Edina, MN 55435, (612) 831-9500, FAX (612) 831-9332

EXERCISE

MATERIALS

Cooperation In The Classroom, Interaction Book Company, 7208 Cornelia Drive, Edina, MN 55435, (612) 831-9500, FAX (612) 831-9332

OBSERVING AND INTERVENING: PURPOSEFUL READING

Read the first question. Find the answer in the text. Discuss the answer with your partner until both of you agree and are able to explain it. Relate the answer to previous learning. Move to the next question and repeat the procedure.

Questions

1. What is observation?

2. What are the two purposes of observation?

3. What is the solution to the major problem in observing?

4. What is the four-step procedure for observing?

5. What actions do you observe?

6. What is a flow chart?

7. Who observes?

8. What is a sampling plan?

9. What are the three observation procedures?

10. How do you construct a formal observation form?

11. How do you construct an observation checklist?

12. How do you plan for unstructured observations?

13. How do you train observers?

14. What is the cycle of immediate diagnosis-feedback-remedation?

15. What are the ten steps of being an observer?

16. What are three reasons for intervening in groups?

17. What are the ten steps of intervening?

18. What are two ways of summarizing data for analysis?

19. What are the six steps of structuring self-monitoring?

20. How would you describe the three rounds of monitoring?

6 : 34

Cooperation In The Classroom, Interaction Book Company, 7208 Cornelia Drive, Edina, MN 55435, (612) 831-9500, FAX (612) 831-9332

THEY WILL NEVER TAKE US ALIVE EXERCISE

1. Form groups of five. One member volunteers to be an observer.

2. Each group member individually completes the **They Will Never Take Us Alive Ranking Task**.

3. The group decides by consensus on the best ranking possible on the **They Will Never Take Us Alive** items. There should be one ranking for the group, every member should agree with the ranking, and every member should be able to explain the rationale behind the ranking of each item.

4. Score the accuracy of the group's ranking by comparing it with the expert's ranking. Find the absolute difference between the group's ranking and the expert's ranking for each item and add them together. The lower the score the more accurate the group's ranking.

5. Using the observer's information, the members' impressions, and the group's accuracy score for the ranking, discuss how effectively the group functioned. Write down your group's conclusions.

6. Share your group's conclusions with the entire class.

Cooperation In The Classroom, Interaction Book Company, 7208 Cornelia Drive, Edina, MN 55435, (612) 831-9500, FAX (612) 831-9332

THEY WILL NEVER TAKE US ALIVE RANKING SHEET

In a recent survey, Dun's Review lists the most perilous products or activities in the United States, based on annual death statistics. Below are listed fifteen of these death-causing hazards. Your task is to rank them in order of their dangerousness according to the number of death's caused each year. Place 1 by the most dangerousness, 2 by the next most dangerous, and so forth.

Item	Your Ranking	Group Ranking	Experts' Ranking	Individual Difference Scores	Group Difference Scores
Swimming					
Railroads					
Police Work					
Home Appliances					
Alcohol					
Nuclear Power					
Smoking					
Motor Vehicles					
Pesticides					
Handguns					
Bicycles					
Firefighting					
Mountain Climbing					
Vaccinations					
Surgery					
Total					

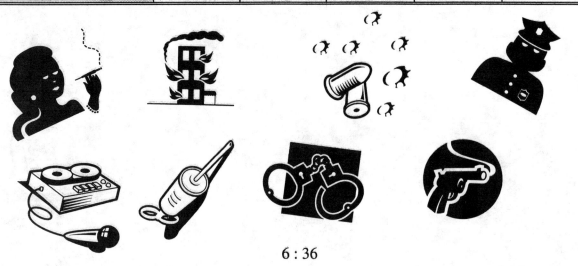

6 : 36

Cooperation In The Classroom, Interaction Book Company, 7208 Cornelia Drive, Edina, MN 55435, (612) 831-9500, FAX (612) 831-9332

COMPLEX PROBLEM SOLVING / DECISION MAKING

Task: Rank items from most important to least important and write out a rationale as to why you ranked the items as you did.

Goal Structures:

1. **Individualistic:** Individual ranking and rationale without interacting with others.

2. **Cooperative:**

   a. One ranking and rationale from the group.

   b. Every member must agree on the ranking and rationale.

   c. Every member must be able to explain the rationale for the ranking.

Criteria For Success: 0 - 20 Excellent, 21 -30 Good, 31-40 Poor, 41+ Terrible.

Individual Accountability:

1. One member will be randomly selected to explain group's ranking and rationale.

2. Each member will explain group's ranking and rationale to a member of another group.

Expected Behaviors:

1. Everyone participates.

2. Summarize and synthesize

3. Ask others for facts and reasoning.

4. Do not change your mind unless you are logically persuaded.

Intergroup Cooperation: When finished, share ranking, information, and reasoning with a nearby group.

6 : 37

Cooperation In The Classroom, Interaction Book Company, 7208 Cornelia Drive, Edina, MN 55435, (612) 831-9500, FAX (612) 831-9332

GROUP SELF-MONITORING

WRITE DOWN TWO WAYS EACH MEMBER HELPED THE GROUP TODAY!

NAME	HELPFUL ACTION	HELPFUL ACTION

GROUP MONITORING

AGREE ON YOUR ANSWERS AND WRITE ON YOUR GROUP PAPER:

1. **What are three specific actions we did that helped us do well on the assignment?**

    a.

    b.

    c.

2. **How did each of us contribute to the group's success?**

    a.

    b.

    c.

3. **What is an action that would help us do even better next time?**

    a.

    b.

    c.

6 : 38

Cooperation In The Classroom, Interaction Book Company, 7208 Cornelia Drive, Edina, MN 55435, (612) 831-9500, FAX (612) 831-9332

Planning For Observing

1. The student actions I wish to observe are:

Cognitive Reasoning	Social Skills

2. The observers will be: _____ Teacher(s)   _____ Students   _____ Visitors

3. The procedure will be: _____ Formal _____ Checklist _____ Informal

Observer: _____ **Date:** _____ **Grade:** _____

Actions	Member 1	Member 2	Member 3	Total
Total				

4. The route through the classroom will be: _____
_____

5. Data will be summarized: _____ Chart/Graph _____ Oral Summary

6. Feedback to: _____ Each Student _____ Each Group _____ Whole Class

7. Students will reflect on:

_____ What do you conclude about (a) your participation in the group and (b) how effectively they learned and helped each other learn?

_____ What actions could you add to increase your own learning and help others learn more?

6 : 39

Cooperation In The Classroom, Interaction Book Company, 7208 Cornelia Drive, Edina, MN 55435, (612) 831-9500, FAX (612) 831-9332

© Johnson, Johnson, & Holubec

SIMULATIONS, ROLE PLAYING, AND OBSERVATION

There are times when you wish to observe students engaging in a skill or pattern of behavior, but it will take far too much time to wait and observe the behavior occurring naturally. To save time, you create a simulation and observe what students do. Simulations and games are increasingly being used as training and assessment procedures. Simulations can vary widely in complexity of issues and number of participants, ranging from relatively simple simulations for an individual or small group to moderately complex computerized simulations requiring a number of groups to participate. For assessment purposes, students are placed within a simulation and their actions are monitored and observed so that behavioral measures of outcomes can be obtained.

Frequently in simulations, students role play the characters. Initial instructions are given, and the role players determine what happens. Role playing is a tool for:

1. Bringing a specific skill and its consequences into focus so it may be practiced.

2. Experiencing concretely the type of interaction under examination.

3. Setting up an imaginary life situation so students can act and react in terms of the assumptions they are asked to adopt, the beliefs they are asked to hold, and the character they are asked to play.

4. Giving students experience in discussing and identifying effective and ineffective behavior.

You, as the coordinator of the simulated role play:

1. Get students in "role." You help involve the role players in the situation by introducing it in such a way that the players are emotionally stimulated. Using name tags and asking the players questions to help them get a feeling for the part are helpful. Introduce the scene to the role players and the observers.

2. Conduct the simulation. While the students are engaged in the role play, you carefully observe and record the frequency of their effective and ineffective actions.

3. Get students out of "role." Always "de-role" after the role playing has ended.

4. Conduct a processing session in which students reflect on what happened and how to behave more effectively.

6 : 40

Cooperation In The Classroom, Interaction Book Company, 7208 Cornelia Drive, Edina, MN 55435, (612) 831-9500, FAX (612) 831-9332

Observation Form

Observer: Date: Grade:

Assignment:

Action					Total
Contributes Ideas					
Describes Feelings					
Encourages Participation					
Summarizes, Integrates					
Checks For Understanding					
Relates New To Old Learning					
Gives Direction To Work					
Total					

Directions For Use: (a) Put the names of the group members above each column. (b) Put a tally mark in the appropriate box each time a group member contributes. (c) Make notes on the back when interesting things happen that are not captured by the categories. (d) Write down one (or more) positive contribution made by each group member.

6 : 41

Cooperation In The Classroom, Interaction Book Company, 7208 Cornelia Drive, Edina, MN 55435, (612) 831-9500, FAX (612) 831-9332

Cooperative Learning: Classroom Observation

Teacher:_____ Date:_____ Observer: _____

Teacher Actions	Implementation	Comments
Objectives	❑ Academics ❑ Social Skills	
Positive Interdependence	❑ Group Goal ❑ Group Celebration/Reward ❑ Resources Shared/Jigsawed ❑ Roles Assigned ❑ Shared Identity	
Group Composition	❑ Random ❑ Teacher Selected	
Seating Arrangement	❑ Clear View/Access to Groupmates, Teacher ❑ Clear View/Access to Materials	
Individual Accountability	❑ Each Student Tested Individually ❑ Students Check Each Other ❑ Random Student Evaluated ❑ Role: Checker for Understanding	
Define Social Skills	❑ Define (T-Chart) ❑ Demonstrate/Model ❑ Guided Practice ❑ Assign As Role	
Observation Of Taskwork And Teamwork	❑ Teacher Monitors And Intervenes ❑ Students Monitor ❑ Formal Observation Form ❑ Informal (Anecdotal) Observation	
Teacher Feedback: Teamwork Skills	❑ Class ❑ Group ❑ Individual ❑ Frequency And Quality Of Use ❑ Charts and Graphs Used ❑ Positive Feedback To Each Student	
Group Processing	❑ Analysis/Reflection: Teamwork & Taskwork ❑ Goal Setting For Improvement ❑ Celebration	
General Climate	❑ Group Products Displayed ❑ Group Progress Displayed ❑ Aids To Group Work Displayed	

6 : 42

Cooperation In The Classroom, Interaction Book Company, 7208 Cornelia Drive, Edina, MN 55435, (612) 831-9500, FAX (612) 831-9332

Teacher Observation Form

Name: _____ **Date:** _____ **Class:** _____

Assignment: _____

Groups	Explaining Concepts	Encouraging Participation	Checking For Under-standing	Organizing The Work
1				
2				
3				
4				
5				

Cooperation In The Classroom, Interaction Book Company, 7208 Cornelia Drive, Edina, MN 55435, (612) 831-9500, FAX (612) 831-9332

WEEKLY OBSERVATION FORM

Teacher: _____ **Date:** _____ **Class:** _____

Assignment: _____

Directions: List the students to be observed in column one, list the social skill each student is supposed to engage in column two, and note the frequency of the use of the skill for each day of the week. Then total the daily frequencies.

Student	Social Skill	Mon	Tues	Weds	Thurs	Fri	Total

Comments:

Weekly Report Form

Name: _____ **Date:** _____ **Class:** _____

Date	On-Task Work	Contributes Ideas	Integrates, Summarizes	Helps Classmates	Completes Assignments
Totals:					

Comments:

Cooperation In The Classroom, Interaction Book Company, 7208 Cornelia Drive, Edina, MN 55435, (612) 831-9500, FAX (612) 831-9332

CHAPTER SEVEN:

GROUP PROCESSING

Introduction

In 1979 a commuter aircraft crashed while landing at an airport on Cape Cod in Massachusetts (reported in Norman, 1992). The pilot died and the co-pilot and six passengers were seriously injured. As the plane was landing, the copilot noted that the plane seemed to be too low, and he told the pilot. The pilot, however, did not respond. The copilot remarked that the glide path seemed rather steep, but the pilot did not respond. The copilot remarked that the descent rate seemed excessive. The pilot did not respond. The pilot, who was also president of the airline, and who had just hired the copilot, hardly ever responded. He was the strong, silent type. He was in charge, and that was that. United States airlines regulations require pilots and copilots to respond to one another, but what was the co-pilot to do. He was new to the company, and the captain was his boss. Moreover, the captain often flew low. What the copilot failed to notice was that the captain was "incapacitated." That is technical term meaning that the captain was unconscious and probably dead from a heart attack. At the investigation the copilot testified that (a) he made all the required call-outs except the "no contact" call and (b) the pilot did not acknowledge any of the calls. Because the captain rarely acknowledged calls, the lack of response did not alert the copilot to the fact that the pilot was dead. It seems strange. There they are flying along and the pilot dies. You would think the copilot would notice.

TEAM
T = Together
E = Everyone
A = Achieves
M = More

What was not established in the cockpit of that plane was a procedure for group processing. The pilot and copilot never discussed the process of flying the plane, did not analyze the nature of their interaction, and did not reflect on their effectiveness as a team. Consequently, when an emergency occurred, the copilot was slow to recognize it. If cooperative learning groups are to function effectively, and student achievement is to be maximized, regular group processing is a necessity.

This chapter presents a framework for ensuring that group processing takes place in an effective manner (see Figure 7.1). We define group processing, discuss procedures for structuring group processing, and give practical suggestions for making group processing effective.

7 : 1

Cooperation In The Classroom, Interaction Book Company, 7208 Cornelia Drive, Edina, MN 55435, (612) 831-9500, FAX (612) 831-9332

Figure 7.1 Small Group And Whole Class Processing

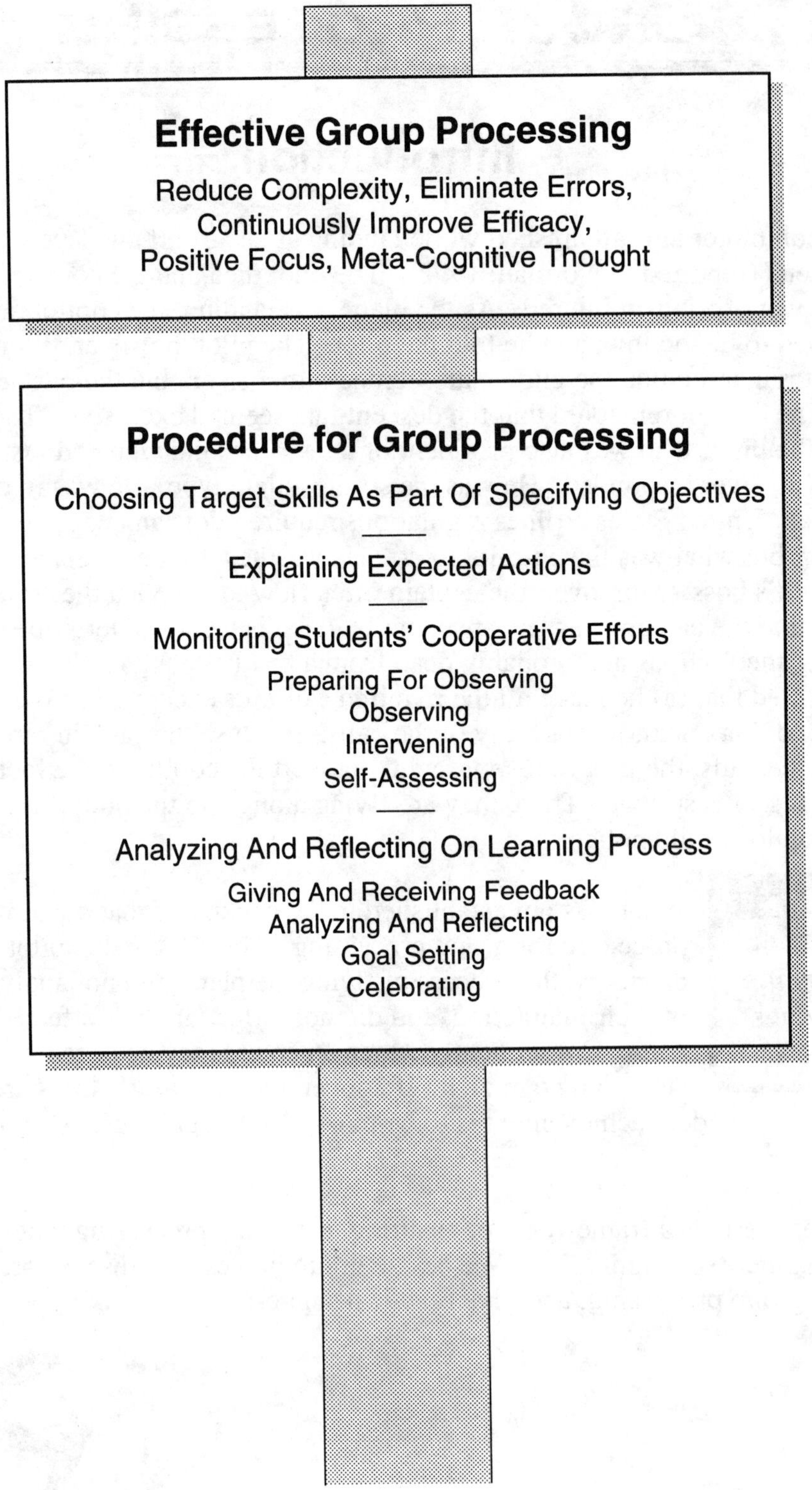

Effective Group Processing

Reduce Complexity, Eliminate Errors,
Continuously Improve Efficacy,
Positive Focus, Meta-Cognitive Thought

Procedure for Group Processing

Choosing Target Skills As Part Of Specifying Objectives

Explaining Expected Actions

Monitoring Students' Cooperative Efforts

Preparing For Observing
Observing
Intervening
Self-Assessing

Analyzing And Reflecting On Learning Process

Giving And Receiving Feedback
Analyzing And Reflecting
Goal Setting
Celebrating

7 : 2

Cooperation In The Classroom, Interaction Book Company, 7208 Cornelia Drive, Edina, MN 55435, (612) 831-9500, FAX (612) 831-9332

The Nature Of Group Processing

We don't seek to be one thousand percent better at any one thing. We seek to be one percent better at one thousand things.

Jan Carlzon, President, Scandinavian Air Systems

An essential component of cooperative learning is group members examining the process by which they are completing assignments and continuously improving it. A **process** is an identifiable sequence of actions (or events) taking place over time aimed at achieving a given goal (Johnson & F. Johnson, 1997). **Group processing** is members reflecting on the group's work and members' interaction to clarify and improve members' efforts to achieve the group's goals and maintain effective working relationships by (a) describing what member actions were helpful and unhelpful and (b) making decisions about what actions to continue or change. The **purposes** of group processing are to:

1. Improve continuously the quality of the group's taskwork and teamwork.

2. Increase individual accountability by focusing attention on each member's responsible and skillful actions to learn and to help groupmates learn.

> **Group Processing**
> Receive Feedback
> Analyze And Reflect
> Set Improvement Goals
> Celebrate

3. Streamline the learning process to make in simpler (reducing complexity).

4. Eliminate unskilled and inappropriate actions (error-proofing the process).

MONITORING	PROCESSING
Prepare For Observation	Students & Groups Receive Feedback
Observe, Supervise Student Observers	Reflect On What Was Helpful And Unhelpful
Summarize Results In Graphs	Set Goals For Improvement
Intervene To Improve Learning	Celebrate Hard Work And Success

Monitoring prepares the way for processing. During monitoring you (the teacher) prepare for observation, observe and supervise the students and visitors who are observing, and summarize and organize the observations (often in charts and graphs) to give to students and other stakeholders (such as parents). When it is needed, you intervene to improve students' taskwork and teamwork.

7 : 3

Cooperation In The Classroom, Interaction Book Company, 7208 Cornelia Drive, Edina, MN 55435, (612) 831-9500, FAX (612) 831-9332

At the end of the lesson, students should engage in group processing. **You (the teacher) structure group processing by** (a) setting aside time for students to reflect on their experiences in working with each other and (b) provide procedures for students to use in discussing group effectiveness (such as, "*List three things your group is doing well today and one thing you could improve*"). You may provide several minutes or so at the end of each group session for immediate processing and a longer period of time every five group sessions or so for a more detailed discussion of the process the group is using to maximize members' learning. Students reflect on and analyze the group session to (a) describe what member actions were helpful and unhelpful in contributing to the joint efforts to achieve the group's goals and (b) make decisions about what actions to continue or change. Group processing occurs at two levels; there is both small group processing and whole-class processing. There are four parts to group processing.

1. **Feedback:** You ensure that each student and each group and the class receives (and gives) feedback on the effectiveness of taskwork and teamwork.

2. **Reflection:** You ensure that students analyze and reflect on the feedback they receive.

3. **Improvement Goals:** You help individuals and groups set goals for improving the quality of their work.

4. **Celebration:** You encourage the celebration of members' hard work and the group's success.

GIVING PERSONAL FEEDBACK IN A HELPFUL, NON THREATENING WAY

_____ 1. Focus feedback on behavior (not on personality traits).

_____ 2. Be descriptive (not judgmental).

_____ 3. Be specific and concrete (not general or abstract).

_____ 4. Make feedback immediate (not delayed).

_____ 5. Focus on positive actions (not negative ones).

_____ 6. Present feedback in a visual (such as a graph or chart) as well as auditory fashion (not just spoken words alone).

7 : 4

Cooperation In The Classroom, Interaction Book Company, 7208 Cornelia Drive, Edina, MN 55435, (612) 831-9500, FAX (612) 831-9332

Giving And Receiving Feedback

You take the first step in structuring group processing when you ensure that learning groups and individual students receive feedback on the quality of their taskwork and teamwork so they can continuously improve both. **Feedback** is information on actual performance that individuals compare with criteria for ideal performance. When feedback is given skillfully, it generates energy, directs the energy toward constructive action, and transforms the energy into action towards improving the performance of the teamwork skills. Student performance improves and the discrepancy between actual and real performance decreases. Increased self-efficacy tends to result. Students tend to feel empowered to be even more effective next time. The following checklist may help in assessing the effectiveness of feedback.

FEEDBACK CHECKLIST

FEEDBACK	YES	NO, START OVER
Is Feedback Given?		Was Not Given Or Received, Start Over
Is Feedback Generating Energy In Students?		Students Are Indifferent, Start Over
Is Energy Directed Towards Identifying & Solving Problems So Performance Is Improved?		Energy Used To Resist, Deny, Avoid Feedback, Start Over
Do Students Have Opportunities To Take Action To Improve Performance?		No, Students Are Frustrated & Feel Like Failures, Start Over

Reflecting On And Analyzing Feedback

You take the second step in structuring group processing when you have students reflect on and analyze the group session they have just completed to discover what helped and what hindered the quality of learning and whether specific behaviors had a positive or negative effect. Varying the procedures for analyzing and reflecting on the data collected about members interactions keep group processing vital and interesting. Ways of doing so include having each group. Ways of doing so include having each group:

1. Plot in a chart the data on members' interaction. Two of the most helpful charting procedures are the Bar Chart and the Run Chart.

2. Do a mind-map representing the secrets to his or her success.

3. Rate themselves on a series of dimensions on a bar chart.

7 : 5

Cooperation In The Classroom, Interaction Book Company, 7208 Cornelia Drive, Edina, MN 55435, (612) 831-9500, FAX (612) 831-9332

4. Give each member 60 seconds to identify three things other members did to help groupmates learn.

5. Discuss the effective use of teamwork skills by members (*"How did other group members encourage participation?" "How did other group members check for understanding?"*). Each group member gives his or her response and then consensus is achieved through discussion.

ENSURING EVERY GROUP MEMBER RECEIVES POSITIVE FEEDBACK

1. Having each group focus on one member at a time. Members tell the target person one thing he/she did that helped them learn or work together effectively. The focus is rotated until all members have received positive feedback.

2. Having members write a positive comment about each other member's participation on an index card. The students then give their written comments to each other so that every member will have, in writing, positive feedback from all the other group members.

3. Having members comment on how well each other member used the social skills by writing an answer to one of the following statements. The students then give their written statements to each other.

❏ *I appreciate it when you...*

❏ *I admire you for...*

❏ *I enjoy it when you...*

❏ *You really helped the group when you...*

This procedure may also be done orally. In this case students look at the member they are complementing, use his or her name, and give their comments. The person receiving the positive feedback makes eye contact and says nothing or "thank you." Positive feedback should be directly and clearly expressed and should **not** be brushed off or denied.

7 : 6

Cooperation In The Classroom, Interaction Book Company, 7208 Cornelia Drive, Edina, MN 55435, (612) 831-9500, FAX (612) 831-9332

SUMMARIZING OBSERVATION DATA: EXAMPLE

Imagine you have finished observing a cooperative learning group with four members. You can either provide direct feedback to each student or you can show them the data and ask them to reach their own conclusions about their participation. If you decide to give direct feedback, you might say:

Helen contributed ten times, Roger seven times, Edythe five times, and Frank twice. Frank encouraged others to participate ten times, Edythe five times, and Roger and Helen twice. Roger summarized five times, Frank twice, and Helen and Edythe once.

If you decided to let the students reach their own conclusions, you might say:

Look at the totals in the rows and columns. What conclusions could you make about:
a. Your participation in the lesson.
b. The effectiveness of the group in completing the assignment.

In summarizing, you might say:

Each of you will wish to set a personal goal for how you can be even more effective tomorrow than you were today. What actions did you engage in most and least? What actions were more and least appropriate and helpful under the circumstances (summarizing right after someone else summarized may be inappropriate and unhelpful)? What actions would have helped the group work more effectively? Decide on a personal goal to increase your effectiveness and share it with the other group members.

OBSERVATION FORM

Students	Contributes Ideas	Encourages Others To Contribute	Integrates, Summarizes	Totals
Frank	II	IIIII IIIII	II	14
Helen	IIIII IIIII	II	I	13
Roger	IIIII II	II	IIIII	14
Edythe	IIIII	IIIII	I	11
Totals	24	19	9	52

Cooperation In The Classroom, Interaction Book Company, 7208 Cornelia Drive, Edina, MN 55435, (612) 831-9500, FAX (612) 831-9332

AVOIDING NEGATIVE FEEDBACK

Working cooperatively in a pair, rank order the following consequences of negative feedback from most important ("1") to least important ("2").

	1. It confirms their apprehension about being evaluated and students will resist being observed in the future.
	2. Criticism carries more weight than does praise. One critical remark often outweighs dozens of positive comments.
	3. People bring more past history to criticism than to praise. Negative feedback taps into past rejection and failure.
	4. Weaknesses take more words to explain than do strengths.
	5. Trust is easy to destroy but hard to build. Criticism often destroys trust.

Processing Without Observation Data

Students need to reflect on and analyze the group session they just completed in order to discover what helped and what hindered the quality of learning and whether specific behaviors had a positive or negative effect. Such reflection and analysis is generally structured by the teacher. **When there is no observational data for the group to analyze or time is very short:**

1. Give group members 30 seconds to identify three things other members did to help others learn. Every member is heard from in a short period of time.

2. Give group members a series of questions concerning their effective use of skills ("*How did other group members encourage participation?*" "*How did other group members check for understanding?*"). Each group member gives his or her response and then consensus is achieved through discussion.

3. Make the last question on an assignment sheet a group-processing question. This signals that the group processing is an integral part of one's learning.

A good way for teachers to stay in touch with the functioning of each learning group is to have each group summarize its processing and place its summary in a folder with its completed academic work. The folder is handed in to the teacher each class session.

Varying the procedures for processing keeps group processing vital and interesting. At the end of the processing, group members should set goals for improving the effectiveness of the group.

Cooperation In The Classroom, Interaction Book Company, 7208 Cornelia Drive, Edina, MN 55435, (612) 831-9500, FAX (612) 831-9332

PROCESSING STARTERS

1. Name three things your group did well in working together. Name one thing your group could do even better.

2. Think of something that each group member did to improve group effectiveness. Tell them what it is.

3. Tell your group members how much you appreciate their help today.

4. Rate yourself from 1 (low) to 10 (high) on (name a cooperative skill like encouraging participation, checking for understanding). Share your rating with your group and explain why you rated yourself the way you did. Plan how to increase the frequency with which group members use this skill.

Whole Class Processing

In addition to small group processing, you should periodically conduct whole-class processing sessions.

1. **You can share your observations with the whole class.** Charting the data to get a continuous record of class improvement is always a good idea. You make a large chart on which you record the frequency with which students' performed each targeted skill. Students can see how much they improved over time. You may wish to give the class a reward when the class total exceeds a preset criterion of excellence. Not only does such a chart visually remind students of the skills they should practice while working in their groups, but continuous improvement becomes a challenge that promotes class cooperation.

2. **You can add together the observation results of the student observers for an overall class total.** You may wish to chart this data.

3. You can ask students to (a) describe things they did to help each other learn, (b) discuss members' answers in the group for a minute or two and arrive at a consensus on an answer, and (c) share their group's answer with the class as a whole. Since this procedure takes some time, three questions may be as many as you will wish to ask.

Students do not learn from experiences that they do not reflect on. If the learning groups are to function better tomorrow than they did today, members must receive feedback, reflect on how the effectiveness of their actions may be improved, and plan how to be even more skillful during the next group session.

Cooperation In The Classroom, Interaction Book Company, 7208 Cornelia Drive, Edina, MN 55435, (612) 831-9500, FAX (612) 831-9332

© Johnson, Johnson, & Holubec

Setting Goals For Improved Functioning

You take the third step in structuring group processing when you encourage students to set improvement goals. After analyzing the observational and self-assessment data, reflecting on its meaning, and giving each other feedback, **group members set improvement goals specifying how they will act more skillfully in the next group session.** Students should publicly announce the behavior they plan to increase. They should write the goal down and review it at the beginning of the next group session. Goal setting is the link between how students did today and how well they will do tomorrow. Goal setting can have powerful impact on students' behavior as there is a sense of ownership of and commitment to actions that a student has decided to engage in (as opposed to assigned behaviors). **Some procedures for goal setting are:**

1. Have students set specific behavioral goals for the next group session. Have each student pick a specific social skill to use more effectively (an "I" focus) and/or have the group reach consensus about which collaborative skill all group members will practice in the next session (a "we" focus). The group can be required to hand in a written statement specifying which social skill each member is going to emphasize during the next work session.

2. In a whole-class processing session, ask each group to agree on one conclusion to the statement, *"Our group could do better on social skills by...,"* and tell their answer to the entire class. You write the answers on the board under the title "goals." At the beginning of the next cooperative learning lesson, you publicly read over the goal statements and remind students what they agreed to work on during this session.

3. Have each student write an answer to one of the following questions before the next cooperative learning session:

   a. "Something I plan to do differently next time to help my group is..."

   b. "The social skill I want to use next time is..."

   c. "How I can help my group next time is..."

   d. "Two things I will do to help my group next time are..."

   e. "One social skill I will practice more consistently next time is..."

4. As an optional activity, have students plan where, outside of class, they can apply the social skills they are learning in class. Ask them to make connections between the cooperative learning groups and the rest of their lives. Have them specify times in the hallway, playground, home, church, or community where they can use the same social skills they are learning in class. Both "I" and "we" focuses are useful.

Cooperation In The Classroom, Interaction Book Company, 7208 Cornelia Drive, Edina, MN 55435, (612) 831-9500, FAX (612) 831-9332

Date _____

We Will _____
(Behavior)

_____ **Times Today**
(Number)

Signed _____ _____

_____ _____

Date _____

Next Time We Will Be

Better At _____
(Behavior)

Signed: _____ _____

_____ _____

7 : 11

Cooperation In The Classroom, Interaction Book Company, 7208 Cornelia Drive, Edina, MN 55435, (612) 831-9500, FAX (612) 831-9332

Celebrating

You take the fourth step in structuring group processing when you have group members celebrate their success and members' efforts to learn. Group processing ends with students celebrating their hard work and the success of their cooperative learning group. Celebrations are key to encouraging students to persist in their efforts to learn (Johnson & Johnson, 1993). Long-term, hard, persistent efforts to learn come more from the heart than from the head. Being recognized for efforts to learn and to contribute to groupmates' learning reaches the heart more effectively than do grades or tangible rewards. Both small-group and whole-class celebrations should take place. Small group processing provides the means to celebrate the success of the group and reinforce the positive behaviors of group members. Individual efforts that contribute to the group's success are recognized and encouraged. Members' actions aimed at helping groupmates learn are perceived, respected, and recognized. It is feeling successful, appreciated, and respected that builds commitment to learning, enthusiasm about working in cooperative groups, and a sense of self-efficacy about subject-matter mastery and working cooperatively with classmates.

A common teaching error is to provide too brief a time for students to process the quality of their cooperation. Students do not learn from experiences that they do not reflect on. If the learning groups are to function better tomorrow than they did today, students must receive feedback, reflect on how their actions may be more effective, and plan how to be even more skillful during the next group session.

COMMON PROBLEMS, POSSIBLE SOLUTIONS

If you have one of these problems, what will you do? Working with a partner, rank order the alternatives from most effective to least effective.

1. **"I do not have enough time to do processing."** When time is running out, try one of these:

   _____ Have students turn to their partners and tell them one thing they did that helped them learn that day (positive feedback).

   _____ Sample the class by having a few students tell the class one thing a partner did that helped them learn that day.

   _____ Have students thank their partners and shake hands or give high-fives.

Cooperation In The Classroom, Interaction Book Company, 7208 Cornelia Drive, Edina, MN 55435, (612) 831-9500, FAX (612) 831-9332

_____ Do the processing and assign the rest of the lesson as homework or assign the processing questions as homework.

_____ Do yesterday's processing at the start of today's cooperative group. Challenge students to improve their group from yesterday.

2. **"Students are not specific enough in their answers."** Value answers may mean trust is low or students are still learning to process. Try having the group write and turn in answers to specific questions, such as:

_____ What are three ways each member helped the group today?

_____ What are three things your group did well in working together? What's one thing that would make your group even better?

_____ What social skills did each member use in the group today? What is one social skill each member will use next time?

_____ How did you help the group today? How will you help even more next time?

3. **"Some students do not help or use poor cooperative skills with the processing."**

_____ Have students individually and privately write their answers to processing questions so they have time to think about it. Have them give these directly to you so they can be more candid than if they were giving feedback in the group.

_____ Assign roles during processing (such as recorder, question-asker, encourager) so everyone has a structured, positive job.

_____ Give students positive sentence starters (*"It helped me today when you..." "One thing I appreciate about you is..."*).

_____ Have the class brainstorm ways in which members can help in groups. Make a poster of the list so students are visually reminded of what to say when giving positive feedback and processing.

_____ Occasionally, sit with a group and guide their processing (modeling), then ask students to rotate leading processing in a similar way.

_____ Formally observe or have a student observer and have the group discuss the resulting data ("What behaviors did we do well? How could we improve?").

7 : 13

Cooperation In The Classroom, Interaction Book Company, 7208 Cornelia Drive, Edina, MN 55435, (612) 831-9500, FAX (612) 831-9332

Continuously Improving Social Skills Quality

To improve the quality of learning in cooperative groups, the process of working together needs to be carefully examined to (a) streamline the learning process to make it simpler (reducing complexity), (b) eliminate unskilled and inappropriate actions (error-proofing the process), and (c) improve continuously students' skills in working as part of a team.

High quality work is based on the continuous improvement of teamwork (and taskwork) skills. You engineer a process through which students assess the current levels of their social skills and plan how to increase them:

❑ You decide which social skill is going to be emphasized in the lesson.

❑ You operationally define the social skill with a T-Chart and teach the social skill to students.

❑ You prepare an observation form, appoint observers, explain the observation form.

❑ You conduct the lesson, observing each of the learning groups, and coaching the student observers. **Observation** is aimed at recording and describing members' behavior as it occurs in the group, that is, to provide objective data about the interaction among group members. The behavior of group members is observed so that students may be given feedback about their participation in the group and so that inferences can be made about the ways in which the group is functioning.

❑ You complete the lesson and structure how the learning groups process members use of the social skill. The data gathered by you and the observers are analyzed as are the self-assessments by the members of how often and how well they individually performed the targeted social skills. The data are recorded and displayed on charts so that individual students and the groups can track their improvement in using the social skill and make informed decisions as to how students' teamwork can be improved. After small group processing, you conduct whole class processing in which you share your feedback to the class as a whole. Class charts are used to record and display the progress in mastering the social skill. Students set goals for improving their social skills during the next group meeting. Finally, the group members celebrate their hard work in mastering social skills.

PROCESSING QUICKIES

Our group is really good at...	The best thing that happened was...
Words to describe our group are...	Today our group discovered...
Today I helped my group by...	We are a super team because...
Today I learned...	Next time we will be better at...

7 : 14

Cooperation In The Classroom, Interaction Book Company, 7208 Cornelia Drive, Edina, MN 55435, (612) 831-9500, FAX (612) 831-9332

Summary

Group processing is the key to continuous improvement. Without group processing, ineffective practices will tend to continue and the potential of the learning group will tend not to be realized. There are four steps to ensuring that students engage in effective group processing. Students must receive feedback on the effectiveness of their actions in trying to learn and help groupmates learn. Students must reflect on the feedback. Students then set improvement goals specifying how they will act more skillfully in the next group session. Finally, students celebrate their hard work and the success of their learning group.

Some of the keys to successful small group processing are allowing sufficient time for it to take place, providing a structure for processing (such as "*List three things your group is doing well today and one thing you could improve*"), emphasizing positive feedback, making the processing specific rather than general, maintaining student involvement in processing, reminding students to use their cooperative skills while they process, and communicating clear expectations as to the purpose of processing.

In order to improve the quality of the group's work, it is also necessary to assess what each group member is learning academically. That is the focus of the next chapter.

Implementation Assignment

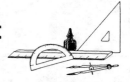

1. Read Chapter 8.

2. Plan how you will use a combination of individual, small group, and whole class processing.

3. Implement the group processing procedures in your classroom. Record the results to share with your base group.

4. Make a journal entry concerning the use of processing procedures.

Cooperation In The Classroom, Interaction Book Company, 7208 Cornelia Drive, Edina, MN 55435, (612) 831-9500, FAX (612) 831-9332

COOPERATIVE LEARNING CONTRACT

Write down your major learnings from reading this chapter and participating in training session one. Then write down how you plan to implement each learning. Share what you learned and your implementation plans with your base group. Listen carefully to their major learnings and implementation plans. You may modify your own plans on the basis of what you have learned from your groupmates. Volunteer one thing you can do to help each groupmate with his or her implementation plans. Utilize the help groupmates offer to you. Sign each member's plans to seal the contract.

MAJOR LEARNINGS	IMPLEMENTATION PLANS

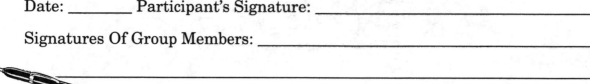

Date: _____ Participant's Signature: _____

Signatures Of Group Members: _____

_____

Cooperation In The Classroom, Interaction Book Company, 7208 Cornelia Drive, Edina, MN 55435, (612) 831-9500, FAX (612) 831-9332

COOPERATIVE LEARNING PROGRESS REPORT

Name: _____ School: _____

Subject Area: _____ Grade: _____

Date	Lesson	Successes	Problems

Describe Critical Or Interesting Incidents:

7 : 17

Cooperation In The Classroom, Interaction Book Company, 7208 Cornelia Drive, Edina, MN 55435, (612) 831-9500, FAX (612) 831-9332

EXERCISE

MATERIALS

INK

7 : 18

Cooperation In The Classroom, Interaction Book Company, 7208 Cornelia Drive, Edina, MN 55435, (612) 831-9500, FAX (612) 831-9332

GROUP PROCESSING: PURPOSEFUL READING

Read the first question. Find the answer in the text. Discuss the answer with your partner until both of you agree and are able to explain it. Relate the answer to previous learning. Move to the next question and repeat the procedure.

Questions

1. What is group processing?

2. What are the four purposes of group processing?

3. What are the four stages of group processing?

4. What is feedback?

5. What are three ways to ensure that all students receive positive feedback?

6. What are the pitfalls of negative feedback?

7. What are three ways to process without observation data?

8. What are three ways to conduct whole class processing?

9. What are four procedures for setting improvement goals?

10. What are group celebrations important?

11. What are the three obstacles to group processing and what are three ways each may be overcome?

12. How do you continuously improve the quality of the use of social skills?

7 : 19

Cooperation In The Classroom, Interaction Book Company, 7208 Cornelia Drive, Edina, MN 55435, (612) 831-9500, FAX (612) 831-9332

PROCESSING POST-TEST

1. Processing is an essential element of cooperation.   True   False

2. In processing, groups discuss how well they are functioning.   True   False

3. Processing helps teach students what social skills are   True   False
   needed and when to use the skill.

4. In processing, students discuss:
   a. Skills not being used by the group
   b. How well skills are implemented
   c. Whether efforts are successful
   d. Plans for improving group skills
   e. All of the above

5. It is best not to tell students the skills you are observing for.   True   False

6. Wait until the group session ends to point out inappropriate   True   False
   group behavior or praise good skill use.

7. Which is **not** a reason to process?
   a. Helps members maintain effective working relationships
   b. Helps students develop cooperative learning skills
   c. Reminds students to practice social skills consistently
   d. Gives the teacher time to regain sanity between lessons.

7 : 20

Cooperation In The Classroom, Interaction Book Company, 7208 Cornelia Drive, Edina, MN 55435, (612) 831-9500, FAX (612) 831-9332

PROCESSING PLAN

To help you remember to do processing, make a chart that will remind you (and/or the class) what to do each day. Example: Monday: "What are three things you did well? What's one thing that would make you even better?"

Monday	
Tuesday	
Wednesday	
Thursday	
Friday	

Ideas To Choose From:

1. As a group, name three things the group did well in working together. Name one thing that would make your group even better. Make a plan for improvement.
2. As a group, list three ways each group member helps the group.
3. As a group, make a list of all the social skills you feel your group has mastered. Pick a social skill to work on until you can also add it to the list.
4. Individually, write three things you like about working in your group. Write one thing that would make your group even better. Write what you will do to help.
5. Individually, write three ways you helped the group today.
6. Individually, make a list of all the social skills you have mastered. Pick a social skill to add to the list and make a plan to work on it. Work on the skill until you can add it to the mastery list.
7. Tell each of your group members something they did which helped you today.
8. Tell each of your group members something you appreciate about them.
9. Get ready for a whole-class discussion on how well the groups are working. Be ready to tell specific behaviors which help you learn and work together well. Be ready to suggest skills to work on to make your groups even better. We will pick one skill as a goal to work on.

7 : 21

Cooperation In The Classroom, Interaction Book Company, 7208 Cornelia Drive, Edina, MN 55435, (612) 831-9500, FAX (612) 831-9332

WAYS TO PROMOTE EFFECTIVE PROCESSING

1. Give students time. Remember they are learning a new skill and must pass through the stages of awkward, phony, mechanical, and automatic.

2. Remember that to build trust, you must build safety. You do this by daily asking students to share the positive things about each other's participation and building a positive feedback environment.

3. Students do not automatically know what are the social skills needed for effective functioning. Have frequent discussions of helpful group behaviors. Display a poster of those behaviors in the classroom so students have a constant visual reminder of what to do. When teaching a specific social skill, remember to post the appropriate T-chart.

4. Emphasize problems in working together are expected and are opportunities for growth and development. After emphasizing the positives within the group, teach the groups to tackle problems as problem-solving tasks. Teach them to define the problem, generate three possible solutions, pick one solution, try it, and if that does not work, try another. Continue until the problem is solved. Go through this procedure with groups until they learn to do it without you.

5. As students specific questions about their group effectiveness instead of general questions. Instead of asking "How well did you work together?" ask questions like:
   a. As a group, name three things the group did well in working together. Name one thing that would make your group even better. Make a plan for improvement.
   b. As a group, list three ways each group member helps the group.
   c. As a group, make a list of the social skills all group members have mastered. Pick a social skill to work on until all members can add it to the list.
   d. Individually, write three things you like about working in your group. Write one thing that would make your group even better. Write what you will do to help.
   e. Individually, write three ways you helped the group today.
   f. Individually, make a list of all the social skills you have mastered. Pick a social skill to add to the list. Plan how to master it. Practice the skill until you can add it to the mastery list.
   g. Tell each group member something he or she did that helped you.
   h. Tell each group member something you appreciate about him or her.

6. Periodically, have whole-class discussions on how well the groups are working. Ask students to tell you specific things that help them learn and work together well. Ask for suggestions of skills to work on to make the groups even better. Have the class pick one as a goal to work on. When they achieve mastery, celebrate!

7 : 22

Cooperation In The Classroom, Interaction Book Company, 7208 Cornelia Drive, Edina, MN 55435, (612) 831-9500, FAX (612) 831-9332

CHAPTER EIGHT:

ASSESSMENT AND EVALUATION

Conducting Assessments

In the time of change, learners inherit the earth, while the learned find themselves beautifully equipped to deal with a world that no longer exists.

Eric Hoffer

In 1955 Edward Banfield lived for nine months in a small town in southern Italy that he called "Montegrano" (Johnson & Johnson, 1996). What Banfield noticed most was the town's alienated citizenry, grinding poverty, and pervasive corruption. He concluded that the primary source of Montegrano's plight was the distrust, envy, and suspicion that characterized its inhabitants' relations with each other. They viewed communal life as little more than a battleground. Town members consistently refused to help one another unless it would result in material gain. Many actually tried to prevent their neighbors from succeeding, believing that others' good fortune would inevitably undercut their own. Consequently, they remained socially isolated and impoverished, unable to cooperate to solve common problems or pool their resources and talents to build viable economic enterprises.

Montegrano's citizens were not inherently more selfish or foolish than people elsewhere. But for a number of complex historical and cultural reasons, they lacked the norms, habits, attitudes, and networks that encourage people to work together for the common good. They lacked what Alexis de Tocqueville called "the habits of the heart." Habits of the heart include taking responsibility for the common good, trusting others to do the same, being honest, having self-discipline, reciprocating good deeds, and perfecting the skills necessary for cooperation and conflict management. The relationship between democracy and such habits is supported by the fact that in the United States, since the early 1960s voter turnout in national elections has fallen by a quarter and the number of citizens saying that *most people can be trusted* has dropped by more than a third.

There is far more to assessment than giving students grades (Johnson & Johnson, 1996). It is vital to assess what students know, understand, and retain over time (academic learning). It is equally important to assess (a) the quality and level of their reasoning processes and (b) their skills and competencies (such as oral and written communication skills and skills in using technology). In today's complex and every changing world, a

8 : 1

Cooperation In The Classroom, Interaction Book Company, 7208 Cornelia Drive, Edina, MN 55435, (612) 831-9500, FAX (612) 831-9332

facts. More than ever, schools need to focus on teaching students appropriate work habits (such as completing work on time and striving for quality work and continuous improvement) and attitudes (such as a love of learning, desire to read good literature, commitment to democracy).

Your Assessment Plan

Given below are generic assessment targets and procedures. In planning your assessment program, check the targets that you wish to assess and then check the procedures you wish to use. Match the procedures with the targets so it is clear how you will assess each target.

What Is Assessed	Procedures Used To Assess
_____ Academic Learning	_____ Goal Setting Conferences
_____ Reasoning Process/Strategies	_____ Standardized Tests
_____ Skills & Competencies	_____ Teacher-Made Tests
_____ Attitudes	_____ Written Compositions
_____ Work Habits	_____ Oral Presentations
	_____ Projects
	_____ Portfolios
	_____ Observations
	_____ Questionnaires
	_____ Interviews
	_____ Learning Logs & Journals
	_____ Student Management Teams

In achieving these complex and long-term responsibilities of the school, teachers need to conduct three types of assessments: **diagnostic** (diagnose students' present level of knowledge and skills), **formative** (monitor progress toward learning goals to help form the instructional program), and **summative** (provide data to judge the final level of students' learning). These assessments need to focus on both the process and the outcomes of learning and instruction. Assessments need to take place in more authentic

8 : 2

Cooperation In The Classroom, Interaction Book Company, 7208 Cornelia Drive, Edina, MN 55435, (612) 831-9500, FAX (612) 831-9332

settings as well as in the classroom. The number of stakeholders in education have increased as the world economic and the interdependence among nations have increased. And the stakes of many of the assessments have increased, as students' futures are more and more determined by what they have learned and how many years of formal education they have completed. As the seriousness of educators' responsibilities have increased, so has the need to use a wider variety of assessment procedures.

ESSENTIAL DEFINITIONS

Form a pair and match the correct definition with each concept. Combine with another pair and check answers.

Concept	Definition
_____ 1. Instruction	a. Change within a student that is brought about by instruction.
_____ 2. Learning	b. Judging the merit, value, or desirability of a measured performance.
_____ 3. Rubric	c. Standards against which the quality and quantity of performances are assessed (what counts or is important).
_____ 4. Assessment	d. Structuring of situations in ways that help students change, through learning.
_____ 5. Criteria	e. Collecting information about the quality or quantity of a change in a student, group, teacher, or administrator.
_____ 6. Evaluation	f. Articulation of gradations of quality and quantity for each criterion, from poor to exemplary.

Assessment Issues

Purpose	Focus	Setting	Stakeholders	Stakes
Diagnostic	Process Of Learning	Artificial (Classroom)	Students-Parents	Low
Formative	Process Of Instruction	Authentic (Real-World)	Teachers, Administrators	High
Summative	Outcomes Of Learning		Policy-Makers	
	Outcomes Of Instruction		Colleges, Employers	

Cooperation In The Classroom, Interaction Book Company, 7208 Cornelia Drive, Edina, MN 55435, (612) 831-9500, FAX (612) 831-9332

Meaningful Assessment

| Involvement In Process | | Use Of Outcomes | |
Less Meaning	More Meaning	Less Meaning	More Meaning
Isolated Goals	Interdependent Goals	Individual Celebration	Joint Celebration
Work Alone	Joint Effort With Others	New Isolated Goals	New Interdependent Goals
Self-Assess Only	Assess Other's Work As Well As One's Own		
Receive Feedback Only	Both Give And Receive Feedback		

Making Assessments Meaningful And Manageable

The two major issues educators face in conducting effective and responsible assessments are making the assessments (Johnson & Johnson, 1996):

1. Meaningful to the various stakeholders.

2. Manageable so they will actually get done.

Many educators forget that the most significant motivating forces for students are to increase their competencies in a way that benefits those they care about. Such personal meaning is created by three factors:

1. **Structuring positive interdependence among students**. It is positive interdependence that creates positive relationships among students, a commitment to each other's learning and well-being, a desire to contribute to the common good, the motivation to strive to be one's best for the sake of others as well as oneself, and the conviction that there is more to life than selfish self-interest.

2. **Involve students in the learning and assessment processes**. Students need to be involved in formulating their learning goals, choosing the paths for achieving the goals, assessing their progress and success, planning how to improve, and implementing their plan, serious management problems arise.

3. **Ensure assessment data is organized in a way that it may be used**. Useful results help students to seek remediation for what they misunderstood, reviews to

Cooperation In The Classroom, Interaction Book Company, 7208 Cornelia Drive, Edina, MN 55435, (612) 831-9500, FAX (612) 831-9332

fill in gaps in what they know, and new learning experiences to take the next steps to advance their knowledge and skills.

These three issues are interrelated. Positive interdependence creates the context for involvement. The involvement creates the ownership of the learning and assessment processes and the motivation to use the assessment results to improve one's understanding and competencies. The more clearly the results point towards the next steps to be taken to increase the quality and quantity of the learning, the more likely students are to engage in the assessment process. Implementing plans to improve learning requires the help of collaborators, which returns the cycle to positive interdependence.

Serious management problems arise in involving students in formulating their learning goals, choosing the paths for achieving the goals, assessing their progress and success, planning how to improve, and implementing their plan. One teacher working by him- or herself can no longer manage the entire assessment system. The most natural sources of help for teachers are students and colleagues. Students provide the most help because they are available at all times. To be constructive participants in the assessment process, however, students need to be organized into cooperative learning groups. Students oriented toward competition or only their own individualistic efforts resist contributing to the others' continuously improvement. To organizational theorists such as Deming, competitive and individualistic structures are "forces for destruction." To provide quality assessment, students have to be as committed to classmates' learning and academic success as they are to their own. Such commitment only comes from clear positive interdependence.

MEANINGFUL ASSESSMENTS		
Positive Interdependence	Involvement	Useful Results
Common Purpose	Setting Goals, Planning Paths To Achieve Goals, Assessing Progress, Planning For Improvement, Implementing Plans	Clarify Of Next Steps To Improve
Positive Relationships	Ownership	Use Of Results
Meaning	Meaning	Meaning

Cooperation In The Classroom, Interaction Book Company, 7208 Cornelia Drive, Edina, MN 55435, (612) 831-9500, FAX (612) 831-9332

Cooperative learning groups provide the setting, context, and environment in which assessment becomes part of the instructional process and students learn almost as much from assessing the quality of their own and their classmates' work as they do from participating in the instructional activities.

1. Cooperative learning allows assessment to be integrated into the learning process. **Continuous assessment requires continuous monitoring and support, which can best be done within cooperative learning groups.**

2. The new assessment practices are so labor intensive that students who are sincerely committed to each other's learning and success may need to be involved.

3. Cooperative learning groups allow more modalities to be used in the learning and assessment process while focusing on more diverse outcomes.

4. Cooperative learning groups allow groupmates to be sources of information in addition to the teacher and the curriculum materials.

5. Involving groupmates in assessment reduces possible biases resulting from the teacher being the sole source of feedback and the heavy reliance on reading and writing as assessment modalities.

6. Cooperative learning groups provide each student help in analyzing assessment data, interpreting the results, and implementing improvement plans.

It is difficult to imagine a class in which cooperative learning groups do not help make the assessment system more manageable or how a comprehensive assessment program can be managed without cooperative learning groups.

This chapter is a summary of the book, **Meaningful and Manageable Assessment through Cooperative Learning** (Johnson & Johnson, 1996). Readers interested in more detail and a wide variety of practice procedures are referred to that book. Assessment begins with setting learning goals.

Assessment Procedures

Assessment begins with setting learning goals. Once students have formulated and agreed to their learning goals, a variety of assessment procedures can be used. The assessment procedures include tests, compositions, presentations, projects, portfolios, observations, interviews, questionnaires, and learning logs and journals.

Cooperation In The Classroom, Interaction Book Company, 7208 Cornelia Drive, Edina, MN 55435, (612) 831-9500, FAX (612) 831-9332

Setting And Managing Learning Goals

Without clear learning and instructional goals, assessment cannot take place (Johnson & Johnson, 1996). The goals are created and re-emphasized in three types of conferences with each student: A **goal-setting conference** is conducted to establish a contract containing the student's learning goals, **progress-assessment conferences** are conducted to review the student's progress in achieving his or her goals, and a **post-evaluation conference** is conducted in which the student's accomplishments are explained to interested parties.

Each student must commit to achieve learning goal that specify what he or she needs to accomplish in the immediate future and his or her responsibilities for helping other students learn. These goals are established in a **goal-setting conference**. The goal setting conference may be between the teacher and the student (T/S), the teacher and the cooperative learning group (T/G), the cooperative learning group and the student (G/S), and a cooperative learning group and another group (G/G). In all cases, the emphasis is on helping students set and take ownership for learning goals that meet the START criteria (specific, trackable, achievable, relevant, transferable). The goal-setting conference contains four steps:

1. Diagnosis of current level of expertise (what does the student now know?).
2. Setting START goals focusing on student's (a) academic achievement, reasoning, social skills, attitudes, and work habits and (b) responsibilities for helping groupmates learn.

START GOALS
S = Specific
M = Measurable, Trackable
A = Challenging But Achieveable
R = Relevant
T = Transfer

3. Organizing support systems and resources to help each student achieve his or her goals successfully.

4. Constructing a plan for utilizing the resources to achieve the goals and formalizing the plan into a learning contract.

The hard truth is that most teachers do not have the time to conference with each individual student, whether it is a goal-setting conference, a progress-assessment conference, or a post-evaluation conference. This does not mean that such conferences cannot happen. Teachers can engineer and supervise such conferences through appropriate use of cooperative learning groups. Groups can regularly have progress-assessment conferences with each member while the teacher listens in or pulls one aside individual students for conferences.

Cooperation In The Classroom, Interaction Book Company, 7208 Cornelia Drive, Edina, MN 55435, (612) 831-9500, FAX (612) 831-9332

My Learning Contract

Learning Goals

My Academic Goals	My Responsibilities For Helping Others' Learn	My Group's Goals
1.		
2.		
3.		
4.		

THE PLAN FOR ACHIEVING MY LEARNING GOALS, MEETING MY RESPONSIBILITIES, AND HELPING MY GROUP IS:

THE TIME LINE FOR ACHIEVING MY GOALS IS:

Beginning Date:

First Road-Mark:

Second Road-Mark:

Third Road-Mark:

Final Date:

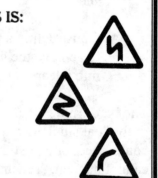

Signatures:

_____   _____

_____   _____

8 : 8

Cooperation In The Classroom, Interaction Book Company, 7208 Cornelia Drive, Edina, MN 55435, (612) 831-9500, FAX (612) 831-9332

Types Of Conferences

Conference	Individual Student	Cooperative Learning Group
Goal-Setting Conference	Each class period, day, week, or instructional unit each student sets personal learning goals and publicly commits him- or herself to achieve them in a learning contract.	Each class period, day, week, or instructional unit each cooperative group sets group learning goals and members publicly commit themselves to achieve them in a learning contract.
Progress-Assessment Conferences	The student's progress in achieving his or her learning goals is assessed, what the student has accomplished so far and what is yet to be done is reviewed, and the student's next steps are detailed.	The group's progress in achieving its learning goals is assessed, what the group has accomplished so far and what is yet to be done is reviewed, and the group's next steps are detailed.
Post-Evaluation Conference	The student explains his or her level of achievement (what the student learned and failed to learn during the instructional unit) to interested parties (student's cooperative learning group, teacher(s), and parents), which naturally leads to the next goal-setting conference.	The group explains its level of achievement (what the group has accomplished and failed to accomplish during the instructional unit) to interested parties (members, teacher(s), and parents), which naturally leads to the next goal-setting conference.

Tests And Examinations

Both standardized and teacher-made tests may be used to assess student learning (Johnson & Johnson, 1996). Standardized tests are often high-stake events for which students need to be carefully prepared. Teacher-made tests are often a routine part of an instructional program to assess quickly and efficiently a broad sampling of students' knowledge. They may be multiple-choice, true-false, matching, short answers, interpretative, or essay. Although there are many effective assessment procedures, testing remains a mainstay in what teachers do. Cooperative learning groups may be used with tests through the GIG (group preparation, individual test, group test), group discussion, and Teams-Games-Tournament procedures.

8 : 9

Cooperation In The Classroom, Interaction Book Company, 7208 Cornelia Drive, Edina, MN 55435, (612) 831-9500, FAX (612) 831-9332

THE GIG PROCEDURE FOR GIVING TESTS

You should frequently give tests and quizzes to assess (a) how much each student knows and (b) what students still need to learn. Whenever you give a test, cooperative learning groups can serve as bookends by preparing members to take the test and providing a setting in which students review the test. Using the following procedure will result in (a) optimizing each student's preparation for the test, (b) making each student accountable to peers for his or her performance on the test, (c) assessing how much each student knows, (d) assessing what students still need to learn, (e) providing students with immediate clarification of what they did not understand or learn, (f) providing students with immediate remediation of what they did not learn, (g) preventing arguments between you and your students over which answer are correct and why. The procedure is.

1. Students prepare for, and review for, a test in cooperative learning groups.

2. Each student takes the test individually, making two copies of his or her answers. Students submit one set of answer to you to grade and keep one set for the group discussion.

3. Students retake the test in their cooperative learning groups.

PREPARING FOR A TEST IN COOPERATIVE GROUPS

Students meet in their cooperative learning groups and are given (a) study questions and (b) class time to prepare for the examination. The task is for students to discuss each study question and come to consensus about its answer. The cooperative goal is to ensure that all group members understand how to answer the study questions correctly. If students disagree on the answer to any study questions, they must find the page number and paragraph in the resource material explaining the relevant information or procedures. When the study/review time is up, the students give each other encouragement for doing well on the upcoming test.

TAKING THE TEST INDIVIDUALLY

Each student takes the test individually, making two copies of his or her answers. The task (and individual goal) is to answer each test question correctly. Students submit one copy of the answers to you (the teacher). You score the answers and evaluate student performance against a preset criterion of excellence. Students keep one copy for the group discussion.

After all group members have finished the test, the group meets to take the test again.

RETAKING THE TEST IN COOPERATIVE GROUPS

Students meet in their cooperative learning groups and retake the test. The **task** is to answer each question correctly. The **cooperative goal** is to ensure that all group members understand the material and procedures covered by the test. Members do so by (a) reaching consensus on the answer for each question and the rationale or procedure underlying the answer and (b) ensuring that all members can explain the answer and the rationale or procedure. The procedure is for members to:

1. Compare their answers on the first question.

2. If there is agreement, one member explains the rationale or procedure underlying the question and the group moves on to question two.

3. If there is disagreement, members find the page number and paragraph in the resource materials explaining the relevant information or procedures. The group is responsible for ensuring that all members understand the material they missed on the test. If necessary, group members assign review homework to each other. When all members agree on the answer and believe other members comprehend the material, the group moves on to question two.

4. The learning groups repeat this procedure until they have covered all test questions.

5. The group members celebrate how hard members have worked in learning the material and how successful they were on the test.

Compositions And Presentations

Every educated person should be able to present what they know in written and oral form. These are difficult competencies and to become skilled writers and presenters, students need to write and present every day. This presents an assessment problem, as someone has to read each composition and listen to each presentation and provide helpful feedback. Using cooperative learning groups to assess members' performances accomplishes four goals at the same time. It allows students to engage in the performance frequently, receive immediate and detailed feedback on their efforts,

Cooperation In The Classroom, Interaction Book Company, 7208 Cornelia Drive, Edina, MN 55435, (612) 831-9500, FAX (612) 831-9332

observe closely the performances of others, and see what is good or lacking in others' performances, and provide the labor needed to allow students to engage in a performance frequently. Two of the most common performances assessed are compositions and presentations. In composition pairs, students are assigned to pairs, discuss and outline each other's composition in their pairs, research their topic alone, in pairs write the first paragraph of each composition, write the composition alone, edit each other's composition, rewrite the composition alone, re-edit each other's compositions, sign-off on partner's composition verifying that it is ready to be handed in, and then process the quality of the partnership. The procedure for presentations is very similar.

Persuasive Argument Composition Rubric

Name: _____   Date: _____   Grade: _____

Title Of Composition: _____

Scoring Scale: Low 1--2--3--4--5 High

Criteria	Score	Weight	Total
Organization: Thesis Statement And Introduction Rationale Presented To Support Thesis Conclusion Logically Drawn From Rationale Effective Transitions		6	(30)
Content: Topic Addressed Reasoning Clear With Valid Logic Evidence Presented To Support Key Points Creativity Evident		8	(40)
Usage: Topic Sentence Beginning Every Paragraph Correct Subject-Verb Agreement Correct Verb Tense Complete Sentences (No Run-Ons, Fragments) Mix Of Simple And Complex Sentences.		4	(20)
Mechanics: Correct Use Of Punctuation Correct Use Of Capitalization Few Or No Misspellings		2	(10)
Scale: 93-100=A, 87 - 85-92=B, 77-84=C		20	(100)

Cooperation In The Classroom, Interaction Book Company, 7208 Cornelia Drive, Edina, MN 55435, (612) 831-9500, FAX (612) 831-9332

Individual And Group Projects

A standard part of most every course is allowing students to be creative and inventive in integrating diverse knowledge and skills. This is especially important in assessing multiple intelligences and the ability to engage in complex procedures such as scientific investigation. Projects allow students to use multiple modes of learning. The use of cooperative learning groups allows projects to be considerable more complex and elaborate than projects completed by any one student.

EXAMPLES OF PROJECTS

Mythological Rap Song: Write and present a rap song about the gods and goddesses in Greek mythology	**Pamphlet:** Select and research a disease and prepare an instructional pamphlet to present to the class.
Select a famous writer, artist, politician, or philosopher from the Renaissance period and become that person on a panel of experts.	Research an international conflict in the world today (for each country a student researchers a different aspect of the country related to the war--history, resolutions, maps, and so forth)
Teaching cycles through gardening (different students are in charge of seeds, fertilizing, and so forth)	**Paint a mural of the history of the earth and humankind (each group takes a section--Greek, Roman, middle ages art)**
Videotape of a community project	Time-line (personal, history, literature, art, geology)
Writing plays, skits, role plays	**School or class newspaper**
Running a school post-office	Mock court
International festival with multi-cultural activity	**Mural based on reading**
Groups write alternative endings with dramatizations	Create a new invention using the computer
Turn a short story or event in history into a movie	**Design an ideal school and have class enact it**
Newscast	Science fair projects

Portfolios

Students become far more sophisticated and educated when they can organize their work into a portfolio that represents the quality of their learning in a course or school year. There is no substitute for having students collect and organize their work samples and write a rationale connecting the work samples into a complete and holistic picture of the student's achievements, growth, and development. The resulting portfolio may feature

Cooperation In The Classroom, Interaction Book Company, 7208 Cornelia Drive, Edina, MN 55435, (612) 831-9500, FAX (612) 831-9332

the student's "best works" or the "process" the student is using to learn. Like all other complex and challenging tasks, students need considerable help in constructing their portfolios and in presenting them to teachers, parents, and other interested stakeholders. Portfolios, therefore, may be more manageable when they are constructed within cooperative learning groups. The group can help each member select appropriate work samples and write a coherent and clear rationale. The portfolio may also include the group's assessment of the student's learning and growth.

An extension of portfolios is to have the student, teacher, and student's cooperative learning group all independently decide on what represents the student's best work and why. They have a conference to compare their assessments and resolve any differences.

Contents Of Portfolios

1. **Cover sheet** that creatively reflects the nature of the student's (or group's) work.

2. **Table of contents** that includes the title of each work sample and its page number.

3. The **rationale** explaining what work samples are included, why each one is significant, and how they all fit together in a holistic view of the student's (or group's) work.

4. The **work samples**.

5. A **self-assessment** written by the student or the group members.

6. **Future goals** based on the student's (or group's) current achievements, interests, and progress.

7. **Other's comments and assessments** from the teacher, cooperative learning groups, and other interested parties such as the parents.

8 : 14

Cooperation In The Classroom, Interaction Book Company, 7208 Cornelia Drive, Edina, MN 55435, (612) 831-9500, FAX (612) 831-9332

COOPERATIVE GROUP PORTFOLIO

What is a cooperative base group?	A **cooperative base group** is a long-term, heterogeneous cooperative learning group with stable membership. It may last for one course, one year, or for several years. Its purposes are to give the support, help, encouragement, and assistance each member needs to make good academic progress and develop cognitively and socially in healthy ways.
What is a group portfolio?	A **group portfolio** is an organized collection of group work samples accumulated over time and individual work samples of each member.
What are its contents?	Cover that creativity reflects group's personality Table of contents Description of the group and its members Introduction to portfolio and rationale for the work samples included. Group work samples (products by the group that any one member could not have produced alone) Observation data of group members interacting as they worked on group projects. Self-assessment of the group by its members. Individual members' work samples that were revised on the basis of group feedback (compositions, presentations, and so forth). Self-assessment of members including their strengths and weaknesses in facilitating group effectiveness and other members' learning. List of future learning and social skills goals for the group and each of its members. Comments and feedback from faculty and other groups

8 : 15

Cooperation In The Classroom, Interaction Book Company, 7208 Cornelia Drive, Edina, MN 55435, (612) 831-9500, FAX (612) 831-9332

Preparing To Use Portfolios

1. Who will construct the portfolios:

    ____ Individual students with teacher input and help.

    ____ Individual students with the input and help of cooperative learning groups.

    ____ Cooperative base groups (whole group work and individual members' work) with teach input and help.

2. What type of portfolio do you want to use?
    ____ Best Works Portfolio   ____ Process/Growth Portfolio

3. What are the purposes and objectives of the portfolio?

    a.

    b.

    c.

4. What categories of work samples should go into the portfolio?

    a.

    b.

    c.

5. What criteria will students or groups use to select their entries?

    a.

    b.

    c.

6. Who will develop the rubrics to assess and evaluate the portfolios?
    ____ Faculty   ____ Students

8 : 16

Cooperation In The Classroom, Interaction Book Company, 7208 Cornelia Drive, Edina, MN 55435, (612) 831-9500, FAX (612) 831-9332

Observing

There is a limit to the information gained by having students turn in completed tests, compositions, projects, and portfolios. Answers on a test and homework assignments handed in and tell teachers whether students can arrive at a correct answer. They cannot, however, inform teachers as to the quality of the reasoning strategies students are using, students' commitment to classmates' success and well-being, or the extent to which students' can work effectively with others. Teachers must find a way to make students' covert reasoning processes overt, demonstrate behaviorally their attitudes and work habits, and show how skillfully they can work with others. Observing students in action thus becomes one of the most important assessment procedures. Observing students has three stages:

1. **Preparing for observing**. Deciding what actions to observe, who will observe, what the sampling plan will be, constructing an observation form, and training observers to use the form.

2. **Observing**. Observations may be formal or informal, structured or unstructured.

3. **Summarizing the data for use by students and other stake-holders**. In summarizing observations, the data may be displayed in bar or run charts, feedback is then given to the students or other interested parties, the recipients reflect on the feedback and set improvement goals.

One of the primary uses of observation procedures is to assess the use of social skills. **First**, you teach students the targeted social skill. You show the need for the skill, define it with a t-chart, set up practice situations in which students can use the skill, ensure that students receive feedback on their use of the skill and reflect on how to improve, and ensure that students persevere in practicing the skill until it becomes automatic. **Second**, you structure cooperative learning situations so students can use the social skills and you can observe their doing so. **Third**, you intervene in the cooperative learning groups to ensure that members are using the social skills appropriately and to recognize them for doing so. **Fourth**, you have students complete checklists or questionnaires to self-diagnose their mastery of the targeted social skills. **Fifth**, you assign students in setting improvement goals to increase their social competence. **Sixth**, you assess students' knowledge of social skills. **Finally**, you report on the level of students' social skills to interested stakeholders, such as the students, parents, and potential employers.

Interviewing

Closely related to observing students in action is interviewing students. Like observing, interviews can make the covert overt through asking students more and more detailed

Cooperation In The Classroom, Interaction Book Company, 7208 Cornelia Drive, Edina, MN 55435, (612) 831-9500, FAX (612) 831-9332

questions about their reasoning processes and strategies. The strengths of the interview is that it is personal and flexible. The personal nature of interviews allows you to build a more positive, supportive, and trusting relationships with each student. The flexibility of interviews allows you to interview either one or a small group of students before, during, and after a lesson and to use the interview for both assessment and teaching purposes. Socrates is an example of a teacher who used interviewing as his major instructional strategy.

Being A Socrates

1. Choose a topic being studied.

2. Develop two or three general questions on what the student knows about the topic to begin an interview.

3. After asking the opening questions, probe what the student knows while looking for inconsistencies, contradictions, or conflicts in what the student is saying.

4. Ask follow-up questions that highlight the conflicts within the student's reasoning and makes the contradictions focal points for the student's attention.

5. Continue the interview until the student has resolved the conflicts by moving towards deeper-level analysis of what he or she knows and arriving at greater and greater insights into the material being studied.

6. Conclude the interview with pointing the student toward further resources to read and study.

Attitude Questionnaires

All learning has affective components and in many ways the attitudes students develop may be more important than their level of academic learning. Getting an "A" in math class, for example, does a student little good if he or she has learned to hate math and never wants to take a math class again. Obviously, loving math and wanting to take math courses throughout one's educational career is far more important than the level of achievement in any one math class. Attitudes largely determine whether students continue to study the subject area, become uninterested, or wish to avoid it in the future. In assessing student attitudes, you (a) decide which attitudes to measure, (b) construct a questionnaire, (c) select a standardized measure if it is appropriate, (d) give the measures near the beginning and end of each instructional unit, semester, or year, (e) analyze and organize the data for feedback to interested stakeholders, (f) give the feedback in a timely

Cooperation In The Classroom, Interaction Book Company, 7208 Cornelia Drive, Edina, MN 55435, (612) 831-9500, FAX (612) 831-9332

and orderly way, and (g) use the results to make decisions about improving the instructional program. In constructing a questionnaire, each question needs to be well-worded and requiring either an open-ended (fill-in-the-blank or free response) or closed-ended (dichotomous, multiple choice, ranking, or scale) response. The questions are then arranged in an appropriate sequence and given an attractive format. A standardized questionnaire, such as the Classroom Life instrument may be used to measure a broader range of student attitudes.

My View Of This Class Is

Answer each question below with your best opinion. Do not leave any questions blank.

1. My general opinion about history is _____.

2. History is my _____ subject.

3. If someone suggested I take up history as my life's work, I would reply

   _____.

4. History is my favorite school subject. ___ True ___ False

5. Do you intend to take another course in history?
   _____ Yes _____ No _____ I'm not sure

6. How interested are you in learning more about history?
   Very interested 1:2:3:4:5:6:7 Very uninterested

7.   **History**
   Ugly 1:2:3:4:5:6:7 Beautiful
   Bad 1:2:3:4:5:6:7 Good
   Worthless 1:2:3:4:5:6:7 Valuable
   Negative 1:2:3:4:5:6:7 Positive

Learning Logs And Journals

Students often do not spend enough time reflecting on what they are learning and how it relates in a personal way to their lives. Learning logs and journals help students document and reflect on their learning experiences. **Logs** tend to emphasize short entries concerning the subject matter being studied. Logs are especially useful in conjunction with informal cooperative learning. **Journals** tend to emphasize more narrative entries

Cooperation In The Classroom, Interaction Book Company, 7208 Cornelia Drive, Edina, MN 55435, (612) 831-9500, FAX (612) 831-9332

concerning personal observations, feelings, and opinions in response to readings, events, and experiences. These entries often connect what is being studied in one class with other classes or with life outside of the classroom. Journals are especially useful in having students apply what they are learning to their "action theories."

ASSIGNING POINT VALUES TO ENTRIES

Points	Criteria
20	Completeness Of Entries
10	Entries Recorded On Time
15	Originality Of Entries
15	Higher-Level Reasoning Demonstrated
15	Connections Made With Other Subject Areas
25	Personal Reflection
100	Total

Total Quality Learning

Total quality learning begins with assigning students to teams and assigning them the task of continuously improving the quality of the processes of learning and assessment. **Continuous improvement** is the ongoing search for changes that will increase the quality of the processes of learning, instructing, and assessing. Each time students write a composition, for example, they should find at least one way to improve their writing skills. The changes do not have to be dramatic. Small, incremental changes are fine.

To improve continuously the processes of learning and assessment, students need to engage in eight steps. **First**, they must form teams. Quality learning is not possible without cooperative learning groups. **Second**, team members analyze the assignment and select a learning process for improvement. **Third**, members define the process to improve, usually by drawing a flow chart or cause-and-effect diagram. **Fourth**, team members engage in the process. **Fifth**, students gather data about the process, display the data, and analyze it. Tools to help them do so include observation forms, Pareto charts, run charts, scatter diagrams, and histograms. **Sixth**, on the basis of the analysis, team members make a plan to improve the process. **Seventh**, students implement the plan by engaging in the learning process in a modified and improved way. **Finally**, the team institutionalizes the changes that do in fact improve the quality of the learning process.

Cooperation In The Classroom, Interaction Book Company, 7208 Cornelia Drive, Edina, MN 55435, (612) 831-9500, FAX (612) 831-9332

One way to enhance the use of total quality learning is through the use of student management teams. A **student management team** consists of three or four students plus the instructor who assume responsibility for the success of the class by focusing on how to improve either the instructor's teaching or the content of the course. The group members monitor the course through their own experience and the comments of classmates. There are four stages of using student management teams: forming the team by recruiting and choosing members, building a cooperative team by structuring the five basic elements, improving the instruction and content of the course, and reaping the long-term gains from the process by carrying on the improvements to the next course.

Teaching Teams And Assessment

The days are gone when a teacher, working in isolation from colleagues, could instruct, assess, and report results by him- or herself. The practices have become so labor intensive and complex that one teacher cannot expect to do them alone. Realistically, colleagial teaching teams are needed to coordinate and continuously improve the instruction, assessment, and reporting process. Teachers need to begin their instruction, assessment, and reporting efforts with forming a colleagial teaching team. This allows them to capitalize on the many ways teams enhance productivity. The team focuses its efforts on continuously improving both student learning and the quality of instruction. The team as a whole conducts the assessment and reporting process by developing rubrics, applying the rubrics effectively, and reporting results to interested audiences. The team then establishes a continuous improvement process focusing on maximizing the quality of instruction of each member. While engaging in the continuous improvement process, the team also engages in continuously retraining aimed at improving the effectiveness of their use of the assessment procedures. The use of colleagial teaching teams provides the framework for developing schoolwide criteria and standards to be used in assessment.

Giving Grades

Teachers need to assess student learning and progress frequently, but they do not need to evaluate or give grades. Assessing involves checking on how students are doing, what they have learned, and what problems or difficulties they have experienced. Grades are symbols that represent a value judgment concerning the relative quality of a student's achievement during a specified period of instruction. Grades are necessary to give students and other interested audiences information about students' level of achievement, evaluate the success of an instructional program, provide students access to certain educational opportunities, and reward students who excel. Grading systems may involve a single grade or multi-grades. It is vital that grades are awarded fairly as they can have considerable influence on students' futures. Being fair includes using a wide variety of assignments to measure achievement. Grades may be supplemented with checklist and

Cooperation In The Classroom, Interaction Book Company, 7208 Cornelia Drive, Edina, MN 55435, (612) 831-9500, FAX (612) 831-9332

narratives to give a more complex and complete summative evaluation of student achievement. Having students work in cooperative groups adds further opportunity to measure aspects of students' learning and assign grades in a variety of ways.

Giving Students Grades in Cooperative Learning

The way grades are given depends on the type of interdependence the instructor wishes to create among students. Norm-referenced grading systems place students in competition with each other. Criterion-referenced grading systems require students to either work individualistically or cooperatively. Here are a number of suggestions for giving grades in cooperative learning situations.

1. **Individual score plus bonus points based on all members reaching criterion:** Group members study together and ensure that all have mastered the assigned material. Each then takes a test individually and is awarded that score. If all group members achieve over a preset criterion of excellence, each receives a bonus. An example is as follows.

Criteria	Bonus	Members	Scores	Bonus	Total
100	15 Points	Bill	100	10	110
90 - 99	10 Points	Juanita	95	10	105
80 - 89	5 Points	Sally	90	10	100

2. **Individual score plus bonus points based on lowest score:** The group members prepare each other to take an exam. Members then receive bonus points on the basis of the lowest individual score in their group. This procedure emphasizes encouraging, supporting, and assisting the low achievers in the group. The criterion for bonus points can be adjusted for each learning group, depending on the past performance of their lowest member. An example is as follows:

Criteria	Bonus	Members	Scores	Bonus	Total
90 - 100	6 Points	Bill	93	2	95
80 - 89	4 Points	Juanita	85	2	87
70 - 79	2 Points	Sally	78	2	80

Cooperation In The Classroom, Interaction Book Company, 7208 Cornelia Drive, Edina, MN 55435, (612) 831-9500, FAX (612) 831-9332

3. **Individual score plus group average:** Group members prepare each other to take an exam. Each takes the examination and receives his or her individual score. The scores of the group members are then averaged. The average is added to each member's score. An example is given below.

Student	Individual Score	Group Average	Final Score
Bill	66	79	145
Juanita	89	79	168
Sally	75	79	154
Benjamin	86	79	165

4. **Individual score plus bonus based on improvement scores:** Members of a cooperative group prepare each other to take an exam. Each takes the exam individually and receives his or her individual grade. In addition, bonus points are awarded on the basis of whether members percentage on the current test is higher than the average percentage on all past tests (i.e., their usual level of performance). Their percentage correct on past tests serves as their base score that they try to better. Every two tests or scores, the base score is updated. If a student scores within 4 points (above or below) his or her base score, all members of the group receive 1 bonus point. If they score 5 to 9 points above their base score, each group member receives 2 bonus points. Finally, if they score 10 points or above their base score, or score 100 percent correct, each member receives 3 bonus points.

5. **Totaling members' individual scores:** The individual scores of members are added together and all members receive the total. For example, if group members scored 90, 85, 95, and 90, each member would receive the score of 360.

6. **Averaging of members' individual scores:** The individual scores of members are added together and divided by the number of group members. Each member then receives the group average as their mark. For example, if the scores of members were 90, 95, 85, and 90, each group member would receive the score of 90.

7. **Group score on a single product:** The group works to produce a single report, essay, presentation, worksheet, or exam. The product is evaluated and all members receive the score awarded. When this method is used with worksheets, sets of problems, and examinations, group members are required to reach consensus on each question and be able to explain it to others. The discussion within the group enhances the learning considerably.

Cooperation In The Classroom, Interaction Book Company, 7208 Cornelia Drive, Edina, MN 55435, (612) 831-9500, FAX (612) 831-9332

8. **Randomly selecting one member's paper to score:** Group members all complete the work individually and then check each other's papers and certify that they are perfectly correct. Since each paper is certified by the whole group to be correct, it makes little difference which paper is graded. The instructor picks one at random, grades it, and all group members receive the score.

9. **Randomly selecting one member's exam to score:** Group members prepare for an examination and certify that each member has mastered the assigned material. All members then take the examination individually. Since all members have certified that each has mastered the material being studied, it makes little difference which exam is scored. The instructor randomly picks one, scores it, and all group members receive that score.

10. **All members receive lowest member score:** Group members prepare each other to take the exam. Each takes the examination individually. All group members then receive the lowest score in the group. For example, if group members score 89, 88, 82, and 79, all members would receive 79 as their score. This procedure emphasizes encouraging, supporting and assisting the low-achieving members of the group and often produces dramatic increases in performance by low-achieving students.

11. **Average of academic scores plus collaborative skills performance score:** Group members work together to master the assigned material. They take an examination individually and their scores are averaged. Concurrently, their work is observed and the frequency of performance of specified collaborative skills (such as leadership or trust-building actions) is recorded. The group is given a collaborative skills performance score, which is added to their academic average to determine their overall mark.

12. **Dual academic and nonacademic rewards:** Group members prepare each other for a test, take it individually, and receive an individual grade. On the basis of their group average they are awarded free-time, popcorn, extra recess time, or some other valued reward.

Summary

Traditionally, assessment procedures have been quite limited. Teachers often notice the light in a student's eye, changes in voice inflections, the "aha" of discovery, the creative insight resulting from collaborating with others, the persistence and struggle of a student determined to understand complex material, the serendipitous use of skills and concepts beyond the context in which they were learned, and reports from parents and other teachers on the changes in a student resulting from a course of study. What has been lacking is a systematic way of collecting and reporting such evidence.

Cooperation In The Classroom, Interaction Book Company, 7208 Cornelia Drive, Edina, MN 55435, (612) 831-9500, FAX (612) 831-9332

Times have changed. The diverse assessment procedures discussed in Johnson and Johnson (1996) and outlined in this book are quite developed and may be used effectively as part of any instructional program. Each has its strengths and its weaknesses. Each can be integrated into ongoing instructional program and managed when they are used as part of cooperative learning. Together, they allow cooperative learning groups to engage in total quality learning and provide a comprehensive and fair means of giving grades.

Implementation Assignment

1. Read Chapter Nine.

2. Make an assessment plan for your cooperative learning groups that includes the new assessment formats and several ideas from this chapter. Bring it to the next class to share with your base group.

3. Use three different ways of assigning grades in your class, make a written assessment of their effectiveness, and bring it to the next class to share with your base group.

4. Have a group celebration in your base group to emphasize how hard all members are working to implement cooperative learning.

Cooperation In The Classroom, Interaction Book Company, 7208 Cornelia Drive, Edina, MN 55435, (612) 831-9500, FAX (612) 831-9332

COOPERATIVE LEARNING CONTRACT

Write down your major learnings from reading this chapter and participating in training session one. Then write down how you plan to implement each learning. Share what you learned and your implementation plans with your base group. Listen carefully to their major learnings and implementation plans. You may modify your own plans on the basis of what you have learned from your groupmates. Volunteer one thing you can do to help each groupmate with his or her implementation plans. Utilize the help groupmates offer to you. Sign each member's plans to seal the contract.

MAJOR LEARNINGS	IMPLEMENTATION PLANS

Date: _____ Participant's Signature: _____

Signatures Of Group Members: _____

_____

Cooperation In The Classroom, Interaction Book Company, 7208 Cornelia Drive, Edina, MN 55435, (612) 831-9500, FAX (612) 831-9332

COOPERATIVE LEARNING PROGRESS REPORT

Name: _____   School: _____

Subject Area: _____   Grade: _____

Date	Lesson	Successes	Problems

Describe Critical Or Interesting Incidents:

8 : 27

Cooperation In The Classroom, Interaction Book Company, 7208 Cornelia Drive, Edina, MN 55435, (612) 831-9500, FAX (612) 831-9332

EXERCISE MATERIALS

8 : 28

Cooperation In The Classroom, Interaction Book Company, 7208 Cornelia Drive, Edina, MN 55435, (612) 831-9500, FAX (612) 831-9332

Creating Rubrics To Assess Student Learning

Step One: Review lesson and type of student performance.

a. Lesson: _____

b. Type Of Student Performance: _____

Step Two: Define the assessment procedure. Indicate on the checklist below the procedures that will be used to assess students' learning.

_____ Goal Setting Conferences   _____ Portfolios

_____ Standardized Tests   _____ Observations

_____ Teacher-Made Tests   _____ Questionnaires

_____ Written Compositions   _____ Interviews

_____ Oral Presentations   _____ Learning Logs & Journals

_____ Homework, Extra-Credit   _____ Student Management Teams

_____ Projects, Experiments, Surveys, Historical Research

Step Three: Develop a set of criteria to use in assessing students performances. The steps for doing so are:

_____ a. Brainstorm a potential list of criteria

_____ b. Rank order the criteria from most important to least important.

Step Four: Develop rubrics. Rubrics are needed to assess the quality and quantity of each student's performance for each criterion.

_____ a. Begin with the criterion ranked most important.

_____ b. Find exemplary and terrible student performances and analyze them to help develop indicators that accurately measure their strengths and weaknesses.

_____ c. List indicators of very poor, poor, middle, good, and very good levels of performance. Define very good and very poor performance and then fill in the middle categories.

_____ d. Communicate rubrics to parents so they can help students with homework.

8 : 29

Cooperation In The Classroom, Interaction Book Company, 7208 Cornelia Drive, Edina, MN 55435, (612) 831-9500, FAX (612) 831-9332

Step Five: Train the students in using the rubric so that they are co-oriented, consistent, and reliable in their use of the rubric. Students have to be able to apply the same rubric in the same way at different times. Different students have to be able to apply the same rubric in the same way. One procedure for training is:

——— a. Students score models of exemplary and substandard work.

——— b. Students score a student performance together as a group, discussing how the performance should be assessed on each criterion.

——— c. Team members score several student performances separately. They compare scoring to see if they are using the rubrics in the same way.

——— d. Compare students' scoring with the teacher's scoring. Discuss any differences until everyone in the class is co-oriented and reliably scores a performance in the same way.

Step Six: Conduct Lesson And Assess Student Performances.

——— a. **Self-Assessment**: Each student assesses his or her own work.

——— b. **Peer Assessment**: Students assess their groupmates' work. At least two team members score each performance. Any differences in the scoring are then discussed until two or more team members agree on the way each student performance is scored.

——— c. **Teacher Assessment**: Teacher assesses each student performance if time allows or assesses samples of students' work if time is short.

Step Seven: On the basis of the assessment, plan how to improve student performances and instructional program.

Step Eight: Continually improve the criteria, the rubrics, and the students' skills in assessing the quality and quantity of their learning. Beware of scoring criteria drift. Periodically recalibrate the teachers and students' use of the scoring rubrics. Search for exemplary criteria, rubrics, and scoring procedures and use them as benchmarks to improve assessment practices.

Cooperation In The Classroom, Interaction Book Company, 7208 Cornelia Drive, Edina, MN 55435, (612) 831-9500, FAX (612) 831-9332

Assessment Rubric

Student: _____ Date: _____ Class: _____

Type Of Performance: _____

Write the indicators for each of the five levels of performance for each criterion.

VERY POOR	POOR	MIDDLE	GOOD	VERY GOOD
Criterion Example: Topic Addressed				
◆ Paper does not address topic.	◆ Opening sentence does not identify the purpose	◆ Opening sentence partially identifies the purpose.	◆ Opening sentence identifies the purpose.	◆ Opening sentence identifies the purpose.
◆	◆ Few aspects of topic are discussed in disorganized ways.	◆ Several aspects are discussed, but not in separate paragraphs.	◆ All aspects of topic are discussed but not in separate paragraphs.	◆ Each paragraph addresses one aspect of the topic.
◆	◆	◆	◆	◆ All aspects of topic are thoroughly discussed.
Criterion One				
◆	◆	◆	◆	◆
◆	◆	◆	◆	◆
◆	◆	◆	◆	◆
Criterion Two				
◆	◆	◆	◆	◆
◆	◆	◆	◆	◆
◆	◆	◆	◆	◆
Criterion Three				
◆	◆	◆	◆	◆
◆	◆	◆	◆	◆
◆	◆	◆	◆	◆

8 : 31

Cooperation In The Classroom, Interaction Book Company, 7208 Cornelia Drive, Edina, MN 55435, (612) 831-9500, FAX (612) 831-9332

Assessment Rubric

Student: _____ Date: _____ Class: _____

Type Of Performance: _____

Write indicators for each of the three levels of performance for each criterion.

INADEQUATE	MIDDLE	EXCELLENT
Criterion Example: Clear Reasoning		
◆ Gives conclusion with	◆ Gives some examples	◆ Consistently gives for
◆ no examples or reasons.	◆ and reasons for each	◆ examples and reasons
◆	◆ conclusion.	◆ each conclusion.
Criterion One		
◆	◆	◆
◆	◆	◆
◆	◆	◆
Criterion Two		
◆	◆	◆
◆	◆	◆
◆	◆	◆
Criterion Three		
◆	◆	◆
◆	◆	◆
◆	◆	◆
Criterion Four		
◆	◆	◆
◆	◆	◆
◆	◆	◆

8 : 32

Cooperation In The Classroom, Interaction Book Company, 7208 Cornelia Drive, Edina, MN 55435, (612) 831-9500, FAX (612) 831-9332

CHAPTER NINE:

THE COOPERATIVE SCHOOL

Introduction

Nothing new that is really interesting comes without collaboration.

James Watson, Nobel Prize Winner (codiscoverer of double helix)

Ford Motor Company knew it had to do something different, dramatically different, to gain back market share from imports. A new mid-sized car was conceived to be Ford's best chance to do so. For years Ford had operated within a mass-manufacturing structure whose motto was "any color as long as it is black." Designers etched out sketches and gave them to manufacturing with the order, "build it!" Sales inherited the car and had to figure out how to sell it. That was the way Ford had always built cars. But not this time. An interdisciplinary team was created made up of designers, engineers, manufacturing and financial executives, and sales and marketing people. Together they created the Taurus, a car whose sales neared one million units in its first four production years and which has consistently won praise from both auto experts and consumers.

Ford is not the only company to switch to cooperative teams. Whereas there is an American myth of progress being spurred on by Lone Rangers, in today's corporations that image is about as current as bustles and spats. From Motorola to AT&T Credit Corporation, self-managing, multi-disciplinary teams are in charge of keeping the company profitable. Teams get things done.

Team development is at the core of the changes necessary to alter the way faculty and students work. It is the way to educate students the right way the first time. Reorganizing students and faculty into teams, however, may not be easy.

Cooperation In The Classroom, Interaction Book Company, 7208 Cornelia Drive, Edina, MN 55435, (612) 831-9500, FAX (612) 831-9332

Figure 9.1 The Cooperative School

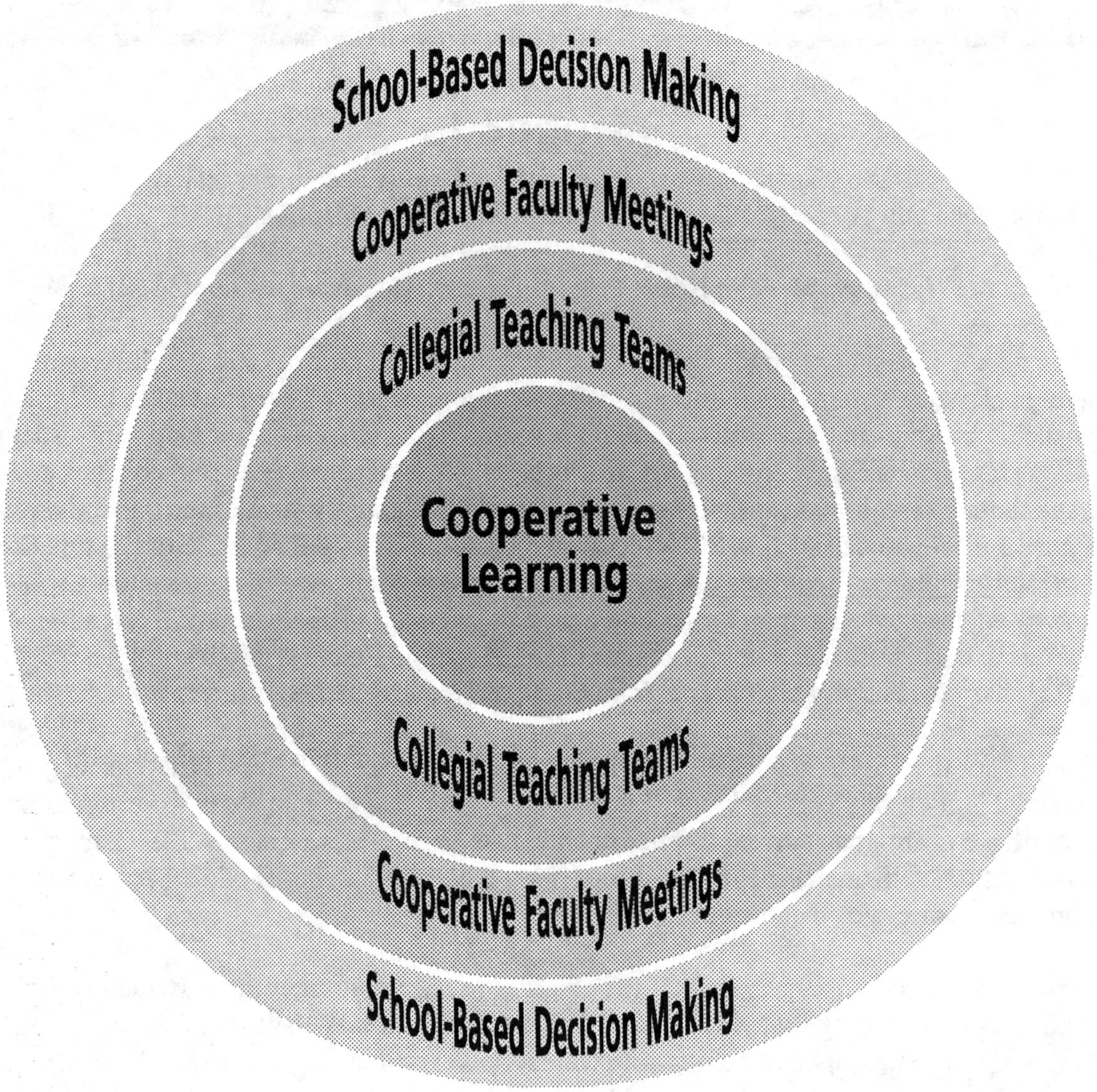

Cooperation In The Classroom, Interaction Book Company, 7208 Cornelia Drive, Edina, MN 55435, (612) 831-9500, FAX (612) 831-9332

The Cooperative School

The worst poverty is the feeling of loneliness and of being unwanted.

Mother Teresa

For nearly a century, schools have functioned as "mass production" organizations that divided work into small component parts performed by individuals who worked separately from and, in many cases, in competition with peers. Teachers have worked alone, in their own room, with their own set of students, and with their own set of curriculum materials. Both teachers and students have been considered to be interchangeable parts in the organizational machine. Students can be assigned to any teacher because teachers are all equivalent and, conversely, teachers can be given any student to teach because all students are considered to be the same.

W. Edwards Deming and others have suggested that more than 85 percent of all the things that go wrong in any organization are directly attributable to the organization's structure, not the nature of the individuals involved. Retraining teachers to use cooperative learning while organizing teachers to mass produce educated students is self-defeating. Changing methods of teaching is much easier when the changes are congruent with (not in opposition to) the organizational structure of the school. In order for schools to focus on the quality of instruction, they need to change from a mass-production, competitive/individualistic organizational structure to a high-performance, cooperative team-based organizational structure known as "the cooperative school." In this structure, work at all levels is organized into whole processes performed by teams focused on joint productivity and continuous improvement (see Johnson & Johnson, 1994).

The **cooperative school** is a team-based, high-performance organizational structure in which teams are used at all levels to increase the productivity and effectiveness of administrators, faculty and staff, and students. In a cooperative school, students work primarily in cooperative learning groups, teachers and building staff work in cooperative teams, and district administrators work in cooperative teams (Johnson & Johnson, 1994). The organizational structure of the classroom, school, and district are then congruent. Each level of cooperative teams supports and enhances the other levels. Structuring cooperative teams is the heart of improving schools and must precede all other improvement initiatives. Effective teamwork is the very center of improving the quality of instruction and education. It forms the hub around which all other elements of school improvement revolves. The primary units of performance in schools need to be teams. Teams are, beyond all doubt, the most direct sources of continuous improvement of instruction and education.

A cooperative school structure begins in the classroom with the use of cooperative learning the majority of the time (Johnson & Johnson, 1994). Work teams are the heart of the team-based organizational structure and cooperative learning groups are the

Cooperation In The Classroom, Interaction Book Company, 7208 Cornelia Drive, Edina, MN 55435, (612) 831-9500, FAX (612) 831-9332

primary work team. Students spend the majority of the day in **formal cooperative learning groups** (students work together for one or several class sessions to achieve shared learning goals and complete specific tasks and assignments) and **informal cooperative learning groups** (students work together in temporary, ad hoc groups that last only for one discussion or class period to achieve joint learning goals) and **cooperative base groups** (students work in long-term groups (lasting for one semester or year) with stable membership whose primary responsibility is to give each member the support, encouragement, and assistance he or she needs to progress academically and develop cognitively and socially in healthy ways). The health of cooperative efforts, however, largely depends on how constructively conflicts among collaborators are managed. In addition, students are taught how to manage conflicts constructively by learning how to engage in **academic controversies** (one student's ideas, information, conclusions, theories, and opinions are incompatible with those of another, and the two seek to reach an agreement) and the peacemaker procedures for **problem-solving negotiations** (procedure by which persons with shared and opposing interests reach an agreement that maximizes joint outcomes and improves their working relationship) and **peer mediation** (a fellow student serves as a neutral person who helps two or more disputants resolve their conflict). Finally, students are taught the **civic values** needed to be part of a learning community.

Quality learning does not take place in isolation, it results from a team effort to challenge each other's reasoning and maximize each other's learning. Cooperative learning is used to increase student achievement, create more positive relationships among students, and generally improve students' psychological well-being. Cooperative learning is also the prerequisite and foundation for most other instructional innovations, including thematic curriculum, whole language, critical thinking, active reading, process writing, materials-based (problem-solving) mathematics, and learning communities. A secondary effect of using cooperative learning is that it affects teachers' attitudes and competencies toward working collaboratively with colleagues. What is promoted in instructional situations tends to dominate relationships among staff members.

The second level in creating a cooperative school is to form colleagial teaching teams, task forces, and ad hoc decision-making groups within the school (Johnson & Johnson, 1994). The use of cooperation to structure faculty and staff work involves (a) **colleagial teaching teams** (two to five faculty members meet to increase their instructional expertise and success in using cooperative learning) and **colleagial study groups** (two to five faculty members meet to read and discuss materials on instructional and assessment procedures that will increase their effectiveness and enhance their use of cooperative learning), (b) faculty meetings in which cooperative procedures are modeled, (c) faculty committees formed to monitor and continuously improve procedures dealing with school life, and (d) school-based decision making . School based decision making begins with the formation of a **teacher task force** which considers a school problem, gather data about the causes and extent of the problem, consider a variety of alternative solutions, make conclusions, and present a recommendation to the faculty as a whole.

9 : 4

Cooperation In The Classroom, Interaction Book Company, 7208 Cornelia Drive, Edina, MN 55435, (612) 831-9500, FAX (612) 831-9332

Ad hoc decision-making teams are formed to (a) listen to the report of a task force, (b) discuss the report and consider whether to accept or modify the task forces' recommendation and (c) inform the entire faculty of their decision. **The whole-faculty decides** on the actions to be taken to solve the problem. The reports of the ad-hoc decision-making teams are combined and the three or four most recommended plans are presented to the faculty. The faculty votes on which plan to adopt. The faculty then implements the plan and the **task force monitors the implementation of the decision** and assesses whether or not the problem is solved.

Faculty meetings represent a microcosm of what administrators think the school should be. The clearest modeling of cooperative procedures in the school may be in faculty meetings. Formal and informal cooperative groups, cooperative base groups, and repetitive structures can be used in faculty meetings just as they can be used in the classroom. In this way, faculty meetings become staff development.

The third level in creating a cooperative school is to implement administrative cooperative teams within the district (Johnson & Johnson, 1994). Administrators are organized into colleagial teams (to increase their expertise and success in leading a cooperative school), task forces, and ad-hoc triads are used as part of the shared decision-making process. In administrative meetings, cooperative procedures dominate to model what the school district should be like. Administrators **support and coach teachers using cooperative learning** to ensure that cooperative learning is used with fidelity, is flexibly adapted to the teachers' students and specific circumstances, and is continuously improved. Finally, administrators **extend cooperation to the community** so that the school, parents, and community are working together to achieve mutual goals.

Team efforts is paramount at every rung of the ladder in modern organizations. Schools are no exception. Students and faculty have to want to belong to teams, they have to contribute their share of the work, and they must take positions and know how to advocate their views in ways that spark creative problem solving. Lone wolves who do not pull with their peers will increasingly find themselves the odd person out.

Colleagial Teaching Teams

In mass-production schools, teachers are isolated from each other and may feel harried, overloaded, and overwhelmed. The isolation and alienation are reduced when teachers form colleagial teaching teams aimed at increasing the quality of instruction in the school. **Teachers generally teach better when they work in colleagial teaching teams to jointly support each other's efforts to increase their instructional expertise.** The purposes of teaching teams include giving teachers ownership of the professional agenda, breaking down the barriers to colleagial interaction, and reducing program fragmentation. The three key activities of a teaching team are (Johnson & Johnson, 1994).

9 : 5

Cooperation In The Classroom, Interaction Book Company, 7208 Cornelia Drive, Edina, MN 55435, (612) 831-9500, FAX (612) 831-9332

© Johnson, Johnson, & Holubec

ORGANIZATIONAL STRUCTURE OF SCHOOLS

OLD PARADIGM	NEW PARADIGM
Mass-Production School	**Team-Based, High-Performance School**
Faculty Work Alone, Barriers Separate Teachers From Each Other	Faculty Work In Colleagial Teaching Teams
Authority Hierarchy	Flat Organizational Structure
Following Procedures Emphasized	Continuous Improvement Of Quality Emphasized
Work Is Segmented Into Small Parts (Subject Areas, Grade Levels)	Team Is Given Responsibility For Whole Process
Teaching Is Standardized	Increased Responsibility And Autonomy Given To Teaching Teams
Faculty, Staff, Students Seen As Interchangeable, Replaceable Parts	Supportive, Committed, Caring Relationships
Certain Percentage Of Failures And Dropouts Accepted	No Student Failures Or Dropouts Accepted
Loosely Coupled School	**Tightly Coupled School**
Goal Ambiguity	Clear, Positively Interdependent Goals
Low Individual Accountability	Individual And Team Accountability
Independent Work	Promotive Interaction
Social Skills Deemphasized	Teamwork Skills Emphasized
No Structured Reflection On Processes Of Teaching And Learning	Frequent Reflection On Processes Of Teaching And Learning
Underlying Competition	**Underlying Cooperation**
Amorphous Competition Pervades Interactions	Cooperation Pervades Interactions

1. **Frequent professional discussions of cooperative learning** in which a common vocabulary is developed, information is shared, successes are celebrated, and problems connected with implementation are solved. Interaction among colleagues is

9 : 6

Cooperation In The Classroom, Interaction Book Company, 7208 Cornelia Drive, Edina, MN 55435, (612) 831-9500, FAX (612) 831-9332

essential for building collaborative cultures in schools (Hargreaves, 1991; Little, 1990). Social support is critical for the ongoing professional development of teachers (Nias, 1984). Expertise in using cooperative learning begins with conceptual understanding of (a) the nature of cooperative learning, (b) how to implement cooperative learning, and (c) what results can be expected from using cooperative learning. Teachers must also think critically about the strategy and adapt it to their specific students and subject areas. In team discussions teachers consolidate and strengthen their knowledge about cooperative learning and provide each other with relevant feedback about the degree to which mastery and understanding have been achieved.

2. **Coplanning, codesigning, copreparing, and coassessing cooperative learning lessons and instructional units.** Once cooperative learning is understood conceptually, it must be implemented. Members of teaching team plan, design, prepare, and assess lesson plans together to share the work of developing the materials and expertise for implementing cooperative learning. Integrated curriculum and thematic teaching depend on coplanning and codesigning. **The cycle of coplanning, parallel teaching, and coprocessing may be followed by one of coplanning, coteaching, and coprocessing.**

3. **Coteaching cooperative lessons.** If faculty are to progress through the initial awkward and mechanical stages to a routine-use, automatic level of mastery, they must (a) receive feedback on the quality of their implementation and (b) be encouraged to persevere in their implementation attempts long enough to integrate cooperative learning into their ongoing instructional practice. The more colleagues are involved in your teaching, the more valuable the help and assistance they can provide. Frequently coteaching cooperative lessons and providing each other with useful feedback provides members with shared experiences to discuss and refer to.

Colleagial teams ideally meet daily. At a minimum, teams should meet weekly. During a typical meeting team members review how they have used cooperative learning since the previous meeting, share a success in doing so, complete a quality chart on their implementation of cooperative learning, set three to five goals to accomplish before the next meeting, establish how each will help the others achieve their goals, learn something new about cooperative learning, and celebrate how hard all members are working (Johnson & Johnson, 1994). Following this agenda ensures that (a) teachers meet with supportive peers who encourage them to learn and grow, (b) continuous training of teachers in how to use cooperative learning is provided, (c) pride of workmanship can be encouraged and self-improvement are recognized and celebrated, and (d) poor workmanship and negativism are discouraged.

Cooperation In The Classroom, Interaction Book Company, 7208 Cornelia Drive, Edina, MN 55435, (612) 831-9500, FAX (612) 831-9332

Form a pair. Rank order the three major activities of colleagial teaching teams from most beneficial ("1") to least beneficial to teachers ("3").

RANK	COLLEAGIAL TEACHING TEAM ACTIVITIES

_____ Frequent professional discussions of cooperative learning

_____ Coplanning, codesigning, copreparing, and coevaluating cooperative learning lessons and instructional units.

_____ Coteaching cooperative lessons.

Continuous Improvement Of Expertise

To have joy one must share it. Happiness was born a twin.

Indian Proverb

For schools to be successful, everyone in the school must be dedicated to continuous improvement in using cooperative learning. In Japan, this mutual dedication is called **kaizen** (a societywide covenant of mutual help in the process of getting better and better, day by day). **Expertise** is reflected in a person's proficiency, adroitness, competence, and skill in structuring cooperative efforts. Cooperation takes more expertise than do competitive or individualistic efforts, because it involves dealing with other people as well as dealing with the demands of the task (i.e., simultaneously engaging in taskwork and teamwork). Expertise is usually gained in an incremental step-by-step manner, using the progressive refinement process over a period of years in a team.

Faculty progressively refine their competence in using cooperative learning through five steps (Johnson & Johnson, 1994). **First, teachers must understand conceptually what cooperative learning is and how it may be implemented in their classrooms.** Teachers must understand the five basic elements of effective cooperation and the teacher's role in using formal and informal cooperative learning and cooperative base groups. They must be able to adapt and refine cooperative learning to fit their unique, idiosyncratic instructional situation. **Second, teachers try out cooperative learning in their classrooms with their students.** Faculty must be willing to take risks by experimenting with new instructional and managing strategies and procedures. **Third, teachers assess how well cooperative learning lessons went and obtain feedback on their teaching from others.** From the progressive refinement point of view, failure and total success never occur. There are simply approximations of what one wants. Teachers refine and fine-tune procedures to get successively closer and closer to the ideal. **Fourth, teachers reflect on what they did and how it may be improved.** The discrepancy between the real and the ideal is considered and plans are made to alter one's

9 : 8

Cooperation In The Classroom, Interaction Book Company, 7208 Cornelia Drive, Edina, MN 55435, (612) 831-9500, FAX (612) 831-9332

behavior in order to get a better match in the future. Quality charts help this reflection process. **Fifth, teachers try out cooperative learning again in a modified and improved way.** Perseverance in using cooperative learning again and again and again is required until the teacher can teach a cooperative lesson routinely and without conscious planning or thought. In is through this progressive refinement process that expertise in using cooperative learning is fine-tuned.

Providing Leadership

Knowing is not enough; we must apply. Willing is not enough; we must do.

Goethe

For the cooperative school to flourish the school has to have leadership. In general, leadership is provided by five sets of actions (Johnson & Johnson, 1994).

1. **Challenging The Status Quo:** The status quo is the competitive-individualistic mass-production structure that dominates schools and classrooms. In the classroom it is represented by lecturing, whole class discussion, individual worksheets, and a test on Friday. In the school it is one teacher to one classroom with one set of students, as well as separating teachers and students into grade levels and academic departments. Leaders challenge the efficacy of the status quo.

2. **Inspiring A Mutual Vision Of What The School Could Be:** Leaders enthusiastically and frequently communicate the dreams of establishing the cooperative school. The leader is the keeper of the dream who inspires commitment to joint goals of creating a team-based, cooperative school.

3. **Empowering Through Cooperative Teams:** This is the most important leadership activities. When faculty or students feel helpless and discouraged, providing them with a team creates hope and opportunity. It is social support from and accountability to valued peers that motivates committed efforts to achieve and succeed. Students are empowered by cooperative learning groups. Faculty members are empowered through colleagial support groups and involvement in site based decision making.

4. **Leading By Example:** Leaders model the use of cooperative strategies and procedures and take risks to increase their professional competence. Actions must be congruent with words. What is advocated must be demonstrated publicly.

5. **Encouraging The Heart To Persist:** Long-term, committed efforts to continuously improve one's competencies come from the heart, not the head. It takes courage and hope to strive for increased knowledge and expertise. It is the social support and concrete assistance from teammates that provides the strength to persist and excel.

9 : 9

Cooperation In The Classroom, Interaction Book Company, 7208 Cornelia Drive, Edina, MN 55435, (612) 831-9500, FAX (612) 831-9332

To implement the cooperative school, leadership that helps faculty do a better job must be provided (Johnson & Johnson, 1994). Leaders do not spend their time in an office talking on the phone, writing memos, and putting out fires. Leaders spend their time "where the action is" (in Japan this is called **genba**). In schools, the action is in classrooms. Thus, leaders have to challenge the status quo of the mass-production organization, inspire a mutual vision of the cooperative school, empower faculty through organizing them in teams, lead by example by using cooperative procedures continually, and encourage faculty's heart to persist by being in the classroom recognizing and celebrating their efforts to teach a perfect lesson every time.

Summary

Through the use of teams a congruent organizational structure is created that promotes quality education by creating a constancy of purpose, being committed to educating every student, focusing on improving the quality of instruction, eliminating competition at all levels, building strong personal relationships, reducing waste, and paying careful attention to implementing the five basic elements on a school and learning group level. Teaching teams provide the setting in which a process of continuous improvement in expertise can take place. Teachers and administrators progressively refine their expertise through a procedure involving action, feedback, reflection, and modified action. Teachers help each other learn an expert system of how to implement cooperative learning that they use to create a unique adaptation to their specific circumstances, students, and needs.

Implementation Assignment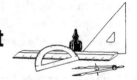

1. Read Chapter Ten.

2. List what you have done during this course to provide yourself with colleagial support for implementing cooperative learning.

3. List what you have done during this course to help colleagues implement cooperative learning.

4. List five things you could do to strengthen your colleagial support group. Do three of these things this week. Bring your lists and a report of the results of your efforts to class to share with your base group.

5. Write down the address and phone numbers of the members of your base group. Call them periodically and encourage their efforts to implement cooperative learning.

Cooperation In The Classroom, Interaction Book Company, 7208 Cornelia Drive, Edina, MN 55435, (612) 831-9500, FAX (612) 831-9332

COOPERATIVE LEARNING CONTRACT

Write down your major learnings from reading this chapter and participating in training session one. Then write down how you plan to implement each learning. Share what you learned and your implementation plans with your base group. Listen carefully to their major learnings and implementation plans. You may modify your own plans on the basis of what you have learned from your groupmates. Volunteer one thing you can do to help each groupmate with his or her implementation plans. Utilize the help groupmates offer to you. Sign each member's plans to seal the contract.

MAJOR LEARNINGS	IMPLEMENTATION PLANS

Date: _____ Participant's Signature: _____

Signatures Of Group Members: _____

_____

9 : 11

Cooperation In The Classroom, Interaction Book Company, 7208 Cornelia Drive, Edina, MN 55435, (612) 831-9500, FAX (612) 831-9332

COOPERATIVE LEARNING PROGRESS REPORT

Name: _____ School: _____

Subject Area: _____ Grade: _____

Date	Lesson	Successes	Problems

Describe Critical Or Interesting Incidents:

9 : 12

Cooperation In The Classroom, Interaction Book Company, 7208 Cornelia Drive, Edina, MN 55435, (612) 831-9500, FAX (612) 831-9332

EXERCISE

MATERIALS

Cooperation In The Classroom, Interaction Book Company, 7208 Cornelia Drive, Edina, MN 55435, (612) 831-9500, FAX (612) 831-9332

HOW WELL DO WE KNOW THIS CHAPTER?

Form a pair. Come to agreement on which definition matches each concept.

	Concept	Definition
	Mass Production Organizations	Organize work at all levels into whole processes performed by teams focused on joint productivity and continuous improvement.
	Team-Based, High-Performance Organizations	Team-based, high-performance organizational structure in which teams are used at all levels to increase the productivity and effectiveness of administrators, faculty and staff, and students.
	Cooperative School	Two to five faculty members meet to read and discuss materials on instructional and assessment procedures that will increase their effectiveness and enhance their use of cooperative learning.
	Colleagial Teaching Teams	A societywide covenant of mutual help in the process of getting better and better, day by day.
	Colleagial Study Groups	Divide work into small component parts performed by individuals who worked separately from and in many cases in competition with peers.
	Kaizen	Two to five faculty members meet to increase instructional expertise and success in using cooperative learning.
	Expertise	Providing social support from and accountability to peers to motivate committed efforts to succeed.
	Leading By Example	A person's proficiency, adroitness, competence, and skill in structuring cooperative efforts.
	Empowering Through Teams	Modeling the use of cooperative procedures so that actions are congruent with words.

9 : 14

Cooperation In The Classroom, Interaction Book Company, 7208 Cornelia Drive, Edina, MN 55435, (612) 831-9500, FAX (612) 831-9332

The Cooperative School: Diagnosis And Goal Setting

Leadership Actions	Where I Am Now	Where I Want To Be
1. Form and maintain colleagial administrative teams.		
2. Use a variety of cooperative procedures in every meeting they structure or lead.		
3. Support and coach teachers who are using cooperative learning.		
4. Extend cooperation to the community to ensure school, parents, and community are working together to achieve mutual goals.		
5. Help teachers form and maintain colleagial teaching teams.		
6. Help teachers form and maintain colleagial study groups.		
7. Lead site-based decision-making by:		
a. Organize and recruit teachers for task forces to consider school problems. Each task force presents a report to the faculty.		
b. Organize faculty into ad-hoc decision-making triads to consider the task force recommendations (agree or modify).		
c. Combine recommendations of ad hoc groups into the top alternatives and faculty votes to decide which one to adopt.		
d. Faculty implement plan and task force monitors to see if it solves the problem. If not, process is repeated.		
8. Organize and structure faculty and staff committees cooperatively		
9. Support and coach teachers in using cooperative learning, academic controversy and peacemaking procedures, and civic values.		

Cooperation In The Classroom, Interaction Book Company, 7208 Cornelia Drive, Edina, MN 55435, (612) 831-9500, FAX (612) 831-9332

School Leadership Worksheet

Your **tasks** are to (1) define each step of providing leadership in your own words, (2) give a colloquial definition of each step, and (3) list two ways you can engage in each step in your school.

Step	Definition	Practical Advice
Challenging The Status Quo		
Inspiring A Mutual Vision		
Empowering Through Teams		
Leading By Example		
Encouraging The Heart To Persist		

Cooperation In The Classroom, Interaction Book Company, 7208 Cornelia Drive, Edina, MN 55435, (612) 831-9500, FAX (612) 831-9332

COLLEAGIAL SUPPORT GROUP MEETING

1. **Membership Grid:** Record in the grid what is shared by each group member. The topics should be personal rather than professional. Examples are: Favorite novel, poem, play, movie, or painting and why it is your favorite; most fun free-time activity; most vivid memory from elementary, junior-high, and high school; most important positive family memory in the last year.

2. **Share A Success:** Think through what cooperative learning lessons and social skills you have taught during the past week. Share a success in using cooperative learning. Listen carefully to the successes shared by your colleagues. Take one good idea from what they did to try in your classroom. Then celebrate as a group.

3. **Goal Setting:** In order to continuously improve your professional expertise and competencies (and to help your colleagues do likewise) set five goals to accomplish this week. One goal should deal with using cooperative learning. One goal should deal with teaching students social skills. One goal should deal with promoting the success of a colleague (another teacher). Two goals should reflect current issues in your classroom.

Goal	Who	How	When/Where
Coop Learning			
Social Skills			
Helped Colleague			

4. **Joint Planning / Contracting:** Each member shares his or her goals for the week. For each goal, another member volunteers to help. How the help will be given and when and where it will take place are noted. The help may range from providing relevant materials to coteaching a lesson. Be specific about the help you will give and when and where you will do so. Make sure that the work is divided so that everyone saves time and energy by being part of the team. Sign the joint planning form of your colleagues

Cooperation In The Classroom, Interaction Book Company, 7208 Cornelia Drive, Edina, MN 55435, (612) 831-9500, FAX (612) 831-9332

to indicate that you understand what they are going to do and you are willing to assist them.

5. **New Content:** Share something new you have learned about the cooperative learning in the last week. This could be summarizing an article you have read, an insight gained from observing a colleague, a summary of a chapter of **Nuts And Bolts Of Cooperative Learning**, or a new way to structure positive interdependence. Guests (such as an innovative teacher, a local businessperson committed to team-based organizations, or the superintendent) may be invited to speak during this part of the meeting. A barrier to creating the cooperative school may be identified and a series of strategies to solving it may be generated.

6. **Celebrate:** Congratulate each member on a good week and send each other off happy, optimistic, and enthusiastic.

Role Of Convener: The role of convener is vital to effective meetings. Rotate this role among members. The convener is in charge of providing the meeting place, gourmet food, any materials required, a procedure for sharing new content, and keeping time so all agenda items are covered in the meeting.

Current Fires: If there is a current crisis in the school or district, save the discussion of it until after all other agenda items have been covered.

Scripting: Take each step of the above agenda and script what you would say to the group to assign the task and structure it cooperatively.

Guided Practice: Role play that you are meeting with a colleagial support group consisting of four of your teachers. Give your statement for structuring each of the meeting's agenda items. Listen to your partner present his or her script. Then work together to create an even better statement.

9 : 18

Cooperation In The Classroom, Interaction Book Company, 7208 Cornelia Drive, Edina, MN 55435, (612) 831-9500, FAX (612) 831-9332

CHAPTER TEN:

REFLECTIONS

Changing Paradigm Of Teaching

"I'm just a cowhand from Arkansas, but I have learned how to hold a team together. How to lift some men up, how to calm down others, until finally they've got one heartbeat together, a team. There's just three things I'd ever say: If anything goes bad, I did it. If anything goes semi-good, then we did it. If anything goes real good, then you did it. That's all it takes to get people to win football games for you."

Bear Bryant, Former Football Coach, University Of Alabama

Like all organizations, schools must adapt to changes in their environment or risk fading away like the dinosaurs. The dinosaurs presumably made good day-to-day adaptations to their environment. They probably made a pretty good choice of what leaves to eat from what trees, and selected the most desirable swamps in which to slosh. At a tactical level of decision, we have no reason to believe that these giant beasts were not reasonably competent. But when faced with major changes in the earth's climate and the resulting changes in plant and other animal life, the dinosaurs were unable to make the fundamental changes required to adapt to the new environmental conditions. Schools may now be faced with new environmental conditions that require them to do what the dinosaurs could not. Schools need to make fundamental changes in the ways students are instructed. The changes are known as the new paradigm of teaching.

Cooperative learning is part of a broader paradigm shift that is occurring in teaching. Essential elements of this paradigm shift are presented in Table 10.1 (Johnson, Johnson, & Holubec, 1992; Johnson, Johnson, & Smith, 1991).

The **old paradigm of teaching** is based on John Locke's assumption that the untrained student mind is like a blank sheet of paper waiting for the instructor to write on it. Student minds are viewed as empty vessels into which teachers pour their wisdom. Because of these and other assumptions, teachers think of teaching in terms of these principal activities:

Cooperation In The Classroom, Interaction Book Company, 7208 Cornelia Drive, Edina, MN 55435, (612) 831-9500, FAX (612) 831-9332

TABLE 10.1: COMPARISON OF OLD AND NEW PARADIGMS OF TEACHING

FACTOR	OLD PARADIGM OF TEACHING	NEW PARADIGM OF TEACHING
Knowledge	Transferred From Faculty To Students	Jointly Constructed By Students And Faulty
Students	Passive Vessel To Be Filled By Faculty's Knowledge	Active Constructor, Discoverer, Transformer of Own Knowledge
Faculty Purpose	Classify And Sort Students	Develop Students' Competencies And Talents
Relationships	Impersonal Relationships Among Students And Between Faculty And Students	Personal Transaction Among Students And Between Faculty And Students
Context	Competitive/Individualistic	Cooperative Learning In Classroom And Cooperative Teams Among Faculty
Assumption	Any Expert Can Teach	Teaching Is Complex And Requires Considerable Training

1. **Transferring knowledge from teacher to students.** The teacher's job is to give it; the student's job to is get it. Teachers transmit information that students are expected to memorize and then recall.

2. **Filling passive empty vessels with knowledge.** Students are passive recipients of knowledge. Teachers own the knowledge that students memorize and recall.

3. **Classifying students by deciding who gets which grade and sorting students into categories** by deciding who does and does not meet the requirements to be graduated, go on to college, and get a good job. There is constant inspection to "weed out" any defective students. Teachers classify and sort students into categories under the assumption that ability is fixed and is unaffected by effort and education.

4. **Conducting education within a context of impersonal relationships among students and between teachers and students.** Based on the Taylor model of industrial organizations, students and teachers are perceived to be interchangeable and replaceable parts in the "education machine."

5. **Maintaining a competitive organizational**

10 : 2

Cooperation In The Classroom, Interaction Book Company, 7208 Cornelia Drive, Edina, MN 55435, (612) 831-9500, FAX (612) 831-9332

structure in which students work to outperform their classmates and teachers work to outperform their colleagues.

6. **Assuming that anyone with expertise in their field can teach without training to do so.** This is sometimes known as the content premise--if you have a Ph.D. in the field, you can teach.

The old paradigm is to transfer the teacher's knowledge to a passive student so that teachers can classify and sort students in a norm-referenced, competitive way. The assumption was that if you have content expertise, you can teach. Many teachers consider the old paradigm the only alternative. Lecturing while requiring students to be passive, silent, isolated, and in competition with each other seems the only way to teach. The tradition of the old paradigm is carried forward by sheer momentum, while almost everyone persists in the hollow pretense that all is well. All is not well. Teaching is changing. The old paradigm of teaching is being dropped for a new paradigm.

The new paradigm of teaching is based on the theory and research that have clear applications to instruction. Educators perhaps should think of teaching in terms of several principal activities.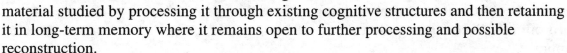

First, knowledge is constructed, discovered, transformed, and extended by students. Teachers create the conditions within which students can construct meaning from the material studied by processing it through existing cognitive structures and then retaining it in long-term memory where it remains open to further processing and possible reconstruction.

Second, students actively construct their own knowledge. Learning is conceived of as something a learner does, not something that is done to a learner. Students do not passively accept knowledge from the teacher or curriculum. Students activate their existing cognitive structures or construct new ones to subsume the new input.

Third, teacher effort is aimed at developing students' competencies and talents. Student effort should be inspired and secondary schools must "add value" by cultivating talent. A "cultivate and develop" philosophy must replace a "select and weed out" philosophy. Students' competencies and talents are developed under the assumption that with effort and education, any student can improve.

Fourth, education is a personal transaction among students and between the teachers and students as they work together. All education is a social process that cannot occur except through interpersonal interaction (real or implied). Learning is a personal but social process that results when individuals cooperate to construct shared understandings and knowledge. Teachers must be able to build positive relationships with students and to create the conditions within which students build caring and

Cooperation In The Classroom, Interaction Book Company, 7208 Cornelia Drive, Edina, MN 55435, (612) 831-9500, FAX (612) 831-9332

committed relationships with each other. The school then becomes a learning community of committed scholars in the truest sense. The more difficult and complex the learning, the harder students have to struggle to achieve, the more important the social support students need. There is a general rule of instruction: The more pressure placed on students to achieve and the more difficult the material to be learned, the more important it is to provide social support within the learning situation. Challenge and social support must be balanced if students are to cope successfully with the stress inherent in learning situations.

Fifth, all of the above can only take place within a cooperative context. When students interact within a competitive context, communication is minimized, misleading and false information often is communicated, helping is minimized and viewed as cheating, and classmates and faculty tend to be disliked and distrusted. Competitive and individualistic learning situations, therefore, discourage active construction of knowledge and the development of talent by isolating students and creating negative relationships among classmates and with teachers. Classmates and teachers need to be viewed as collaborators rather than as obstacles to students' own academic and personal success. Teachers, therefore, structure learning situations so that students work together cooperatively to maximize each other's achievement. Ideally, administrators would in turn create a cooperative, team-based organizational structure within which faculty work together to ensure each other's success (Johnson & Johnson, 1993).

Sixth, teaching is assumed to be a complex application of theory and research that requires considerable teacher training and continuous refinement of skills and procedures. Becoming a good teacher takes at least one lifetime of continuous effort to improve.

The primary means of achieving the new paradigm of teaching is to use cooperative learning. Cooperative learning provides the means of operationalizing the new paradigm of teaching and provides the context within which the development of student talent is encouraged. Carefully structured cooperative learning ensures that students are cognitively, physically, emotionally, and psychologically actively involved in constructing their own knowledge and is an important step in changing the passive and impersonal character of many classrooms.

1 Types Of Cooperative Learning

Now that you have mastered the use of formal cooperative learning groups, there are a number of steps you might consider. **The first step is to expand your use of cooperative learning to include three types of cooperative learning (Johnson, Johnson, & Holubec, 1988b): formal cooperative learning groups, informal cooperative learning groups, and cooperative base groups.**

Cooperation In The Classroom, Interaction Book Company, 7208 Cornelia Drive, Edina, MN 55435, (612) 831-9500, FAX (612) 831-9332

Formal Cooperative Learning Groups

Formal cooperative learning groups may last for several minutes to several class sessions to complete a specific task or assignment (such as solving a set of problems, completing a unit, writing a report or theme, conducting an experiment, and reading and comprehending a story, play, chapter, or book). This book has focused on formal cooperative learning groups. Any course requirement or assignment may be reformulated to be cooperative rather than competitive or individualistic through the use of formal cooperative learning groups. **Gaining expertise in using formal cooperative learning groups provides the foundation for gaining expertise in using informal and base groups.**

Informal Cooperative Learning Groups

Informal cooperative learning groups are temporary, ad hoc groups that last for only one discussion or one class period. Their **purposes** are to focus student attention on the material to be learned, create an expectation set and mood conducive to learning, help organize in advance the material to be covered in a class session, ensure that students cognitively process the material being taught, and provide closure to an instructional session. They may be used at any time, but are especially useful during a lecture or direct teaching. The length of time students can attend to a lecture before their minds drift away is estimated to be from 12 to 15 minutes.

During direct teaching the instructional challenge for the teacher is to ensure that students do the intellectual work of organizing material, explaining it, summarizing it, and integrating it into existing conceptual networks. This may be achieved by having students do the advance organizing, cognitive process what they are learning, and provide closure to the lesson. Breaking up lectures with short cooperative processing times will give you less lecture time, but will enhance what is learned and build relationships among the students in your class. It will help counter what is proclaimed as the main problem of lectures: "The information passes from the notes of the teacher to the notes of the student without passing through the mind of either one."

The following procedure may help to plan a lecture that keeps students actively engaged intellectually. It entails having **focused discussions** before and after a lecture (bookends) and interspersing **turn-to-your-partner** discussions throughout the lecture.

1. **Focused Discussion 1**: Plan your lecture around a series of questions that the lecture answers. Prepare the questions on an overhead transparency or write them on the board so that students can see them. Students will discuss the questions in pairs. The discussion task is aimed at promoting **advance organizing** of what the students know about the topic to be presented and creates an **expectation set** and a learning mood conductive to learning.

Cooperation In The Classroom, Interaction Book Company, 7208 Cornelia Drive, Edina, MN 55435, (612) 831-9500, FAX (612) 831-9332

2. **Turn-To-Your-Partner Discussions**: Divide the lecture into 10 to 15 minute segments. Plan a short discussion task to be given to pairs of students after each segment. The task needs to be short enough that students can complete it within three or four minutes. Its purpose is to ensure that students are actively thinking about the material being presented. **It is important that students are randomly called on to share their answers after each discussion task.** Such **individual accountability** ensures that the pairs take the tasks seriously and check each other to ensure that both are prepared to answer. Each discussion task should have four components: **formulate** an answer to the question being asked, **share** your answer with your partner, **listen** carefully to his or her answer, and to **create** a new answer that is superior to each member's initial formulation through the processes of association, building on each other's thoughts, and synthesizing. Students will need to gain some experience with this procedure to become skilled in doing it within a short period of time.

3. **Focused Discussion 2**: Give students an ending discussion task to provide closure to the lecture. Usually students are given five or six minutes to summarize and discuss the material covered in the lecture. The discussion should result in students integrating what they have just learned into existing conceptual frameworks. The task may also point students toward what the homework will cover or what will be presented in the next class session. Until students become familiar and experienced with the procedure, **process** it regularly to help them increase their skill and speed in completing short discussion tasks.

Informal cooperative learning gets students actively involved in processing what they are learning. It also provides time for you to gather your wits, reorganize your notes, take a deep breath, and move around the class listening to what students are saying. Listening to student discussions provides you with direction and insight into (a) students' levels of reasoning and (b) how the concepts you are teaching are being grasped by your students.

Base Groups

Base groups are long-term, heterogeneous cooperative learning groups with stable membership. **The primary responsibility of members is to provide each other with the support, encouragement, and assistance they need to make academic progress.** The base group verifies that each member is completing the assignments and progressing satisfactorily through the academic program. Base groups may be given the task of letting absent group members know what went on in the class when they miss a session and bring them up to date. The use of base groups tends to improve attendance, personalize the work required and the school experience, and improve the quality and quantity of learning. The base group provides permanent and caring peer relationships in which students are committed to and support each other's educational success.

Base groups last for at least a semester or year and preferably for several years. The larger the class and the more complex the subject matter, the more important it is to have

Cooperation In The Classroom, Interaction Book Company, 7208 Cornelia Drive, Edina, MN 55435, (612) 831-9500, FAX (612) 831-9332

base groups. Learning for your groupmates is a powerful motivator. Receiving social support and being held accountable for appropriate behavior by peers who care about you and have a long-term commitment to your success and well-being is an important aspect of growing up and progressing through school.

It is important that some of the relationships built within cooperative learning groups are permanent. School has to be more than a series of "ship-board romances" that last for only a semester or year. In elementary, junior-high, high-schools, and colleges students should be assigned to permanent base groups. The base groups should then be assigned to most classes so that members spend much of the day together and regularly complete cooperative learning tasks. Doing so can create permanent caring and committed relationships that will provide students with the support, help, encouragement, and assistance they need to make academic progress and develop cognitively and socially in healthy ways.

When used in combination, these formal, informal, and base cooperative learning groups provide an overall structure to classroom life. The use of informal and base groups are described in depth in:

2 Teaching Students' Social Skills

The second step in adding to your expertise in using cooperative learning is to teach students additional social skills. There are many sources of further social skills to be taught to students, including **Advanced Cooperative Learning** (Johnson, Johnson, & Holubec, 1992), **Reaching Out** (Johnson, 1997), and **Joining Together** (Johnson & F. Johnson, 1997).

3 Integrated Use Of All Three Goal Structures

The third step in increasing your expertise in using cooperative learning is to use all three goal structures within an integrated way. While the dominant goal structure within any classroom should be cooperation (which ideally would be used about 60 - 70 percent of the time), competitive and individualistic efforts are useful supplements. Competition may be used as a fun change-of-pace during an instructional unit that is predominantly structured cooperatively and individualistic learning is often productive when the information learned is subsequently used in a cooperative activity. The integrated use of cooperative, competitive, and individualistic learning is described in depth with in Johnson and Johnson (1994) and Johnson, Johnson, and Holubec (1992).

10 : 7

4 Utilizing Creative Conflict

The fourth step is to promote the creative use of conflict in the classroom and school. Cooperation and conflict go hand-in-hand. The more group members care about achieving the group's goals, and the more they care about each other, the more likely they are to have conflicts with each other. How conflict is managed largely determines how successful cooperative efforts tend to be. In order to ensure that conflicts are managed constructively, students must be taught two procedures and sets of skills:

1. **Use Academic Controversies To Facilitate Achievement And Cognitive and Social Development** (Johnson & Johnson, 1995b): In order to maximize academic learning and higher-level reasoning, engage students in intellectual conflicts. Organize students into cooperative learning groups of four. Divide them into two pairs. Give one pair the pro position and the other the con position on the issue being studied. Students research and prepare positions, make a persuasive presentation of their position, refute the opposing position while rebutting attacks on their own position, view the issue from both perspectives, and create a synthesis or integration of the best reasoning on both sides.

2. **Implement The Peacemaker Program** (Johnson & Johnson, 1995a): First, you teach students what is and is not a conflict. Second, you teach students how to engage in problem-solving negotiations. Students are taught to state what they want and how they feel, explain the reasons why they want and feel as they do, accurately understand the opposing perspective, create a number of optional agreements that maximize joint outcomes, and reach an agreement as to which option to adopt. Third, you teach students how to mediate. When students cannot successfully negotiate a constructive resolution to their conflicts, mediators are available to end hostilities, ensure commitment to the mediation process, facilitate negotiations, and formalize the agreement.

The combination of knowing how to manage intellectual disagreements and how to negotiate/mediate conflicts among students' wants, needs, and goals ensures that the power of cooperative efforts will be maximized. The productivity of learning groups increases dramatically when members are skilled in how to manage conflicts constructively.

5 Empowering Staff Through Cooperative Teams

The fifth step is to create a cooperative school. What is good for students is even better for staff. A cooperative school is one in which cooperative learning dominates the classroom and cooperative teams dominate staff efforts (Johnson & Johnson, 1993). It is social support from and accountability to valued peers that motivates committed efforts

Cooperation In The Classroom, Interaction Book Company, 7208 Cornelia Drive, Edina, MN 55435, (612) 831-9500, FAX (612) 831-9332

to succeed. Empowering individuals through cooperative teamwork is done in three ways: (1) **colleagial support groups** (to increase teachers' instructional expertise and success), (2) **task forces** (to plan and implement solutions to school-wide issues and problems such as curriculum adoptions and lunchroom behavior), and (3) **ad hoc decision-making groups** (to use during faculty meetings to involve all staff members in important school decisions). How to structure and use these three types of cooperative teams may be found in Johnson and Johnson (1994).

Creating A Learning Community

Frances Hodgson Burnett, in her book, The Secret Garden, stated, *Where you tend a rose, a thistle cannot grow.* Schools should tend roses. They do so by creating a learning community characterized by cooperative efforts to achieve meaningful goals. In a recent review of the research (**Within Our Reach: Breaking the Cycle of Disadvantage**) Lisbeth Schorr concludes that the most important attribute of effective schools is caring. Educational historians David Tyack and Elizabeth Hansot (1982) concluded that the theme that runs through all successful schools is that students, teachers, administrators, and parents share a sense of community and a "socially integrating sense of purpose."

A **community** is a limited number of people who share common goals and a common culture (Johnson, Johnson, Stevahn, & Hodne, 1997). The smaller the size of the community, the more personal the relationships, and the greater the personal accountability. Everyone knows everyone else. Relationships are long-term and have a future rather than being temporary brief encounters. Instruction becomes personalized. The students are thought of as citizens, and the teachers are thought of as the community leaders. A sense of belonging tends to boost the desire to learn. The learning community becomes an extended family where mutual achievement and caring for one another are important. With citizenship in the community comes an ethical code that includes such rules as (a) be prepared for classes each day, (b) pay attention in class, (c) be your personal best, and (d) respect other people and their property. In order to create a learning community, students (and teachers) need to be organized into cooperative teams.

Expertise is difficult to attain without the help of a colleagial teaching team. Long-term, persistent efforts to improve continuously come from the heart, not the head. A colleagial teaching team will provide you with the support and joint commitment essential to maintaining a love affair with teaching. Through implementing cooperative learning in your classes and being a contributing member of a teaching team, a true learning community of scholars may be created for both your students and yourself.

Cooperation In The Classroom, Interaction Book Company, 7208 Cornelia Drive, Edina, MN 55435, (612) 831-9500, FAX (612) 831-9332

Classroom / School Management: The Three Cs

It is time for classroom management systems to move beyond behaviorism (with its emphasis on self-interest and behaving in order to achieve extrinsic rewards and avoid punishments) to positive learning environment (with its emphasis on intrinsic motivation to contribute to own and other's well being and success and to the overall common good) (Johnson & Johnson, 1998; Johnson, Johnson, Stevahn, & Hodne, 1997). The latter is built on three interrelated programs: **cooperative community, constructive conflict resolution, and civic values**. To establish a learning community, cooperation must be carefully structured at all levels in the school. To maintain the learning community, constructive conflict resolution procedures must be taught to all members of the school. To guide and direct the cooperation and constructive conflict resolution, civic values must be inculcated in all school members. While each of the Cs may be discussed and implemented separately, together they represent a gestalt in which each enhances and promotes the others.

Cooperation creates a structure within which faculty, students, and parents work together to educate the students. The more cooperative the structure, the more committed and dedicated faculty, students, and parents are to providing quality education. The greater the commitment to the school's goals, the more frequent and intense the **conflicts** around how best to achieve the goals and coordinate behavior. When the controversy and problem-solving negotiation procedures are used skillfully, the conflicts lead to higher-level reasoning, the utilization of diverse perspectives, creative insights, synthesis of different positions, high quality and novel solutions, and trusting, supportive, and caring relationships. **Civic values**, that highlight the need to work together toward the common good and maximize joint (not individual) benefits, are the glue that holds the school together and defines how members should act towards each other.

The Three Cs result in students being more autonomous individuals who can regulate and control their own actions by monitoring, modifying, refining, and changing how they behave in order to act appropriately and competently. Students who work effectively with others and resolve conflicts with skill and grace and who have internalized civic values have a developmental advantage that increases their future academic and career success, improves the quality of their relationships with friends, colleagues, and family, and generally enhances their life-long happiness.

Together the three Cs are a complete management program for creating effective and nurturing schools where few management problems occur and the well-being of students and other members of the learning community is promoted.

10 : 10

Cooperation In The Classroom, Interaction Book Company, 7208 Cornelia Drive, Edina, MN 55435, (612) 831-9500, FAX (612) 831-9332

Looking Forward

At the end of this book you are at a new beginning. Years of experience in using cooperative learning in your classroom are needed to gain expertise in its use. While you are using cooperative learning there is much more to learn about its use. The addition of informal cooperative learning activities and long-term permanent base groups will increase the power and effectiveness of cooperation in your classroom. Teaching students more and more sophisticated social skills will improve how well they work together to maximize their learning. Supplementing the use of cooperative learning with appropriate competitions and individualistic assignments will further enrich the quality of learning within your classroom. Structuring academic controversies within your cooperative learning groups will move students to higher levels of reasoning and thinking while providing a considerable increase in energy and fun. Teaching students how to negotiate their differences and mediate each other's conflicts will accelerate their skills in managing conflicts within cooperative learning groups. Finally, moving cooperation up to the school and district levels by structuring staff into cooperative teams will create a congruent organizational structure within which both faculty and students will thrive.

In Retrospect

There is an old story about 12 men in a lifeboat. One of the men announced that he had decided to bore a series of holes in the bottom of the boat. "*You can't do that*," the other eleven men cried. "*Why not?*" the man answered. "*I've divided the boat into twelve equal parts. Each of us has part of the boat. We can do anything to our part of the boat we want to. I've decided to drill holes in the bottom of my part. You do anything you want with your part. It's your right!*" Many people see the world in these terms. They are unaware of their interdependence with others and the ways that their actions spread out like ripples in a pond to touch others.

Cooperation is the "*air*" of society that we constantly breathe--it is completely necessary but relatively unnoticed. We notice changes in the air, a whiff of perfume or a blanket of smog, but these are the rare instances. Like the perfume, the time we are locked (or licked) in competition and the things we achieve "on our own" stand out and are remembered because they are different from the majority of our efforts, which are cooperative. Just as the parochial myth that "smog is what most air is like, and we need to learn to live with it" can grow in the minds of those who live in a large city, so egocentric myths like "*it's a survival-of-the-fittest society*" have grown and have nourished by those who ignore the many cooperative aspects of their lives, while concentrating on those aspects that are competitive. In American society (and schools) we share a common language, we drive on the appropriate side of the street, we take turns going through doors, we raise families, we seek friendship, we share the maintenance of life through an intricate division of labor. This is not to say that the skills

10 : 11

Cooperation In The Classroom, Interaction Book Company, 7208 Cornelia Drive, Edina, MN 55435, (612) 831-9500, FAX (612) 831-9332

of competitive and individualistic efforts are unimportant. They are important, but only within the larger context of cooperation with others. A person needs to know when it is appropriate to compete or work individualistically and when to cooperate. Unfortunately, instruction in schools at present stresses competitive and individualistic efforts without much attention to the skills needed to facilitate effective cooperation. To encourage a positive learning environment and to promote the outcomes of schools, we must realize that cooperation is the forest--competitive and individualistic efforts are but trees.

As the authors look back on the aspects of our growing up together, we realize that we may have misled you. The competition between us was a rather small part of the time we spent together. What made the instances of competition bearable was our partnership and the constant supportive cooperation within our family, and later with our friends and our families. Without cooperation and the skills that it requires, life in a society or a school would not be possible.

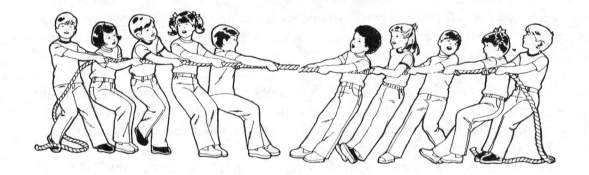

Cooperation In The Classroom, Interaction Book Company, 7208 Cornelia Drive, Edina, MN 55435, (612) 831-9500, FAX (612) 831-9332

Review and Celebration

The greatest rewards come only from the greatest commitment.

Arlene Blum, Mountain Climber and Leader, American Women's Himalayan Expedition

Task 1: Review of Progress

Meet in your base groups. Every member should have his or her:

1. Journal.
2. Case studies.
3. Log sheet.
4. Lesson plans of lessons and units taught.
5. Completed implementation assignments.

Task: Group members have ten minutes to summarize their implementation of cooperative learning. The summary should include personal learnings as recorded in their journals, the impact of the cooperative lessons on the students being followed for case studies, the number and type of lessons they have conducted, and their overall experiences in teaching cooperative skills to students. Once all members have summarized their implementation of cooperative learning, the group makes at least three conclusions about their experiences to share with the entire class. This is a **cooperative** activity, everyone should participate, listen carefully to groupmates, provide support and encouragement, and celebrate the group's effort in implementing cooperative learning into their classrooms and schools.

Task 2: Sharing Successes

Stay in your base groups. Your **task** is to share your successes in implementing cooperative learning and help each groupmates do the same. Work **cooperatively** in answering the following questions:

1. How have your students benefited from cooperative learning?

2. What cooperative lesson was most successful?

3. Which student benefited most from working cooperatively?

4. What cooperative lesson was most important to you personally?

Cooperation In The Classroom, Interaction Book Company, 7208 Cornelia Drive, Edina, MN 55435, (612) 831-9500, FAX (612) 831-9332

Task 3: Cooperative Learning Review Quiz

Divide your base group into pairs. Your **task** is to answer each question in the Review Quiz correctly. Work **cooperatively**. Each pair takes the quiz together, one answer for the pair, with both members in agreement and able to explain each answer. When finished, reform as a base group and take the Review Quiz again. If there is any disagreement as to the answer to a question, find the page number in the book the answer appears on and clarify until all members are in agreement and can explain the answer.

Task 4: Basic Concepts Review

Divide your base group into pairs. Starting with Chapter One, identify the basic concepts in each chapter and ensure both pair members can correctly define each one. When finished, reform as a base group and compare the concepts identified for each chapter and their definitions. If there is disagreement as to the definitions, identify what page the definition is on and clarify the definition until all members of the group agree and are able to explain it. Make sure all base group members can define each concept.

Task 5: Planning Your Cooperative Learning Future

Your **tasks** are to (1) diagnose your current level of expertise in using cooperative learning and (2) make a plan for increasing your expertise. The diagnosis and plan must be in writing and signed by all base group members.

Work **cooperatively** Meet in your base group and ensure all members (a) have completed the above two tasks and (b) agree with each member's diagnosis and plan (noted by the signatures on each member's plan).

In diagnosing where you stand in gaining expertise in cooperative learning consider:

1. The long-term goals of being able to:

    a. Take any lesson in any subject area and teach it cooperatively.

    b. Use cooperative learning at the routine-use level.

    c. Use cooperative learning at least 60 percent of the time.

Cooperation In The Classroom, Interaction Book Company, 7208 Cornelia Drive, Edina, MN 55435, (612) 831-9500, FAX (612) 831-9332

d. Be a member of an ongoing colleagial support groups.

2. The amount of training you have received.

3. The amount of experience you have in using cooperative learning.

4. The effectiveness of your colleagial support group in encouraging and assisting members' implementation efforts.

5. Your ability to experiment, take risks, and generally stay on the edge of your comfort zone in order to increase your expertise.

6. The quality and quantity of the feedback you are receiving on your implementation efforts.

7. The quality and quantity of your reflections and problem solving on the feedback received.

8. Your persistence in using cooperative learning again and again.

9. Your experience in encouraging and assisting your colleagues' efforts to implement cooperative learning.

What are your next steps in increasing your expertise in cooperative learning? Your plan should include a:

1. List of units coming up in which cooperative learning should be used.

2. List of cooperative skills you plan to teach to your students.

3. Plan for:

a. Forming and maintaining a colleagial support group in your school to focus on cooperative learning.

b. Your own skill development in working cooperatively with colleagues.

c. A **time schedule** as to when cooperative skills will be taught and perfected by your students while you provide opportunities for the use of the skills, feedback on how well each student is performing the skill, and encouragement for each student to continue practicing the skill.

Cooperation In The Classroom, Interaction Book Company, 7208 Cornelia Drive, Edina, MN 55435, (612) 831-9500, FAX (612) 831-9332

    d. The phone numbers of your base group members and the time you will call each one and give him or her a report on your progress.

Task 6: Whole Class Review By Drawing Names

The purpose of this activity is to provide a fun review of the course. The instructor will ask a question and then draw a participant's name from a hat. The participant named must give an interesting and truthful answer.

Task 7: Thanking Your Learning Partners

Seek out the people who have helped you learn how to implement cooperative learning. **Thank them.**

ACTION PLAN	
1. Your Next Steps:	
a.	c.
b.	d.
2. Support From Whom	**In What Ways**
a.	
b.	
c.	
d.	
3. Realities To Be Faced:	
a.	c.
b.	d.

4. Your Vision Of The Cooperative Classroom And School:

Cooperation In The Classroom, Interaction Book Company, 7208 Cornelia Drive, Edina, MN 55435, (612) 831-9500, FAX (612) 831-9332

GLOSSARY

Ad hoc decision-making groups: Faculty members listen to a recommendation, are assigned to small groups, meet to consider the recommendation, report to the entire faculty their decision, and then participate in a whole-faculty decision as to what the course of action should be.

Arbitration: The submission of a dispute to a disinterested third person who makes a final judgment as to how the conflict will be resolved. A form of third-party intervention in negotiations in which recommendations of the person intervening are binding on the parties involved.

Base group: A long-term, heterogeneous cooperative learning group with stable membership.

Benchmarking: Establishing operating targets based on best known practices.

Bumping: A procedure used to ensure that competitors are evenly matched. It involves (a) ranking the competitive triads from the highest (the three highest achievers are members) to the lowest (the three lowest achievers are members), (b) moving the winner in each triad up to the next highest triad, and (c) moving the loser down to the next lowest triad.

Cohesiveness: All the forces (both positive and negative) that cause individuals to maintain their membership in specific groups. These include attraction to other group members and a close match between individuals' needs and the goals and activities of the group. The attractiveness that a group has for its members and that the members have for one another.

Colleagial teaching teams: Small cooperative groups (from two to five faculty members) whose purpose is to increase teachers' instructional expertise and success.

Competition: A social situation in which the goals of the separate participants are so linked that there is a negative correlation among their goal attainments; when one student achieves his or her goal, all others with whom he or she is competitively linked fail to achieve their goals.

Conceptual/adaptive approaches to cooperative learning: Teachers are trained in how to use a general conceptual framework to plan and tailor cooperative learning lessons specifically for their students, circumstances, curricula, and needs.

Conflict-of-interests: When the actions of one person attempting to maximize his or her needs and benefits prevent, block, interfere with, injure, or in some way make less effective the actions of another person attempting to maximize his or her needs and benefits.

Controversy: When one person's ideas, information, conclusions, theories, and opinions are incompatible with those of another, and the two seek to reach an agreement.

Co-op Co-op: A complex cooperative learning script in which each group is assigned one part of a class learning unit, each group member is assigned part of the work and then presents it to the group, the group synthesizes the work of its members, and the group presents the completed project to the class.

Cooperation: Working together to accomplish shared goals and maximize own and other's success. Individuals perceiving that they can reach their goals if and only if the other group members also do so.

G : 1

Cooperation In The Classroom, Interaction Book Company, 7208 Cornelia Drive, Edina, MN 55435, (612) 831-9500, FAX (612) 831-9332

Cooperation imperative: We desire and seek out opportunities to operate jointly with others to achieve mutual goals.

Cooperative curriculum package: Set of curriculum materials specifically designed to contain cooperative learning as well as academic content.

Cooperative Integrated Reading And Composition (CIRC): A set of curriculum materials to supplement basal readers and students read, write, spell, and learn language mechanics in pairs and fours but are evaluated individualistically.

Cooperative learning: Students working together to accomplish shared learning goals and maximize their own and their groupmates' achievement.

Cooperative learning scripts: Standard content-free cooperative procedures for either conducting generic, repetitive lessons or managing classroom routines that proscribe students actions step-by-step.

Cooperative learning structures: See cooperative learning scripts.

Cooperative school: Team-based, high-performance organizational structure specifically applied to schools, characterized by cooperative learning in the classroom, colleagial teaching teams and school-based decision making in the building, and colleagial administrating teams and shared decision-making at the district level.

Delusion of individualism: Believing that (1) they are separate and apart from all other individuals and, therefore, (2) others' frustration, unhappiness, hunger, despair, and misery have no significant bearing on their own well-being.

Deutsch, Morton: Social psychologist who theorized about cooperative, competitive, and individualistic goal structures.

Direct/prescriptive approach to cooperative learning: Teachers are trained to use prepackaged lessons, curricula, strategies, and activities in a lock-step prescribed manner (step 1, step 2, step 3).

Egocentrism: Embeddedness in one's own viewpoint to the extent that one is unaware of other points of view and of the limitations of one's perspectives.

Expert system: An understanding of a conceptual system that is used to engineer effective applications in the real world.

Expertise: A person's proficiency, adroitness, competence, and skill.

Feedback: Information that allows individuals to compare their actual performance with standards of performance.

Fermenting skills: Skills needed to engage in **academic controversies** to stimulate reconceptualization of the material being studied, cognitive conflict, the search for more information, and the communication of the rationale behind one's conclusions.

Forming skills: Management skills directed toward organizing the group and establishing minimum norms for appropriate behavior.

Cooperation In The Classroom, Interaction Book Company, 7208 Cornelia Drive, Edina, MN 55435, (612) 831-9500, FAX (612) 831-9332

Formulating skills: Skills directed toward providing the mental processes needed to build deeper level understanding of the material being studied, to stimulate the use of higher quality reasoning strategies, and to maximize mastery and retention of the assigned material.

Functioning skills: Skills directed toward managing the group's efforts to complete their tasks and maintain effective working relationships among members.

Formal cooperative group: A learning group that may last for several minutes to several class sessions to complete a specific task or assignment (such as solving a set of problems, completing a unit, writing a theme or report, conducting an experiment, or reading and comprehending a story, play, chapter or book.

Genba: Where the action is.

Goal: A desired place toward which people are working, a state of affairs that people value.

Goal structure: The type of social interdependence structured among students as they strive to accomplish their learning goals.

Group: Two or more individuals in face-to-face interaction, each aware of his or her membership in the group, each aware of the others who belong to the group, and each aware of their positive interdependence as they strive to achieve mutual goals.

Group investigation: A complex cooperative learning script in which students form cooperative learning groups according to common interests in a topic, develop a division of labor in researching the topic, synthesizing the work of group members, and presenting the finished product to the class.

Group processing: Reflecting on a group session to (a) describe what member actions were helpful and unhelpful and (b) make decisions about what actions to continue or change.

Horizontal teams: A number of teachers from the same grade level or subject area are given responsibility for a number of students for one year or one semester.

Individual accountability: The measurement of whether or not each group member has achieved the group's goal. Assessing the quality and quantity of each member's contributions and giving the results to all group members.

Individualistic goal structure: No correlation among group members' goal attainments; when group members perceive that obtaining their goal is unrelated to the goal achievement of other members. Individuals working by themselves to accomplish goals unrelated to and independent from the goals of others.

Informal cooperation group: A temporary, ad hoc group that lasts for only one discussion or one class period. Its purposes are to focus student attention on the material to be learned, create an expectation set and mood conductive to learning, help organize in advance the material to be covered n a class session, ensure that students cognitively process the material being taught, and provide closure to an instructional session.

Jigsaw: The work of a group is divided into separate parts that are completed by different members and taught to their groupmates.

G : 3

Cooperation In The Classroom, Interaction Book Company, 7208 Cornelia Drive, Edina, MN 55435, (612) 831-9500, FAX (612) 831-9332

Learning goal: A desired future state of demonstrating competence or mastery in the subject area being studied, such as conceptual understanding of math processes, facility in the proper use of a language, or mastering the procedures of inquiry.

Lewin, Kurt: Father of group dynamics; social psychologist who originated field theory, experimental group dynamics, and applied group dynamics.

Maintenance of use: Continual, long-term use of cooperative learning over a period of years.

Means interdependence specifies the actions required on the part of group members to achieve their mutual goals and rewards. There are three types of means interdependence: resource, task, and role.

Mediation: When a third person intervenes to help resolve a conflict between two or more people. A form of third-party intervention in negotiations in which a neutral person recommends a nonbinding agreement.

Motivation: A combination of the perceived likelihood of success and the perceived incentive for success. The greater the likelihood of success and the more important it is to succeed, the higher the motivation.

Negotiation: A process by which persons with shared and opposing interests who want to come to an agreement try to work out a settlement by exchanging proposals and counterproposals.

Norms: The rules or expectations that specify appropriate behavior in the group; the standards by which group members regulate their actions.

Outcome interdependence: When the goals and rewards directing individuals' actions are positively correlated, that is, if one person accomplishes his or her goal or receives a reward, all others with whom the person is cooperatively linked also achieve their goals or receive a reward. Learning goals may be actual, based on involvement in a fantasy situation, or based on overcoming an outside threat.

Perspective taking: Ability to understand how a situation appears to another person and how that person is reacting cognitively and emotionally to the situation.

Positive environmental interdependence: When group members are bound together by the physical environment in some way.

Positive fantasy interdependence: When students imagine that they are in an emergency situation (such as surviving a ship wreak) or must deal with problems (such as ending air pollution in the world) that are compelling but unreal.

Positive goal interdependence: When students perceive that they can achieve their learning goals if, and only if, all other members of their group also attain their goals.

Positive identity interdependence: When the group establishes a mutual identity through a name, flag, motto, or song.

Positive interdependence is the perception that you are linked with others in a way so that you cannot succeed unless they do (and vice versa), that is, their work benefits you and your work benefits them.

Positive outside enemy interdependence: When groups are placed in competition with each other; group members then feel interdependent as they strive to beat the other groups.

G : 4

Cooperation In The Classroom, Interaction Book Company, 7208 Cornelia Drive, Edina, MN 55435, (612) 831-9500, FAX (612) 831-9332

Positive resource interdependence: When each member has only a portion of the information, resources, or materials necessary for the task to be completed, and members' resources have to be combined in order for the group to achieve its goal. Thus, the resources of each group member are needed if the task is to be completed.

Positive reward interdependence: When each group member receives the same reward for achieving the goal.

Positive role interdependence: When each member is assigned complementary and interconnected roles that specify responsibilities that the group needs in order to complete a joint task.

Positive task interdependence: When a division of labor is created so that the actions of one group member have to be completed if the next team member is to complete his or her responsibilities. Dividing an overall task into subunits that must be performed **in a set order** is an example of task interdependence.

Procedural learning: Learning conceptually what the skill is, when it should be used, how to engage in the skill, practicing the skill while eliminating errors, until an automated level of mastery is attained.

Promotive interaction: Actions that assist, help, encourage, and support the achievement of each other's goals.

Routine-use level: Automatic use of a skill as a natural part of one's behavioral repertoire.

School-based decision-making: Task force considers a school problem and proposes a solution to the faculty as a whole, small ad-hoc decision making groups consider the proposal, the entire faculty decides what to do, the decision is implemented by the faculty, and the task force assesses whether or not the problem is solved.

Self-efficacy: The expectation of successfully obtaining valued outcomes through personal effort; expectation that if one exerts sufficient effort, one will be successful.

Self-regulation: Ability to act in socially approved ways in the absence of external monitors.

Social dependence: When Person A's outcomes are affected by Person B's actions, but the reverse is not true.

Social facilitation: The enhancement of well-learned responses in the presence of others. Effects on performance resulting from the presence of others.

Social independence: When individuals' outcomes are unaffected by each other's actions.

Social interaction: Patterns of mutual influence linking two or more persons.

Social interdependence: When each individuals' outcomes are affected by the actions of others.

Social loafing: A reduction of individual effort when working with others on an additive group task.

Social skills: The interpersonal and small group skills needed to interact effectively with other people.

Cooperation In The Classroom, Interaction Book Company, 7208 Cornelia Drive, Edina, MN 55435, (612) 831-9500, FAX (612) 831-9332

Social skills training: A structured intervention designed to help individuals improve their interpersonal skills.

Student Team Learning (STAD): A modification of TGT that is basically identical except that instead of playing an academic game, students take a weekly quiz. Teams receive recognition for the sum of the improvement scores of team members.

Sunburst Integrated Co-Op Learning Geometry Course: A combination of a geometry curriculum, an interactive computer program, discovery learning, and cooperative learning.

Support: Communicating to another person that you recognize his or her strengths and believe he or she has the capabilities needed to productively manage the situation.

Synthesizing: Integrating a number of different positions containing diverse information and conclusions into a new, single, inclusive position that all group members can agree on and commit themselves to.

Team: A set of interpersonal relationships structured to achieve established goals.

Team-Assisted-Individualization (TAI): A highly individualized math curriculum for grades 3 to 6 in which students work individualistically to complete math assignments using self-instructional (programmed learning) curriculum materials and have their answers checked, and help given, by groupmates.

Teams-Games-Tournaments (TGT): An instructional procedure in which cooperative groups learn specified content and then compete with each other in a tournament/game format to see which group learned the most.

T-chart: Procedure to teach social skills by specifying the nonverbal actions and verbal phrases that operationalize the skill.

Transfer: Teachers using in their classes what they learned about cooperative learning in training sessions.

Vertical teams: A team of teachers representing several different subject areas are given responsibility for the same students for a number of years.

Cooperation In The Classroom, Interaction Book Company, 7208 Cornelia Drive, Edina, MN 55435, (612) 831-9500, FAX (612) 831-9332

REFERENCES

Aronson, E. (1978). **The jigsaw classroom.** Beverly Hills, CA: Sage Publications.

Astin, A., Green, K., & Korn, W. (1987). **The American freshman: Twenty year trends.** Los Angeles: University of California at Los Angeles, Higher Education Research Institute.

Astin, A., Green, K., Korn, W., & Shalit, M. (1986). **The American freshman: National norms for fall 1986.** Los Angeles: University of California at Los Angeles, Higher Education Research Institute.

Berman, P., & McLaughlin, M. (1978). **Federal programs supporting educational change, Vol. VIII: Implementing and sustaining innovations.** Santa Monica, CA: Rand Corporation.

Blake, R., & Moulton, J. (1961). Comprehension of own and outgroup positions under intergroup competition. **Journal of Conflict Resolution, 5,** 304-310.

Blake, R., & Mouton, J. (1974). Designing change for educational institutions through the D/D Matrix. **Educational and Urban Society, 6,** 179-204.

Blumberg, A., May, J., & Perry, R. (1974). An inner-city school that changed--and continued to change. **Education and Urban Society, 6,** 222-238.

Bower, S. (1960). **Early identification of emotionally handicapped children in school.** Springfield, IL: Thomas.

Campbell, J. (1965). **The children's crusader: Colonel Francis W. Parker.** PhD dissertation, Teachers College, Columbia University.

Cartwright, D., & Zander, A. (Eds.). (1968). **Group dynamics.** New York: Harper & Row.

Cohen, E. (1986). **Designing groupwork.** New York: Teachers College Press.

Conger, J. (1988). Hostages to fortune: Youth, values, and the public interest. **American Psychologist, 43,** 291-300.

Crawford, J., & Haaland, G. (1972). Predecisional information seeking and subsequent conformity in the social influence process. **Journal of Personality and Social Psychology, 23,** 112-119.

Dansereau, D. (1985). Learning strategy research. In J. Segal, S. Chipman, and R. Glaser (Eds.). **Thinking and learning skills, Vol. 1: Relating instruction to research.** Hillsdale, NJ: Lawrence Erlbaum Associates, Inc.

Deutsch, M. (1949a). An experimental study of the effects of cooperation and competition upon group processes. **Human Relations, 2,** 199-232.

Deutsch, M. (1949b). A theory of cooperation and competition. **Human Relations, 2,** 129- 152.

Deutsch, M. (1962). Cooperation and trust: Some theoretical notes. In M. R. Jones (Ed.), **Nebraska symposium on motivation,** 275-319. Lincoln, NE: University of Nebraska Press.

Cooperation In The Classroom, Interaction Book Company, 7208 Cornelia Drive, Edina, MN 55435, (612) 831-9500, FAX (612) 831-9332

Deutsch, M. (1973). **The resolution of conflict**. New Haven, Conn.: Yale University Press.

Deutsch, M. (1975). Equity, equality, and need: What determines which values will be used as the basis for distributive justice. **Journal of Social Issues, 31**, 137-149.

Deutsch, M. (1979). A critical review of equity theory: An alternative perspective on the social psychology of justice. **International Journal of Group Tensions, 9**, 20-49.

DeVries, D., & Edwards, K. (1973). Learning games and student teams: Their effects on classroom process. **American Educational Research Journal, 10**, 307-318.

DeVries, D., & Edwards, K. (1974). Student teams and learning games: Their effects on cross-race and cross-sex interaction. **Journal of Educational Psychology, 66**, 741-749.

DeVries, D., Slavin, R., Fennessey, G., Edwards, K., & Lombardo, M. (1980). **Teams-games-tournament**. Englewood Cliffs, NJ: Educational Technology.

Dewey, J. (1924). **The school and society.** Chicago: University of Chicago Press.

Dishon, D., & O'Leary, P. (1981). Teaching students to work in groups: Cooperative learning in the classroom. In P. Roy (Ed.), **Structuring cooperative learning experiences in the classroom: The 1982 handbook**. Edina, MN: Interaction Book Company.

Dishon, D., & O'Leary, P. (1984). **A guidebook for cooperative learning**. Holmes Beach, FL: Learning Publications.

Gibbs, J. (1987). **Tribes**. Santa Rosa, CA: Center Source Publications.

Glasser, W. (1986). **Control theory in the classroom**. New York: Harper & Row.

Gronlund, N. (1959). **Sociometry in the classroom**. New York: Harper.

Harkins, S., & Petty, R. (1982). The effects of task difficulty and task uniqueness on social loafing. **Journal of Personality and Social Psychology, 43**, 1214-1229.

Hartup, W. (1976). Peer interaction and the behavioral development of the individual child. In E. Schloper and R. Reicher (Eds.), **Psychopathology and child development**. New York: Plenum.

Hartup, W., Glazer, J., & Charlesworth, R. (1967). Peer reinforcement and sociometric status. **Child Development, 38**, 1017-1024.

Hill, G. (1982). Group versus individual performance: Are N + 1 heads better than one? **Psychology Bulletin, 91**, 517-539.

Horowitz, F. (1962). The relationship of anxiety, self-concept, and sociometric status among 4th, 5th, and 6th grade children. **Journal of Abnormal and Social Psychology, 65**, 212-214.

Hwong, N., Caswell, A., Johnson, D. W., & Johnson, R. (1993). Effects of cooperative and individualistic learning on prospective elementary teachers' music achievement and attitudes. **Journal of Social Psychology, 133**, 53-64.

Cooperation In The Classroom, Interaction Book Company, 7208 Cornelia Drive, Edina, MN 55435, (612) 831-9500, FAX (612) 831-9332

Ingham, A., Levinger, G., Graves, J., & Peckham, V. (1974). The Ringelmann effect: Studies of group size and group performance. **Journal of Personality and Social Psychology, 10**, 371-384.

Johnson, D. W. (1970). **The social psychology of education.** New York: Holt, Rinehart & Wilson.

Johnson, D. W. (1971). Role reversal: A summary and review of the research, **International Journal of Group Tensions, 1**, 318-334.

Johnson, D. W. (1974). Communication and the inducement of cooperative behavior in conflicts. **Speech Monographs, 41**, 64-78.

Johnson, D. W. (1975a). Affective perspective-taking and cooperative predisposition. **Develpmental Psychology, 11**, 869-870.

Johnson, D. W. (1975b). Cooperativeness and social perspective taking. **Journal of Personality and Social Psychology, 31**, 241-244.

Johnson, D. W. (1979). **Educational psychology.** Englewood Cliffs, NJ: Prentice-Hall.

Johnson, D. W. (1980a). Constructive peer relationships, social development, and cooperative learning experiences: Implications for the prevention of drug abuse. **Journal of Drug Education, 10**, 7-24.

Johnson, D. W. (1980b). Group processes: Influences of student-student interactions on school outcomes. In J. McMillan (Ed.), **Social psychology of school learning**. New York: Academic Press.

Johnson, D. W. (1981). Student-student interaction: The neglected variable in education. **Educational Researcher, 10**, 5-10.

Johnson, D. W. (1991). **Human relations and your career** (3rd ed.). Englewood Cliffs, NJ: Prentice-Hall.

Johnson, D. W. (1997). **Reaching out: Interpersonal effectiveness and self-actualization** (6th ed.). Needham Heights, MA: Allyn & Bacon.

Johnson, D. W., & Ahlgren, A. (1976). Relationship between students' attitudes about cooperative learning and competition and attitudes toward schooling. **Journal of Educational Psychology, 68**, 29-102.

Johnson, D. W., & Johnson, F. (1997). **Joining together: Group theory and group skills** (6th ed.). Englewood Cliffs, NJ: Prentice-Hall.

Johnson, D. W., & Johnson, R. (1974). Instructional goal structure: Cooperative, competitive, or individualistic. **Review of Educational Research**, **44**, 213-240.

Johnson, D. W., & Johnson, R. (1977). **Controversy in the classroom** (Video). Edina, MN: Interaction Book Company.

Johnson, D. W., & Johnson, R. (Eds.) (1978). Social interdependence within instruction. **Journal of Research and Development in Education, 12**(1).

R : 3

Cooperation In The Classroom, Interaction Book Company, 7208 Cornelia Drive, Edina, MN 55435, (612) 831-9500, FAX (612) 831-9332

Johnson, D. W., & Johnson, R. (1978). Cooperative, competitive, and individualistic learning. **Journal of Research and Development in Education, 12**, 3-15.

Johnson, D. W., & Johnson, R. (1979). **Conflict in the classroom: Controversy and learning.** Review of Educational Research, 49, 51-70.

Johnson, D. W., & Johnson, R. (1980). **Belonging** (Video). Edina, MN: Interaction Book Company.

Johnson, D. W., & Johnson, R. (1980). Integrating handicapped students into the mainstream. **Exceptional Children, 46**, 89- 98.

Johnson, D. W., & Johnson, R. (1982). Healthy peer relationships: A necessity not a luxury. In P. Roy (Ed.), **Structuring cooperative learning: The 1982 handbook**. Edina, MN: Interaction Book Company.

Johnson, D. W., Johnson, R. (1983). **Circles of learning** (Video). Edina, MN: Interaction Book Company.

Johnson, D. W., & Johnson, R. (1983). The socialization and achievement crisis: Are cooperative learning experiences the solution? In L. Bickman (Ed.), **Applied Social Psychology Annual 4**, 119-164, Beverly Hills, CA: Sage.

Johnson, D. W., & Johnson, R. (Eds.) (1984). **Structuring cooperative learning: The 1984 handbook of lesson plans for teachers**. Edina, MN: Interaction Book Company.

Johnson, D. W., & Johnson, R. (1985a). Mainstreaming hearing-impaired students: The effect of effort and interpersonal attraction. **Journal of Psychology, 119**, 31-44.

Johnson, D. W., & Johnson, R. (1985b). The internal dynamics of cooperative learning groups. In R. Slavin, S. Sharan, S. Kagan, R. Hertz-Lazarowitz, C. Webb, & R. Schmuck (Eds.). **Learning to cooperate, cooperating to learn.** New York: Plenum Press.

Johnson, D. W., & Johnson, R. (1986). Impact of classroom organization and instructional methods on the effectiveness of mainstreaming. In C. Meisel (Ed.), **Mainstreaming handicapped children.** Hillsdale, NJ: Lawrence Erlbaum.

Johnson, D. W., & Johnson, R. (1987a). **Creative conflict.** Edina, MN: Interaction Book Company.

Johnson, D. W., & Johnson, R. (1987b). Research shows the benefits of adult cooperation. **Educational Leadership, 45**(3), 27-30.

Johnson, D. W., & Johnson, R. (1988). Critical thinking through structured controversy. **Educational Leadership**, May, 58-64.

Johnson, D. W., & Johnson, R. (1989). **Cooperation and competition: Theory and research.** Edina, MN: Interaction Book Company.

Johnson, D. W., & Johnson, R. (1991). **Teaching students to be peacemakers** (Video). Edina, MN: Interaction Book Company.

Cooperation In The Classroom, Interaction Book Company, 7208 Cornelia Drive, Edina, MN 55435, (612) 831-9500, FAX (612) 831-9332

Johnson, D. W., & Johnson, R. (1992b). **Positive interdependence: The heart of cooperative learning.** Edina, MN: Interaction Book Company.

Johnson, D. W., & Johnson, R. (1992c). **Positive interdependence: The heart of cooperative learning** (Video). Edina, MN: Interaction Book Company.

Johnson, D. W., & Johnson, R. (1993). **Leading the cooperative school** (2nd Edition). Edina, MN: Interaction Book Company.

Johnson, D. W., & Johnson, R. (1975/1994). **Learning together and alone: Cooperative, competitive, and individualistic learning** (4th ed.). Englewood Cliffs, NJ: Prentice-Hall.

Johnson, D. W., & Johnson, R. (1995a). **Teaching students to be peacemakers** (3rd ed.). Edina, MN: Interaction Book Company.

Johnson, D. W., & Johnson, R. (1995b). **My mediation notebook** (3rd ed.). Edina, MN: Interaction Book Company.

Johnson, D. W., & Johnson, R. (1995c). **Creative controversy: Intellectual challenge in the classroom** (3rd Ed.). Edina, MN: Interaction Book Company.

Johnson, D. W., & Johnson, R. (in press). Cooperative learning, values, and culturally plural classrooms. In M. Leicester, C. Modgill, & S. Modgil (Eds.). **Values, the classroom, and cultural diversity**. London: Cassell PLC.

Johnson, D. W., & Johnson, R. (in press). The three Cs of school and classroom management. In H. Freiberg (Ed.), **Beyond behaviorism: Changing the classroom management paradigm**. Boston: Allyn & Bacon.

Johnson, D. W., & Johnson, R., & Anderson, D. (1978). Relationship between student cooperative, competitive, and individualistic attitudes toward schooling. **Journal of Psychology, 100**, 183-199.

Johnson, D. W., Johnson, R., & Holubec, E. (1987). **Structuring cooperative learning: The handbook of lessons plans for teachers**. Edina, MN: Interaction Book Company.

Johnson, D. W., Johnson, R., & Holubec, E. (1992). **Advanced cooperative learning** (2nd ed.). Edina, MN: Interaction Book Company.

Johnson, D. W., Johnson, R., & Holubec, E. (1993). **Circles of learning** (4th ed.). Edina, MN: Interaction Book Company.

Johnson, D. W., Johnson, R., Ortiz, A., & Stanne, M. (1991). Impact of positive goal and resource interdependence on achievement, interaction and attitudes. **Journal of General Psychology, 118**, 341-347.

Johnson, D. W., Johnson, R., & Smith, K. (1991). **Active learning: Cooperative in the college classroom.** Edina, MN: Interaction Book Company.

Johnson, D. W., & Johnson, R., & Maruyama, G. (1983). Interdependence and interpersonal attraction among heterogeneous individuals: A theoretical formulation and a meta-analysis of the research. **Review of Educational Research, 53**, 5-54.

Cooperation In The Classroom, Interaction Book Company, 7208 Cornelia Drive, Edina, MN 55435, (612) 831-9500, FAX (612) 831-9332

Johnson, D. W., Johnson, R., & Smith, K. (1986). Academic conflict among students: Controversy and learning. In R. Feldman, (Ed.). **Social psychological applications to education**. London: Cambridge University Press.

Johnson, D. W., Johnson, R., Stanne, M. & Garibaldi, A. (1990). The impact of leader and member group processing on achievement in cooperative groups. **The Journal of Social Psychology, 130**, 507-516.

Johnson, D. W., Johnson, R., Stevahn, L., & Hodne, P. (1997). The three Cs of safe schools. **Educational Leadership, 55**(2), 8-13.

Kagan, S. (1988). **Cooperative learning.** San Juan Capistrano, CA: Resources for Teachers.

Kohn, A. (1986). **No contest**. Boston: Houghton Mifflin.

Kouzes, J., & Posner, B. (1987). **The leadership challenge.** San Francisco: Jossey-Bass.

Lamm, H., & Trommsdorff, G. (1973). Group verses individual performance on tasks requiring ideational proficiency (Brainstorming): A review. **European Journal of Social Psychology, 3**, 361-388.

Langer, E., & Benevento, A. (1978). Self-induced dependence. **Journal of Personality and Social Psychology, 36**, 886-893.

Latane, B., Williams, K., & Harkins, S. (1979). Many hands make light the work: The causes and consequences of social loafing. **Journal of Personality and Social Psychology, 37**,822-832.

Laughlin, P., & McGlynn, R. (1967). Cooperative versus competitive concept as attainment as a function of sex and stimulus display. **Journal of Personality and Social Psychology, 7**, 398-402.

Lawrence, G. (1974). **Patterns of effective inservice education: A state of the art summary of research on materials and procedures for changing teacher behaviors in inservice education.** Tallahassee: Florida State Department of Education.

Lew, M., Mesch, D., Johnson, D. W., & Johnson, R. (1986a). Positive interdependence, academic and collaborative-skills group contingencies and isolated students. **American Educational Research Journal, 23**, 476-488.

Lew, M., Mesch, D., Johnson, D. W., & Johnson, R. (1986b). Components of cooperative learning: Effects of collaborative skills and academic group contingencies on achievement and mainstreaming. **Contemporary Educational Psychology, 11**, 229-239.

Lewin, K. (1935). **A dynamic theory of personality.** New York: McGraw-Hill.

Lewin, K. (1948). **Resolving social conflicts.** New York: Harper.

Lippitt, R., & Gold, M. (1959). Classroom social structure as a mental health problem. **Journal of Social Issues, 15**, 40-58.

Little, J. (1981). **School success and staff development in urban desegregated schools.** Paper presented at the American Educational Research Association Convention, Los Angeles, CA: April, 1981.

Cooperation In The Classroom, Interaction Book Company, 7208 Cornelia Drive, Edina, MN 55435, (612) 831-9500, FAX (612) 831-9332

Little, J. (1987). Teachers as colleagues. In V. Koehler (Ed.), **Educator's handbook: A research perspective** (pp. 491-518). New York: Longman.

Little, J. (1990). The persistance of privacy: Autonomy and initiative in teachers' professional relations. **Teacher's College Record, 9**, 509-536.

Lorber, N. (1966). Inadequate social acceptance and disruptive classroom behavior. **Journal of Educational Research, 59**, 350-362.

Male, M., Johnson, R., Johnson, D., & Anderson, M. (1988). **Cooperative learning and computers: An activity guide for teachers**. Santa Cruz, CA: Ed. Apple-cations.

Maller, J. (1929). **Cooperation and competition: An experimental study in motivation.** New York: Teachers College, Columbia University.

May, M., & Doob, L. (1937). Competition and cooperation. **Social Science Research Council Bulletin (No. 25)**. New York: Social Science Research Council.

Mayer, A. (1903). Uber einzel und gesamtleistung des schul kindes. **Archiv fur die Gesamte Psychologie, 1**, 276-416.

McLaughin, M., & Marsh, D. (1978). Staff development and school change. **Teachers College Record, 80**, 69-94.

McKeachie, W., Pintrich, P., Lin, Y., & smith, D. (1986). **Teaching and learning in the college classroom.** Ann Arbor, MI: University of Michigan.

Mesch, D., Johnson, D. W., & Johnson, R. (1988). Impact of positive interdependence and academic group contingencies on achievement. **Journal of Social Psychology, 128**, 345- 352.

Mesch, D., Lew, M., Johnson, D. W., & Johnson, R. (1986). Isolated teenagers, cooperative learning and the training of social skills. **Journal of Psychology, 120**, 323-334.

Miller, L., & Hamblin, R. (1963). Interdependence, differential rewarding, and productivity. **American Sociological Review, 28**, 768-778.

Moede, W. (1927). Die richtlinien der leistungs-psycholgie. **Industrielle Psychotechnik, 4**, 193-207.

Montagu, A. (1965). **The human revolution.** New York: World Publishing Company.

National Association of Secondary School Principals (1984). **The mood of American youth.** Reston, VA: Author.

Napier, R., & Gerschenfeld, M. (1981). **Groups: Theory and experience**. Boston: Houghton-Mifflin.

Norman, D. (1992). **The turnsignals of cars are their facial expressions.** Reading, MA: Addison-Wesley.

Orlick, T. (1982). **Cooperative sports and games book**. New York: Pantheon.

Cooperation In The Classroom, Interaction Book Company, 7208 Cornelia Drive, Edina, MN 55435, (612) 831-9500, FAX (612) 831-9332

Nias, J. (1984). Learing and acting the role: Inschool support for primary teachers. **Educational Review, 33**, 181-190.

Norman, D. (1992). **Turn signals are the facial expression of automobiles.** Reading, MA: Addison-Wesley,

Pepitone, E. (1980). **Children in cooperation and competition.** Lexington, MA: Lexington Books.

Petty, R., Harkins, S., Williams, K., & Latane, B. (1977). The effects of group size on cognitive effort and evaluation. **Personality and Social Psychology Bulletin, 3**, 575-578.

Putnam, J., Rynders, J., Johnson, D. W., & Johnson, R. (1989). Collaborative skill instruction for promoting positive interactions between mentally handicapped and nonhandicapped children. **Exceptional Children, 55**, 550-557.

Rhoades, J., & McCabe, M. (1985). **Simple cooperation.** Willits, CA: ITA.

Rosenshine, B., & Stevens, R. (1986). Teaching functions. In M.C. Wittrock (Ed), **Handbook of research on teaching** (3rd ed., pp. 376-391). New York: Macmillan.

Salomon, G. (1981). Communication and education: Social and psychological interactions. **People & Communication, 13**, 9-271.

Sarason, I., & Potter, E. (1983). **Self-monitoring, cognitive processes, and performance.** Seattle: University of Washington, mimeographed report.

Schmuck, R. (1963). Some relationships of peer liking patterns in the classroom to pupil attitudes and achievement. **School Review, 71**, 337-359.

Schmuck, R. (1966). Some aspects of classroom social climate. **Psychology in the School, 3**, 59-65.

Schmuck, R., & Schmuck, P. (1983). **Group processes in the classroom.** Dubuque, Iowa: Wm. C. Brown.

Schniedewind, N., & Davidson, E. (1987). **Cooperative learning, cooperative lives.** Dubuque, Iowa: Wm. C. Brown.

Seligman, M. (1988, October). Boomer blues. **Psychology Today, 22**, 50-55.

Sharan, S. (1980). Cooperative learning in small groups. **Review of Educational Research, 50**, 241-271.

Sharan, S., & Hertz-Lazarowitz, R. (1980). **A group-investigation method of cooperative learning in the classroom.** Technical report, University of Tel Aviv, Tel Aviv, Israel.

Sharan, S., & Sharan, Y. (1976). **Small-group teaching.** Englewood Cliffs, N.J.: Educational Technology Publications.

Sheingold, K., Hawkins, J., & Char, C. (1984). I'm the thinkist, you're the typist: The interaction of technology and the social life of classrooms. **Journal of Social Issues, 40**, 49-61.

Slavin, R. (1980). Cooperative learning. **Review of Educational Research, 50**, 315-342.

Cooperation In The Classroom, Interaction Book Company, 7208 Cornelia Drive, Edina, MN 55435, (612) 831-9500, FAX (612) 831-9332

Slavin, R. (1985). An introduction to cooperative learning research. In R. Slavin, et al., (Eds.), **Learning to cooperate, cooperating to learn.** New York: Plenum Press.

Slavin, R., Leavey, M., & Madden, N. (1982). **Team-assisted individualization: Mathematics teacher's manual.** Johns Hopkins University, Center for Social Organization of Schools.

Slavin, R., Sharan, S., Kagan, S., Lazarowitz, R., Webb, C., & Schmuck, R. (Eds.). (1985). **Learning to cooperate, cooperating to learn**. New York: Plenum.

Stevens, R., Madden, N., Slavin, R., and Farnish, A. (1987). Cooperative integrated reading and composition: Two field experiments. **Reading Research Quarterly, 4**, 433-454.

Stevenson, H., & Stigler, J. (1992). **The learning gap.** New York: Summit.

Tjosvold, D. (1986). **Working together to get things done.** Lexington, MA: D. C. Heath.

Tjosvold, D., & Johnson, D. W. (1983). **Productive conflict management**. New York: Irvington.

Triplett, N. (1898). The dynamogenic factors in pacemaking and competition. **American Journal of Psychology, 9**, 507-533.

Turk, S., & Sarason, I. (1983). **Test anxiety and causal attributions.** Seattle: University of Washington, unpublished report.

Van Egmond, E. (1960). **Social interrelationship skills and effective utilization of intelligence in the classroom**. Doctoral dissertation, University of Minnesota.

Webb, N., Ender, P., & Lewis, S. (1986). Problem-solving strategies and group processes in small group learning computer programming. **American Educational Research Journal, 23**, 243-261.

Wheeler, R., & Ryan, R. (1973). Effects of cooperative and competitive classroom environments on the attitudes and achievement of elementary school students engaged in social studies inquiry activities. **Journal of Educational Psychology, 65**, 402-407.

Williams, K. (1981). **The effects of group cohesiveness on social loafing.** Paper presented at the annual meeting of the Midwestern Psychological Association, Detroit.

Williams, K., Harkins, S., & Latane, B. (1981). Identifiability as a deterrent to social loafing. Two cheering experiments. **Journal of Personality and Social Psychology, 40**, 303-311.

Wilson, R. (1987). Toward excellence in teaching. In L. M. Aleamoni (Ed.), **Techniques for evaluating and improving instruction** (pp. 9-24). San Francisco: Jossey-Bass.

Winget, P. (Ed.). (1987). **Integrating the core curriculum through cooperative learning: Lesson plans for teachers**. Sacramento, CA: California State Department of Education.

Wittrock, M. (1990). Generative processes of comprehension. **Educational Psychologist, 24**, 345-376.

Yager, S., Johnson, D., & Johnson, R. (1985). Oral discussion, group-to individual transfer, and achievement in cooperative learning groups. **Journal of Educational Psychology, 77**, 60- 66.

Cooperation In The Classroom, Interaction Book Company, 7208 Cornelia Drive, Edina, MN 55435, (612) 831-9500, FAX (612) 831-9332

INDEX

Cooperation In The Classroom, Interaction Book Company, 7208 Cornelia Drive, Edina, MN 55435, (612) 831-9500, FAX (612) 831-9332

Structures, Scripts

Cooperation In The Classroom, Interaction Book Company, 7208 Cornelia Drive, Edina, MN 55435,
  (612) 831-9500, FAX (612) 831-9332